Mike Leigh

Contemporary Film Directors

Edited by James Naremore

The Contemporary Film Directors series provides concise, well-written introductions to directors from around the world and from every level of the film industry. Its chief aims are to broaden our awareness of important artists, to give serious critical attention to their work, and to illustrate the variety and vitality of contemporary cinema. Contributors to the series include an array of internationally respected critics and academics. Each volume contains an incisive critical commentary, an informative interview with the director, and a detailed filmography.

*A list of books in the series appears
at the end of this book.*

Mike Leigh |

Sean O'Sullivan

**UNIVERSITY
OF
ILLINOIS
PRESS**
URBANA
CHICAGO
AND
SPRINGFIELD

Frontispiece: Mike Leigh on the set of *Another Year,* 2009.
Photograph by Simon Mein, copyright Thin Man Films Ltd.

Library of Congress Cataloging-in-Publication Data

O'Sullivan, Sean, 1965–

Mike Leigh / Sean O'Sullivan.

p.   cm. — (Contemporary film directors)

Includes filmography.

Includes bibliographical references and index.

ISBN 978-0-252-03638-5 (cloth) — ISBN 978-0-252-07819-4 (pbk.)

1. Leigh, Mike, 1943—Criticism and interpretation.

I. Title.

PN1998.3.L445O88   2011

791.43'0233092—dc22   2011004552

Contents

Acknowledgments |

Mike Leigh has been an ideal subject as both filmmaker and fellow—from his warm response to my first letter of inquiry to the many hours he donated to talk about cinema, art, and the world. I am deeply indebted to him for all his contributions to the welfare of this study. Helen Grearson and Abbie Browne at Thin Man Films offered unceasingly helpful and cheerful logistical assistance.

James Naremore's sharp-eyed editorial suggestions and his vast patience were vital to this project. Joan Catapano and the staff at the University of Illinois Press have been a pleasure to work with in shaping the manuscript into a book.

My colleagues and friends at Clemson and Ohio State offered the best kind of advice—sympathetic and direct—as my arguments developed. I never would have embarked on this study without the initial invitation of Barton Palmer. Jared Gardner helped bring me to the department that is my invigorating home, and his brightness and technical legerdemain have proven invaluable. Lorraine Cashman offered her generous perspective on revisions, and Ray Cashman staged a transatlantic rescue.

Two eminent figures provided timely jolts, at either end of the process. Murray Pomerance's active intervention kept the book on course, and D. A. Miller's exhortation made the final section of the essay possible.

Stanley Cavell's *Pursuits of Happiness* was the book that first showed me just how much there is to see, hear, and indeed pursue in the movies. I am delighted that he served as one of the manuscript's initial readers, and I can only hope that some of his senses of viewing the world find influential effects in these pages.

Alex Woloch's warm convictions always provided bracing encouragement, from the most casual of conversations to his active endorsement in teaching sections of the essay. Christian Keathley is the fellow newcomer we dream of having when we begin our lives as faculty members: smart, purposeful, and astoundingly present at all times. My deepest thanks to both these gentlemen of letters and images.

Gwen O'Sullivan Romagnoli transcribed the many hours of interviews, proofread industriously, and served as beneficent counselor throughout. A writer is truly blessed to have a mother so able in all the tasks she volunteers to perform.

I owe Hannah Eigerman so much for her sustained heroics, as we shared the making of this book. Given the centrality of pregnancy in Mike Leigh's films, it is fitting that Hannah was expecting our first child when I embarked on this venture. Now Rory, and the sequel Eve, are here to see it in covers. I love them all dearly (even more than chairs and stuff).

The first two sections of the essay contain excerpts from my interviews with Mike Leigh—excerpts separate from the interview that follows the essay. All quotations are taken from interviews conducted in July and October of 2004.

Mike Leigh

The Nature of Contrivance |

It is time to reclaim Mike Leigh from the kindly ghetto in which he has been placed by his well-meaning enthusiasts. I intend to reclaim him, over the course of this book, as a practicing theorist—a filmmaker deeply invested in cinema's formal, conceptual, and narrative dimensions. Leigh is typically considered an unassuming crafter of little movies, an English social realist who has called himself "a Third World filmmaker from this obscure island off the French coast" (Movshovitz 57) and who has written little or nothing that we would consider theory, or even criticism. I would argue that the recurrent simplifications of what Leigh's cinema is, and what Leigh's cinema does, result in part from the mode in which he works, or the mode in which he is said to work: realism. When his films are praised, it is because they are "authentic," whatever that means; when his films are attacked, it is because they fail to live up to some restrictive code of realism, a code to which he has never really claimed to subscribe. According to received wisdom, realists don't theorize; realists merely reflect. This is an absurd provincialism, and yet it remains the coin of the realm.

Films are composed of two elements: images and sounds. But Mike Leigh's images and sounds are rarely discussed. In the ancient conversation about form and content, content appears to be the only thing that matters in Leigh's cinema. The only formal aspect that does get attention is Leigh's famously unusual collaborative process, whereby the director and his actors create the characters and narrative from scratch over many months of improvisation. Just as the formal approach that distinguished the preparation of Alfred Hitchcock's movies—his elaborate storyboards—has served to draw attention to Hitchcock's interest in composition and editing, so has the prehistory of Leigh's films conditioned their reception. Unlike Hitchcock's case, however, where the story of storyboarding makes form more prominent, the story of Leigh's improvisatory approach has valorized content to the exclusion of form, celebrating the putative ideology of this system and diverting attention from Leigh's films as independent art objects. This phenomenon applies not only to images and sounds but to the third defining element of narrative cinema, storytelling structure, or what is often subdivided into character and plot. Instead of hearing about character and plot, we hear about people and events. As the story goes, Mike Leigh is not a craftsman, not a hewer of shapes and ideas, but a "wizard" whose films have "the feel of life" and celebrate "a sense of the real"; the "substance" of his films "is not to be found at the surface of events or in the way in which he handles form, but in the lives of his people, as people" (Jones xi, Carney and Quart 239, Watson iii, Clements, *Improvised,* 69). Whatever Leigh's purchase on verisimilitude, our discussion of that purchase remains in thrall to the question of cause (the film behind the film) at the expense of the question of effect (the film as we see and hear it). If someone who had never heard of Leigh sat down to watch one of his films, he or she would have no idea, based on the images and sounds that were produced, that the film had been made through idiosyncratic means. We need to separate the romance from the result. It is time that we stopped thinking of Mike Leigh as a shaman and started thinking of him as a filmmaker.

We can draw a parallel from the field of art history, where so-called realists are also often misunderstood. Michael Fried has worked to recover the French painter Gustave Courbet as a complex and subtle practicing theorist of art, against the Courbet public, which has portrayed him as a mechanic holding the mirror up to nature. As Fried argues: "Commentaries on Courbet's art, as on that of other realist painters (Thomas Eakins, for example), have often focused on questions of subject matter, either narrowly or broadly construed. And it has also meant that discussion has tended to proceed on the unexamined assumption that a realist painting's representation of a given scene was to all intents and purposes determined by the 'actual' scene itself, with the result that features of the representation that ought to have been perceived as curious or problematic, as calling for reflection and analysis, have either been made invisible (the usual outcome) or, if registered at all, have been attributed to reality rather than to art" (Fried 3). These assertions about the constructedness of realist enterprises hold true for any art form or discipline, but they still need to be argued, not only in the case of Gustave Courbet but in the case of Mike Leigh. The "curious or problematic," the choices that call "for reflection and analysis," have been elided, or noted only as flaws in the imitation of the real.

When I asked Leigh about his cinema, and about perhaps the most famous single image in his oeuvre, the shot of two women in a café in *Secrets and Lies* (1996), a daughter and mother at the moment of awkward reunion, here is what he said: "They are not naturalistic literal quasi-documentary films—they are very heightened. That café scene has as much to do with Beckett and Hopper, has more to do with Beckett and Hopper, than it has to do with a literal investigation into two women around Covent Garden on a Saturday night in the summer of 1995."

To people familiar with Leigh's early work in the theater, or with his first generation of films, the name of Beckett will not be surprising, given Leigh's often minimalist plots and the recurrent sensibility of loss and disconnection. Surely Samuel Beckett is no one's idea of a diaphanous realist, eschewing artifice and tapping straightforwardly into a "sense of the real" or "the feel of life." Likewise, one can hardly look at Edward Hopper's "Nighthawks" or "Morning Sun"—to say nothing of a nearly abstract canvas like "Rooms by the Sea"—and claim that the world we see in his paintings has not been altered in some way: framed, tinted, angled, shifted, accented to shape a version of reality. The artifice of that shot from *Secrets and Lies* goes beyond matters of visual composition; in fact, the shot troubles the "reality" of its supposed verisimilitude. As Leigh added: "That wide shot in the café in itself is a massive contrivance, because anybody's who's been to London will know perfectly well that if you walk down that way toward Covent Garden, you wouldn't find a café as empty as that. So, that in itself was a complete contrivance." "Contrivance" is a key term for Leigh, one critical not only for art in general but for his art in particular.

Of course, Beckett and Hopper do share an interest in the bric-a-brac of the everyday, and they brood over the ephemeral, and that certainly accounts in part for Leigh's interest in them. I should make clear that, with all my emphasis on form and contrivance and design, I am not trying to make a pitch for Mike Leigh as an exponent of the rococo or even baroque. He is not Tim Burton or Baz Luhrmann. There are compelling reasons to dip into the language of realism when considering his films. To a large degree, this is because the characters and subjects of his drama are those often associated with a realist perspective: the unemployed, the class-bound, the adrift—all the individuals and stories forgotten by the bogeyman of Hollywood. And Leigh has always insisted that the instruments of cinema—camera, *mise-en-scène*, music—should be motivated by the dramatic environments that they are representing. My quarrel is not with the rhetoric of realism as such; indeed, it is exactly Leigh's rhetoric of realism that I mean to address. We need to move away from the notion that Leigh's style is, in Ray Carney's words, "unrhetorical in the extreme" (Carney and Quart 241).

Leigh's enthusiasts like to discuss the back story. And certainly Leigh's process is remarkable. His method begins by gathering actors and embarking on several months of what is sometimes called rehearsal, or what Leigh prefers to call "preparatory work." He works with each actor individually, asking her or him to draw on a list of up to one hundred people that the actor has met as possible sources for the character that will be created—a list from which Leigh will select a final roster of candidates. Gradually, a history of that character is explored and created through research and improvisation, and Leigh brings different embryonic characters into contact with one another. Paul Clements has helpfully outlined Leigh's five central rules:

1. All action is the result of the characters' motivations.
2. In order for motivation to exist, the characters' individual and collective reality must be credible.
3. Each improvisation, as a real event for the characters, grows organically out of what has gone before.
4. The actors must not know the motivations of other actors' characters.
5. The improvisations are discussed always in terms of real events and never as "scenes." (Clements, *Improvised*, 37–38)

The balance between realism and artifice is remarkable. On the one hand, actors immerse themselves in their roles as almost nowhere else in the film or theater. If a character has a specific trade or profession, such as Natalie the plumber in *Life Is Sweet* (1990), the actor playing that character, in this case Claire Skinner, takes the time to learn and practice that trade or profession. The actors are ignorant of the background, plot developments, and often even the existence of other characters—as illustrated by the fact that the central surprises of *Secrets and Lies* and *Vera Drake* (2004) were revealed, to the shock of many of the actors involved, in the process of creating the story of each film. When socializing during the preparatory process, actors are strictly forbidden from discussing their work or their characters with each other. So on this side of the equation, the likeness to the real world is crucial—we don't know what's happening outside of ourselves, we don't know why other people do things, and we have no idea how the script of our lives will develop. On the other side of the equation, actors treat their characters as characters; Leigh insists that they come out of character so that they can look at what has happened objectively. When he is shooting, Leigh gives his cast a final instruction to "warm up," and they go into character for a short time before the camera rolls. This ability to move in and out of character signals an approach halfway between the precise line reading of traditional British training in Shakespeare and the complete immersion of the American strain of Method acting. And Leigh operates throughout as Daedalus in the workshop, constructing the object, moving characters and potential plots into collision with each other, deciding who gets to live and die and how things begin and end. For all the illusion of democracy, or even anarchy, that commonly attaches itself to discussion of Leigh's films, in many ways they are as despotically made as anything by Alfred Hitchcock or Stanley Kubrick.

Again, the tension between the endless possibilities of life and the circumscribed direction of art is manifest in every page of Leigh's skeletal shooting scripts. The denouement of *Naked* (1993) involves a number of major developments of character and plot, an extended confrontation that unfolds over twenty-one minutes of screen time. The final shooting script describes those twenty-one minutes in only eight words: "Sandra's Flat (Day Int/Ext Friday)—Enter Sandra." As Leigh has done on several films, he stopped shooting at that point in production, sent the crew home for over a week, and worked out with the actors exactly how the film would conclude. When the crew returned, there were still no words on the page. But Leigh and the cast had painstakingly determined not only what would happen but what the dialogue and blocking would be. There is virtually no on-camera improvisation on a Leigh set, in contrast with the vast majority of films, in or out of Hollywood, where multiple takes not only serve camera and sound but allow actors to play with their lines. In a Mike Leigh film, the characters, and what they say and do, are laminated before they are recorded. This volatile mixture of uncertainty and precision in the making of his films is often central to what the films explore. And the volatile mixture of uncertainty and precision in the *finished* films is of far greater import than the volatile mixture of uncertainty and precision in the *making* of the films, because if all these fascinating eccentricities simply produced "a load of rubbish" (to use Leigh's own phrase), then what importance would the gestation have? The process matters only in terms of the results. For example, until *Happy-Go-Lucky* (2008), there were almost no small children in his films, beyond a few extras used for context or scene-setting. This is due in part to the nature and demands of the process, since young people do not have the professional training, breadth of experience, or logistical capacity to devote to the round-the-clock preparatory months that Leigh requires. But the procedural aspect of this is of little final interest; what is of interest is the way in which the absence of small children acts as a flashpoint for innumerable issues of character, plot, image, and sound, as a central catalyst for the ideas, questions, and problems of Leigh's finished movies.

There are two dominant critical camps, in regard to his cinema. The first and most influential camp is the exceptionalists. Their perspective accentuates the distinctiveness of Leigh's creative process and the consequent purity or authenticity of his finished works. This narrative of slow, careful nurturing makes for a happy story in times anxious about multinational globalization; Leigh stands for the organic in a world of genetically modified filmmaking. This has contributed to critics' emphasis on the "reality" of his work; responses to his films are often festooned with such words as "true" and "honest," as if the films were simplifying devices rather than meticulously judged constructs. In this view, other films announce, "Somebody made this." By contrast, Leigh's films announce, "This was not made. This is." Exceptionalists have celebrated Leigh as a facilitator of "this is," linking the collectivist parable of the films' conception with the relative plotlessness of the films' stories to carve a utopian image of what movies should be—pure, honest, the whole laundry list of virginity. Leigh's films, by this reckoning, offer a kind of realism and authenticity (codes for art that cares about content and not form) that is supposedly lacking from recent cinema. Here is Stephen Holden of the *New York Times* on *Vera Drake* (2004): "The *purest* ensemble movie of the season is the British director Mike Leigh's gloomy period piece. . . . The list of *perfectly calibrated* supporting performances would include a dozen names" (emphases added; Holden E1). "Pure" and "perfect," words usually reserved to describe mountain spring water, are used to separate Leigh from his maculate peers.

A second camp is the generalists. The generalists wish to associate Leigh with a tradition of British cinema that often goes by the name of social realism, which traces its roots to the documentary movements of the 1930s, the Free Cinema of the 1950s, and the New Wave of the 1960s and whose most prominent contemporary practitioner would be Ken Loach. Generalists choose to define Leigh by his cinematic nationality; and, even more narrowly, that nationality is defined by its fondness for an agenda of reform, one that indicts the English class system, often by caricaturing the well-to-do or petty capitalists in favor of the noble working class—especially in the wake of the cataclysmic revolution personified by Margaret Thatcher. Generalists insist on finding an agenda in all his films, and they are often offended by it.[1] Providing an example is Holden's *New York Times* colleague Manohla Dargis, in her own review of *Vera Drake*. Dargis praises the film by juxtaposing it with recent work like *Secrets and Lies* and *Career Girls* (1997), which apparently failed because Leigh, "like his filmmaking compatriot Ken Loach . . . sometimes betrays his art for some political finger-wagging. That the two filmmakers are, of course, often just preaching to the adoring, approving choir makes such grandstanding especially tedious" (Dargis, "When a Motherly," E1). Leaving aside the idea that politics is a betrayal of art, *Secrets and Lies* and *Career Girls* are freer of overt politics than virtually any British film of the last two decades and would be among the last candidates for preachiness to be found in Leigh's oeuvre. Indeed, *Vera Drake*—with its focus on abortion—might more closely approximate finger-wagging than any of the films on Dargis's list. So fixed are the categories through which Leigh is judged that actual distinctions between films no longer matter. Mike Leigh has become the sum of our perceptions of him.[2]

The exceptionalists and the generalists come together in the first sentence of David Denby's *New Yorker* capsule review of *Vera Drake*, distilling into five words all the banalities of current conversation about Mike Leigh: "In its limited way, perfect" (Denby 50). "Limited" because constricted by its modest artistic ambitions (hampered in part by that "Third World" of cinema, the United Kingdom); "perfect" because nobler in process and intent than mass-produced contemporary cinema. Given the ubiquity of such language in discussions of Leigh, it is easy to overlook the fact that a line like "in its limited way, perfect" makes no sense whatsoever. What on earth is a "perfect" film? "Perfect" is not praise but a prison sentence, since it forecloses discussion by removing *Vera Drake* from the realm of possibility, accident, and interpretation— the oxygen of art and of cultural conversation. "Perfect" allows us to forget about the choices of art and simply bask in their results, as if they were somehow self-evident; to return to Fried on Courbet's paintings, this way of thinking "has made close scrutiny of what they offer to be seen appear to be beside the point" (3). Fried's tricky phrase—what the paintings "offer to be seen"—is only half the story when it comes to cinema, since we also need to pay attention to what Leigh's films offer to be *heard*; the argument applies doubly in our case. The last part of that phrase of Fried's—"beside the point"—is just as crucial, since this idea of a "point," which one might extrapolate as a "message" or "purpose," is just as toxic as the language of perfection. Hence the other half of the seesaw, the belief that these films are "limited." To some degree, that word belongs to a long tradition that simultaneously celebrates realism while diminishing its effects. Because realist art objects do not appear to be difficult or obscure, their ambition must surely be a tempered one, content to capture stories and people through a single prism. Such criticism is typically directed at genre art, such as comic operas (a form dear to Mike Leigh's heart). It is rather odd to think of realism as genre art and therefore "limited" and modest, given that the genre of realism is limited to everything that exists.

This rhetoric of limited perfection represents a distortion of the language of the high priest of cinematic realism himself, André Bazin. Here are the famous last words of his 1949 essay on Vittorio De Sica's *Bicycle Thieves* (1948): "*Ladri di Biciclette* is one of the first examples of pure cinema. No more actors, no more story, no more sets, which is to say that in the perfect aesthetic illusion of reality there is no more cinema" (Bazin, "*Bicycle Thief*," 60). "Pure" and "perfect," ready to be recycled by Leigh's champions fifty-five years later. Bazin's elevated vocabulary worked powerfully in 1949 as a corrective to cinematic schematism, but the current conversation about Mike Leigh has drained that vocabulary of meaning. In "The Evolution of the Language of Cinema," Bazin praises the films of Erich von Stroheim, where "reality lays itself bare like a suspect confessing under the relentless examination of the commissioner of police" (27)—a phrase that anticipates the second half of *Vera Drake*, where a veiled discussion of the meaning of the real takes place between a suspect and a policeman. Bazin's simile ascribes an active role to the director and the camera: after all, a policeman uses a bag of tricks to get the suspect to confess, and it is precisely the fact that Mike Leigh operates by deploying a bag of tricks and not waiting for limited-but-perfect revelations. We must always connect realism to aesthetics—or we risk finding ourselves in a version of the Courbet problem.

Consider W. S. Gilbert, as he defends his dramatic philosophy in Leigh's *Topsy-Turvy* (1997). When his partner, Arthur Sullivan, accuses him of dwelling too heavily on such "contrived devices" as magic potions and magic lozenges, Gilbert harrumphs: "Every theatrical performance is a contrivance, by its very nature." We all know this, but many have chosen not to know it, in the case of Leigh. Leigh readily acknowledges that the climactic, central moment of *Vera Drake*—when the Sunday dinner celebrating an engagement and a pregnancy tragically coincides with the arrival of the policeman who will subject Vera to relentless examination—is a contrivance, perpetrated by him as author. During my interviews with him, Leigh expressed impatience with the notion that this dramatic contrivance might represent a breach of contract, a sordid commingling of the dirty work of plot in the sacred grove of pure realism. Leigh's process is just as much a contrivance as any other. Why is the process of researching and exploring and improvising over several months, and shaping stories as the preparatory work, any less artificial than the classical Hollywood system of castes of actors, writers, and directors serving at the behest of producers? Perhaps because so little seems to happen in many of Leigh's films—the fact that we get not, as Hitchcock said of his own cinema, "life with the dull bits cut out" (qtd. in Truffaut 103) but the dull bits of life—their evolution seems more authentic. But if artifice simply means making, why is making dull bits any less an act of making than making exciting bits? We need to recover words like "contrivance," "artifice," and "design" in order to see and hear what Leigh offers to be seen and heard.

Before elaborating what I argue Leigh is, rather than what he is not, let us linger with Gilbert and Sullivan. The central drama of *Topsy-Turvy* articulates the struggle between Gilbert, a man happy to concoct "trivial soufflés" (as Sullivan calls them), and Sullivan, a man intent on exploring "the realms of human emotion and probability"—in conventional terms, the first man is a hack, and the second man is *un vrai artiste*. The critical consensus has looked to ascribe one version of Gilbert and one version of Sullivan to Mike Leigh, as follows. Leigh, in his introduction to the screenplay of *Topsy-Turvy*, deems the comic operas that the partnership produced "profoundly trivial" (Leigh, *Topsy*, vii)—a fitting oxymoron. It is precisely the combination of the trivial and the profound, though in somewhat different slants of those words, that people have celebrated in Leigh's films; they dwell on the trivial—on "trivial" lives of "trivial" people, replete with "trivial" moments—and find the profound in the trivia of everyday life. Gilbert and Leigh, according to this approach, are happy to be artists of minutiae. And Leigh, like Sullivan, wants to dedicate himself to "the realms of human emotion and probability"—honesty, purity, and so forth.

I, too, would like to extrapolate some of Gilbert and some of Sullivan in order to reconsider Leigh—but a very different Gilbert and a very different Sullivan from the ones I have just sketched. We need to realign Leigh with Gilbert the artificer, the careful shaper of language, actions, and images. The scene in *Topsy-Turvy* that shows Gilbert painstakingly and dictatorially directing three actors through the precise grammar, phrasing, and exhibition of his dialogue bears much closer resemblance to Leigh's directing method, as contriving craftsman, than the common image of Leigh genially overseeing a be-in.[3] And we need to rescue not the Sullivan who was Romantic enough to think that his grand opera *Ivanhoe* would be more important than *Princess Ida* but the Sullivan who was ambitious enough to want to write grand opera. Leigh considers all his films, in one way or another, as "epic"—including such perhaps unlikely candidates as *Vera Drake* and a short entitled *The Short and Curlies* (1987). This might seem an especially surprising description for the latter project, which on the face of it looks like a trivial soufflé based on body ailments and silly jokes. What matters is that we think of Leigh not as perfect or limited but as restless and expansive.

How to Watch a Mike Leigh Movie: *The Short and Curlies*

Let me outline the major narrative and stylistic elements central to Leigh, the practicing theorist. An ideal place to begin, in terms of narrative issues, is with a neglected aspect of his career, *The Five-Minute Films*. Leigh made these short stories, each five minutes long, for the BBC in 1975—that is, in the relative infancy of his cinematic development. Previously, he had made one theatrical feature, *Bleak Moments* (1971), and one film for television, *Hard Labour* (1973). Here is how Leigh described the premise of *The Five-Minute Films* when I interviewed him:

> I thought it was a cracking idea, and I would have done about forty
> of them or fifty—so you'd see them all the time, and sometimes you
> might see a character you never saw again, sometimes you might see

somebody popping up for a moment and then be a main character in another one, or there'd be a couple of ones that would run on to a narrative. It would be a whole microcosm of the world. There was a debate about whether they should be shown at the same time or they should be dotted around the channel, like currants in the pudding, as Tony Garnett, the producer, called it.

As it happened, five of these five-minute films were produced as a pilot venture, and they were not broadcast until 1982, by which time Leigh had become a British televisual institution. Leigh explains the compositional impulse behind them: "The liberating thing from an artistic and filmmaking point of view—the thing that you couldn't do within the context of a single piece—is to actually do all sorts of different things *stylistically*" (Movshovitz 8). If we define style narrowly in terms of camera and *mise-en-scène,* then the five completed films do not exhibit a great variety of styles. But it we define style as narrative structure, an investigation of the machinery and possibilities of storytelling, then these films offer a bonanza of experiments, covering an astonishing amount of territory within a limited number of episodes. The organizing principle of this collection would be the same as that of Italo Calvino's *Invisible Cities* or, in film terms, Peter Greenaway's encyclopedic *The Falls* (1980); given the loosest of frameworks, the playful artist concocts a series of variations on a theme, each variation operating independently yet commenting on the enterprise as a whole. This is conceptual art, or postmodern art—hardly the province of a sober realist.

At first glance, that premise may seem more exciting than the finished products, since the content of these films looks just like the humdrum stuff that sober realists are always churning out. Consider the subjects of these five stories: A couple decides to have a baby. Two men walk to a car. A youth meets his probation officer. Two men make sausage rolls while one man washes a window. Three women sit around drinking. But if we dig into this array of the ordinary, a more complicated set of subjects emerges. The first film, *The Birth of the Goalie of the 2001 F.A. Cup Final,* covers in ten vignettes an arc of six years, as a man tries to persuade his partner to get pregnant; she finally consents, and a boy is born while the father-to-be is playing for his weekend soccer team. The very brief final scene jumps ahead in time, showing in long shot the father and the boy kicking a ball around in a park, surrounded by large apartment buildings. As a storytelling gambit, the contrast with the second film, *Old Chums,* could not be more blatant. *Old Chums* consists of a large, boorish man (Terry) running into a handicapped acquaintance (Brian), who moves around on crutches; they talk about family and old times as Brian laboriously makes his way to his tiny, specially equipped car and then drives off to go see a movie. If *Birth of the Goalie* is an exercise in expanding the five-minute rubric into half a decade of story development, *Old Chums* unfolds in real time, with no chitchat elided. One film doesn't give us nearly enough information, given the range of its events; the other film gives us entirely too much information. This initial pair works as a kind of thesis and antithesis, at a basic level of narrative.

But there is more going on here than simply two extremes in the dimension of storytelling time. *The Birth of the Goalie* emphasizes plot, through one of the oldest plots of fiction—the decision to have, and the process of having, children. Indeed, plot is all that we are given here. We have no access to the psychology of the man and the woman; his desire to have a child, and her reluctance to have a child, exist as premises without exploration; their dialogue and their blank affects give us little sense of these individuals or of their marital history. Indeed, it is not even clear if they are married. And what are these characters' names? The closing credits label them as "Father" and "Mother"—curious, since neither fits that description until the very end of the film. Those names are functions of plot and not of individuated identity. *The Birth of the Goalie* exhibits a hypertrophy of plot, to the almost complete exclusion of character—a film that leaves the protagonists of its central incident completely opaque.

The ironic contrast with *Old Chums* is apparent in the name of the movie that Brian drives off to see: *Blazing Inferno.* Nothing could be further from the plot-driven widescreen spectacle implied by that title than a mundane event—walking to a car—decorated with small talk. That small talk consists of a bewildering assortment of names—at least twenty-three, if we include the chatty Terry and the taciturn Brian. Names come up in *The Birth of the Goalie* only when the prospective parents run through lists of possible names for their child; names in that film are simply labels, without reference to specific people. In *Old Chums,* however, Terry and Brian discuss (in order of appearance) Terry's parents; Terry's wife, Shirley, and their kids; Terry's brother-in-law and his two children; Brian's mum; Pete; Phil Jones; Frankie Payne; Mocca; Taffy Evans; Roz Whitely; Margaret; Sandra with the big feet; the two twins; Cynthia Lambert; and "some rich bloke," Cynthia Lambert's husband. Who are all these people? Who knows? The names of these characters from past and present, families and mates and old girlfriends, fizz past us in fractions of recollection and anecdote, making us aware of the extent of the known universe of people inhabited by these two "ordinary" men. Brian is uncomfortable with Terry not only because of his imposing attitude and physique but because clearly some of these people from the past dredge up recollections and episodes that are less than pleasant, presumably of sexual adventure or misadventure. What recollections or episodes? What moments of plot? We can only guess.

If *The Birth of the Goalie* offers a hypertrophy of plot at the expense of character, then *Old Chums* offers a hypertrophy of character at the expense of plot. It is as if Leigh were standing at the console of narrative, deliberately turning each knob—character and plot—to its lowest and highest extreme in alternating cases. Even the titles emphasize this schism. *The Birth of the Goalie of the 2001 F.A. Cup Final* advertises event and plot, and the action-filled world of sports, while ignoring personality; *Old Chums* speaks to personal history, to specific memories that may lead nowhere other than into the minds of the film's two characters. This dissection of character and plot, of the DNA of narrative, would return on a larger scale a decade later, when Leigh made two adjacent films—*Meantime* (1983) and *Four Days in July* (1985)—that enact successively a narrative restricted to character and a narrative restricted to plot—or, more precisely, to characters starved of plot and characters overwhelmed by plot.

The Five-Minute Films are perhaps most significant as an enterprise of stories and characters linked by conceit rather than causality. What, may we ask, happened to Leigh's stated interest in representing "a whole microcosm of the world" by slicing it into small pieces, in thinking about the balance between miniature narratives and global narratives? That question is a complex one. One immediate answer is that the enterprise of *The Five-Minute Films* returns most forcefully in some of Leigh's later films as a series of loosely connected stories, of characters organized not by any knowledge of each other but by a shared narrative context or device. In *Secrets and Lies,* we get brief glimpses, some only a few moments long, of a series of people having their portraits taken at Maurice Purley's studio; in *All or Nothing* (2002), we get brief glimpses, some only a few moments long, of a series of people sitting in Phil Bassett's taxi; in *Vera Drake*, we get brief glimpses, all more than a few moments long, of a series of women getting abortions at the hands of the title character. The portrait sitters, the cab fares, and the abortion clients have nothing in common, beyond the one thing they have in common. But these ten-second films, or thirty-second films, or one-minute films briskly open up new characters and places and plots, cracking open the master narrative that surrounds them and forcing us, as in science fiction, to glimpse wormholes that lead us into and out of *Secrets and Lies* and *All or Nothing* and *Vera Drake,* throwing into doubt the centrality of the "main story" we are following. Mike Leigh did not give up being Calvino or Greenaway when he turned from nationally known TV director to world-renowned auteur; it is our job to find the Calvino and Greenaway embedded in the daily and the real.

| | |

I am proposing three terms or concepts to understand how Leigh makes movies—three terms that will serve as a basic lexicon for navigating what, in Fried's terms, Leigh's films offer to be seen. The first term is the "unbroken shot," a long take that articulates, to borrow David Bordwell's terms, the difference between a director watching something and a director staging something. A long take can suggest a rhetoric of presence, of self-announcing diegetic intervention, as with the intricate opening of Orson Welles's *Touch of Evil.* Conversely, a long take, especially when used as a fixed wide shot, can suggest a rhetoric of absence—giving the appearance of merely "watching." As Bordwell argues in *Figures Traced in Light,* "staging" connotes a director who uses the guise of a passive camera to construct a specific kind of shot—often a shot that "engages in a delicate play of balance and counterbalance" (200). Leigh's unbroken shots, produced for much of his career by a fixed camera, often do not draw attention to themselves as cinematic material; we may be in them for a long time without realizing we are in them. It is fitting that Bordwell's language for this kind of shot—"unmoving take," "unbudging long take," "static long take" (5, 29, 231)—puts pressure on the apparently absent (the "un-") or the dormant (the "static"). Leigh's unbroken shots keep us at bay by not giving us the structure, psychological proximity, and narrative clarification afforded by an edited sequence, while also inviting us in, asking us to probe an image-world that somehow warrants a shot that lasts longer than it "should." The "action," such as it is, may take a long time to develop, or it may not develop at all, or it may lie beyond the margin of the frame. I will be addressing a number of unbroken shots over the course of the book. For now, I will point out that Leigh is particularly fond of such shots at the beginnings and ends of his films, and in films such as *Four Days in July* and *Topsy-Turvy,* which both begin and end with unbroken shots, the dialogue between those bookends often raises specific questions about the film between them in a way not dissimilar from the methods of the embedded, centrifugal series of mini-narratives I have cited in *Secrets and Lies, All or Nothing,* and *Vera Drake.*

The second term is the "side-by-side," which in its basic incarnation offers a shot of two people in conversation, framed head-on, their bodies oriented toward us and not each other. Just as the unbroken shot is not simply a long take, the side-by-side is not simply a two-shot, because the side-by-side presents two people in parallel, while a two-shot usually presents two people either facing each other or at angles that convince us that they could be engaged in conversation. If the unbroken shot can carry with it the force of verisimilitude, of simply watching, the side-by-side carries a feeling of artifice, of something not quite familiar. The side-by-side has as much to do with positioning two people for the camera as it has to do with allowing us to see and hear a conversation unfold; in some way, the conversational side-by-side suggests the mannered cinema of Georges Méliès, where action is constructed to face the audience. We need to stress the tinge of artifice, of design, that often colors the side-by-side, in contradistinction with the illusion of reality that colors the unbroken shot. I should point out that, in conjunction with this basic recipe of the side-by-side—two people in conversation—Leigh also constructs important variants, not least side-by-sides of other similarly shaped objects, such as buildings, a visual element that is central to the story of *Grown-Ups* (1980) and *High Hopes* (1988). Side-by-sides need not necessarily be visual, as married couples or siblings who share first initials (such as Nicola and Natalie in *Life Is Sweet,* Maurice and Monica in *Secrets and Lies,* and the family of Rachel and Rory and Penny and Phil in *All or Nothing*) also often reflect two linked but disconnected characters. And I will be discussing Leigh's eight most recent feature films as a series of side-by-sides, as adjacent pairs that are deep into conversation with each other. In each instance, the side-by-side puts two similarly dissimilar or dissimilarly similar entities alongside one another, engaged in a debate about not only a point within the story but also a thematic or structural question of the story. I claim that these literal moments of side-by-side figuration, which, like all my terms, also exist in metaphorical or allegorical modes, present oppositions not only between characters but between ideas of character, ideas of representation, and ideas of the world.

The third term is the "centaur," which connects to the unbroken shot in that information is compressed into one shot that might more commonly be dispersed into two or more, and to the side-by-side in that it involves the collision of two distinct entities. At its most literal level, a centaur shot shows one part of one character's body and a different part of another character's body, squeezed into the frame simultaneously. We

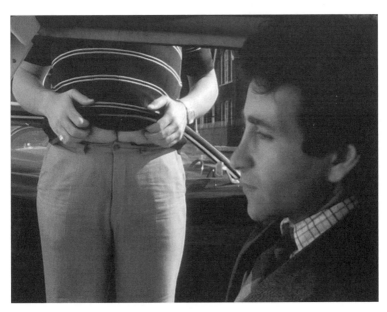

Figure 1. The centaur: body and mind
(Terry and Brian) in *Old Chums.*

can see a prominent example of this deliberately awkward construction in *Old Chums,* when at one point during Brian and Terry's conversation, Brian's head, which is inside the car, dominates the right side of the frame, in close-up, while Terry's midsection, which is outside the car, and which Terry has revealed to scratch his exuberant gut, dominates the left side of the frame, at medium distance. So we have one man from the top of his head to the middle of his sternum, and another man from his chest to his knees. If the viewer cannot avoid noticing this odd configuration, since Brian is startled by Terry's lack of couth and turns away from him in disgust, in effect creating a perpendicular tension between the two men. If the side-by-side presents two bodies or objects that are somehow linked while staying independent of each other, the visual centaur presents parts of two bodies integrated into one image; in one case, the unease of disconnection, in the other, the unease of connection. While there are other visual centaurs in Leigh's cinema, these are less frequent than the side-by-side and the unbroken shot, and the centaur's real force comes out in its more figurative associations, in ideas or fantasies of two separate beings momentarily joined into one. This fantasy of splicing is given clearest voice in *Career Girls,* when the two main characters, Hannah and Annie, sit down to dinner and Hannah says, regarding their respective faults and strengths, "Well, you see, if we could be a combination, we'd be the perfect woman, wouldn' we? Unfortunately, we can't." The fact that "Hannah" and "Annie" are etymologically the same name underscores their interrelatedness. The title, *Career Girls,* does more than just convey a problematic term for professional women—it makes a centaur of adulthood and childhood, of the conforming, economic space of "career" and the eccentric, psychological space of "girls."

I want to highlight another version of the centaur: the pregnant woman. We see a number of pregnant women in the films, at all stages of development, and this actual centaur, of two beings sharing the same body, is an important touchstone. Just as important, however, are discussions of pregnancies—future and past as well as present—along with a kind of centaur of absence or omission, the woman who has had an abortion. Babies, small children, and young teenagers are virtually absent as individualized characters in Leigh's films, and so pregnancy without issue becomes a defining conceit—pregnancy as the specter of infinite possibility, without resolution of that possibility. The issues of pregnancy and abortion have been most widely discussed, for obvious reasons, in the context of *Vera Drake,* but in many ways that film represents a culmination of a collection of dilemmas and questions, just as, in a very different way, does *Topsy-Turvy.* We will turn, at the end of this introduction, to a prominent instance of the pregnant woman, and to the way in which that centaurical creature points us to things beyond the mere fact of pregnancy itself.

The unbroken shot, the side-by-side, and the centaur share the screen at some key moments, bringing all their meanings together into noisy conversation. I have already cited the café scene from *Secrets and Lies.* Let us juxtapose it with a somewhat less famous but equally complicated image from *Topsy-Turvy,* in which the two principals sit down to discuss their next opera in a side-by-side conversation that evolves as an unbroken shot nearly three and a half minutes long. In this instance, we have two people conversing over coffee or tea, the person on the left presenting a script that the person on the right considers an improbable fiction; they are engaged in an argument about what constitutes a story that one would want to believe. Look back at the café shot from *Secrets and Lies,* a side-by-side unbroken shot that lasts for eight minutes. We see the precursor to the scene from *Topsy-Turvy*: two people conversing over coffee or tea, the person on the left presenting a script that the person on the right considers an improbable fiction. In the later case, the person on the left is W. S. Gilbert; the person on the right is Sir Arthur Sullivan. In the earlier case, the person on the left is Hortense Cumberbatch, an optometrist; the person on the right is Cynthia Purley, who works in a cardboard-box factory. In the later case, the script is a comic opera about a magic potion in the Sicilian mountains; in the earlier case, the script is the collection of Hortense's adoption papers, and we are witnessing the moment where Hortense reveals herself to her birth mother, and her birth mother, at first, thinks this must be a mistake, a story that makes no sense—it is the kind of topsy-turvy, babies-switched-at-birth scenario that Sullivan will later refuse to buy. Few viewers, on seeing these two films, would confuse the cultivated Sir Arthur Sullivan with the impetuous Cynthia Purley; this visual rhyme, however, asks us to confuse them, or to think about how their elements of cinema connect. Cynthia Purley will begin to relent

Figure 2. The side-by-side centaur
in the unbroken shot: Hortense and Cynthia
in *Secrets and Lies*.

in her opposition to Hortense's script before this shot is finished and
will gradually try to connect with her daughter over the course of the
film; but the performance style of Brenda Blethyn on the right, which
stresses the register of hysteria, and the performance style of Marianne
Jean-Baptiste on the left, which maintains a sheath of reserve, hold out

Figure 3. The side-by-side centaur in the
unbroken shot: Gilbert and Sullivan in *Topsy-Turvy*.

not a promise of final reconciliation but an extended dialogue between possibly incompatible ideas of performance. Likewise, Sir Arthur Sullivan will begin to relent in his opposition to Gilbert's script—more precisely, Gilbert will provide a new script, called *The Mikado.* But this new venture does nothing to address the representational objections that Sullivan has voiced, and the idea of performance (of human emotion and probability) personified by Sullivan is never made compatible with the idea of performance (of coincidence and the implausible) personified by Gilbert.

The centaurical tensions here are equally complicated. It is not, in the case of *Secrets and Lies,* simply that Hortense is Cynthia's child; the centaur needs to be more narrowly defined than the pairing of a woman and a person who used to be in the woman's womb. Cynthia is specifically denying, at the start of this scene, that there was ever a centaurical connection between them. Even as Cynthia eventually recalls, over the course of the shot, the event that made Hortense, the mother refuses to share that information with her daughter, and even at the end of the film—when all the secrets seem to get disclosed and all the lies corrected—the one thing we never discover is the identity of Hortense's father or the story of her conception. If Hortense and Cynthia are separate beings that have been brought into collision by this moment, then the shot from *Topsy-Turvy* shows us two symbiotic beings on the verge of splitting apart. "Gilbert and Sullivan" is itself a centaurical formulation, and the visual rhyme between these unbroken, side-by-side, centaur shots applies not only to the issue of the contested script. Just as Hortense, by her profession, is connected to the world of the eye, so Gilbert, by his vocation as theater director and creator of visual spectacle, is connected to the world of the eye; just as Cynthia, by her logorrhea and distinctive plaintive voice, is connected to the world of the ear, so Sullivan, by his vocation as composer, is connected to the world of the ear. Hortense, through her reserved demeanor and vocational training, exemplifies the art of precision, as does Gilbert, through his microscopic attention to the details of his plays' staging, verbal rhythms, and performance; Cynthia, through her impetuous behavior and emotional fragility, exemplifies the art of uncertainty, as does Sullivan, through his belief in the mysteries of inspiration and his sudden refusal to fulfill his contract. Precision and uncertainty, the combustible elements that Leigh employs to make his films, are exhibited here as the subjects *of* his films.

| | |

How do the narrative and the stylistic come together? We can ask this question of *The Short and Curlies,* which, like *The Five-Minute Films,* offers a turning point in Leigh's career. *The Short and Curlies* represented his route back to the big screen after a decade and a half in television. Made in 1987, it was financed by Film Four as a kind of hors d'oeuvre for *High Hopes,* Leigh's first theatrical release in seventeen years. Just as that earlier series of shorts demonstrated the range of ideas and spaces (and games) that he wanted to pursue, this later short film allows us to see the simultaneous jostling of "realist," or observational, elements that have always defined Leigh's work with the conceptual Leigh, the problem-poser, the artificer trying out another combination of tricks.

As I have said, *The Short and Curlies* appears to be a trivial soufflé. (The film is available as an extra on the Criterion DVD of *Naked.*) The story, which unfolds over eighteen minutes, is a four-hander that follows two couples. The first couple consists of the terse, ironically named Joy (Sylvestra Le Touzel), who toils as a sales assistant in a pharmacy, and the gangly, talkative Clive (David Thewlis), who begins the film by chatting Joy up. Clive gradually wears down her defenses over a series of encounters at work, pub, and home; by the end of the film, they are on the brink of marriage. The second couple consists not of two people courting but of two people who already live together—a dithery middle-aged mother, Betty (Alison Steadman), who cuts hair for a living, and her sullen adult daughter, Charlene (Wendy Nottingham). The two couples first intersect when Joy visits Betty at her salon, in what becomes a series of visits to get her hair washed, shaped, dyed, and modeled—like an embedded version of the *Five-Minute Films,* a theme with variations on the subject of hair, central to the main narrative but also indulged for its own sake, as an incomplete and playful taxonomy. We get glimpses of Betty and Charlene's awkward home life, which fails either to improve or worsen, while Joy and Clive's relationship progresses nicely (with one significant dip in the middle).

This is another of Leigh's experiments in storytelling: alongside the oldest tale in the world (boy meets girl), with all the traditional notes of tension, expectation, anxiety, and fulfillment, we have the meandering situation of mother and daughter, where a great deal is unspoken, or at least unexplained. This contrasting pair of pairs in some way resembles the first two of the *Five-Minute Films*, as the Joy/Clive story moves inexorably along a familiar plotline from first encounter to wedding day, while the Betty/Charlene story seems to have no plot at all. That is, until the end, when the final scene unexpectedly reveals a significantly pregnant Charlene—who, in her conversations with Betty, has disavowed any interest in going out on the town or in having a boyfriend—walking slowly to Betty's shop and sitting glumly in the salon while Betty does Joy's hair in advance of her big event.

We will return to the perplexing peripeteia of the Charlene story. For now, let us consider the body ailments and dirty jokes. The central engine of the film, even more than matters of plot and character, is the delightful conceit of people talking at cross-purposes; indeed, it is difficult to discuss "dialogue" as such in *The Short and Curlies*, because words are deployed not from any genuine desire to communicate but rather from the compulsion to articulate, almost autistically, an obsessive frame of mind. Joy cannot stop talking about remedies for, or failures of, the human body, and she exhibits an expert's familiarity with over-the-counter solutions to the nagging trivial somatic breakdowns of everyday life. She shares this fixation with Betty, and between them they invoke such topics as vaginal dryness, diarrhea, unexplained itches, mouth ulcers, constipation, blisters, varicose veins, the flu, menstrual complaints, vomiting, and skin blemishes—in addition to "a gorgeous cat dying dead in the road" with all its innards on display, a sight that makes Betty "queasy." The film begins with Clive entering the pharmacy to request "something for a sore throat," and that is in many ways the first and last time that he and Joy speak the same language. Clive's preferred mode of discourse is not the body but the mind—the province of language, and specifically jokes. When Joy, in her perpetually taciturn manner, suggests "a pastille," he seizes the opportunity for his first pun and asks, "Do you have any crayons?" She stares blankly, almost accusingly, at this attempt at humor, thereby initiating a pattern of lovemaking that will define the course of their relationship. This shared noncommunication is on display most beautifully on their first date, when she laconically comments on current and prospective physiological problems while he lobs in such discontinuous remarks as, "I was on the telly last night; I'll sleep anywhere when I've had a few drinks," and, "Two peanuts were walking down the road; one was assaulted." Here Leigh crashes the real and the artificial, the mimetic and the implausible, into one another. There is, on the one hand, nothing implausible about the monomania of each character; on the other hand, each evinces the kind of single, limiting tic that we would expect from one of Dickens's minor characters. We are neither in the sphere of documentary nor in the sphere of the absurd; we are at the deliberately uneasy intersection of the two.

That issue of minor characters needs to be emphasized. Their minorness is not simply a function of the brevity of the film but of the characters' behavioral styles. We will see characters such as Sandra in *Naked* and the estate manager in *Meantime,* whose eccentric and immediately defining ways of speaking or talking or moving mark them out as comic, supporting players. These characters manifest Leigh's interest and background in cartooning and caricature, again not unlike that most renowned of British narrative caricaturists, Charles Dickens. But the supporting players in those other films always play off some core "realist" characters, whose behaviors may be idiosyncratic without being what we might call flat.[4] At times, Leigh taxes our willingness to accede to the putative realism of those core characters, as in the case of Cynthia in *Secrets and Lies,* or Phil in *All or Nothing*; despite behavioral patterns that verge on caricature, that suggest minority, each of these characters clearly operates at the center of a story. Their considerable screen time grants them the status of major characters within the shape of the narrative (with the implicit understanding, in Leigh's cinema, that other characters could just as easily be worthy of that status, as we will see with the portrait sitters or cab fares or abortion clients). And gradually, the respective plots of *Secrets and Lies* and *All or Nothing* transport Cynthia and Phil fully from minority to majority. This is not because they are more "important" to the world of the film at the end than they were at the start, but because their comic, in some ways artificial, behavior gets smoothed out, integrated into what we might deem a plausible style; so Cynthia's seemingly permanent hysteria diminishes, and Phil's monosyllabic inwardness begins to thaw. This process, which we might call normalizing, is not a way of describing these characters that Leigh would particularly like, since he has always insisted that all his characters are real, even those that might be considered to live at the very cusp of viability, like Aubrey in *Life is Sweet,* the Boothe-Braines in *High Hopes,* or Jeremy/Sebastian in *Naked.*

My point is not that one couldn't find a Cynthia or a Phil or a Sandra or a Wayne in "the real world" but rather that, by the behavioral codes of "realist" narrative, and certainly by the behavioral codes of central characters compared with these "artificial" characters, the likes of Cynthia and Phil and Sandra and Wayne give the *appearance* of being artificial. This is the exit strategy from the seemingly landlocked debate about Leigh's characters—the debate that pits those who insist on the fundamental reality of all the people in his world against those who complain that these one-dimensional characters represent a failure. And this exit strategy is central to my initial claim that Leigh is a practicing theorist; in this case, he is asking how we make epistemological transactions between characters who are real in the real world and characters who are real within certain conventions of realism. The films interrogate the tension between minor and major not simply through chains of barely glimpsed worlds (the portrait sitters in *Secrets and Lies*) but through ranges of behavior that call into question how and why we construct for ourselves definitions of what a "true" or "believable" character, or person, might be. Once more, the artificial and the real bump into each other, like Gilbert and Sullivan sitting on a couch, discussing their next story.

Let us return to this issue in the context of *The Short and Curlies.* What is even more noteworthy than this narrative composed exclusively of minor characters is that two of those characters, Joy and Clive, seem to transcend the boundaries of caricature at one point, only to return within those boundaries. We see the couple in bed, after their first sexual experience, lying quietly and uncomfortably next to one other. Joy worries that she "might have put the cap in upside down," and Clive, irked, replies that he was wearing a condom. The idea that a young man might turn off the charm once he's made a conquest is hardly a new one, but it is startling to see the perpetually cheery and joking Clive-caricature suddenly turn into just another self-obsessed male—that is, someone from the territory of real life (again, as determined by fictional conventions of what caricature and real life look like). He gets up from the bed and, out of frame, casually tosses a shirt toward Joy, so that it lands on her face. This unexpectedly cruel act of dismissal not only alters our perception of Clive; it alters our perception of Joy. It is not so much that she behaves differently here. Rather, it is that now we have a reason to feel sorry for her, when we have not quite felt for her at all, in the way that we tend to feel for "real" characters; and that feeling carries on in the next two scenes, when we see her engage in the time-honored, and therefore "real," rituals of washing that man out of her hair (by rinsing her dye job at the salon) and eating comfort food alone at home. This might look like the smoothing-out I have described with Cynthia and Phil, the alignment of figures of artifice with the world of reality.

But then Clive reappears, bringing apologetic flowers while Joy is getting yet another haircut, and their last scene together is a minute-long unbroken shot of the two them at either end of a couch: the iconic Leigh position. Clive is back to cracking silly jokes, and Joy is back to vaguely tolerating, and secretly enjoying, them. Clive and Joy have gone from minor to major to minor, from "artificial" to "real" to "artificial," breaking all kinds of rules about storytelling and verisimilitude along the way. This marriage not only of two people but of two apparently antithetical aesthetic practices offers an uneasy synthesis of the side-by-side and the centaur—of the figure of the adjacent and the figure of the commingled. Side-by-sides have dominated the film, starting from the "and" in the title that connects "short" with "curlies," an anticipation of many of Leigh's recent films, whose titles suggest the side-by-side or centaur in some way: secrets *and* lies, the centaurical career girls, topsy colliding with turvy, all *or* nothing, and most provocatively, *Vera Drake,* a centaurical examination of first and last names. From the opening credits of *The Short and Curlies* (where the screen is split between a garishly colored left half and a black right half), to the initial shot of a concrete pillar dividing a parking lot, to the semi-detached house where Joy lives, to the many shots framing two people at either side of the image, we get juxtapositions without reconciliation, or with only the illusion of reconciliation. Marriage, that oldest comic reconciliation, is represented here in the persons of Clive and Joy, and the conventional closure might look like the victory of the artificial over the real, or the structural over the likely. But this particular marriage more closely imitates life than a realist, or unresolved, resolution might; Clive and Joy each return to an autistic version of the self, thereby discrediting the universal fiction of two people commingling identities in a shared existence.

But I have left out a character, perhaps the most important character in the film. If we know Joy by her obsession with medications, if we know Betty by her obsession with sex and physical decay, if we know Clive by his obsession with jokes, how do we know Charlene? We could say that Betty and Clive are the chatty ones, and Joy and Charlene are the quiet ones. But that pairing breaks down, because Joy's relative economy of language finds a recurring, recognizable idiom, while Charlene says very little at all; she utters a total of forty-one words in the film, and those words largely amount to "Yeah," "No," and "I'm all right." That opacity alone distinguishes her, and her glum face suggests an interiority (a "realness") that the other characters seem, with their minor-character limitations, to lack. (That interiority becomes literalized at the end of the movie when her interior, namely her womb, swells and shows itself in a way distinct from the absent interior of the other characters.) She is so withdrawn from the life around her that she almost seems to belong to a different narrative altogether, as if she were an alien being merely visiting this world of three obsessives. Her status as metacharacter, for most of the film, is underscored in *The Short and Curlies'* most full-fledged two-character side-by-side, at least by my strictest definition: two characters oriented toward the camera, engaged in conversation, facing in parallel directions, and therefore not facing each other. Charlene and Betty are watching a movie on television; Betty, who has been ogling and commenting on the two lead actors in the film (which we can hear but not see), exclaims, "Ooh, I could go for a man like that," and she asks Charlene for her preference. Asked to choose between two actors put on display—that is, put into side-by-side comparison—Charlene replies, "Neither of them." The fact that a character, herself displayed in a side-by-side frame, should refuse to choose one compared character over another, during a rare moment when a filmed narrative appears within a Mike Leigh filmed narrative—well, this is as close to self-reflexivity as we're going to get. (Not to mention the fact that Betty—who, unlike her daughter, is sitting in the dark—chooses "the dark one.")

And why does this matter? Leigh, during one of my discussions with him, made quite clear where he stands on this issue: "[My films] are not a catalogue of references; they are not decodable, enigmatic cuneiform of any kind. They are simply what they are, to be understood in terms of the human experience." So much for the arid postmodern joke, as such.

But this is not a postmodern joke; or, rather, it is a postmodern joke that is alive with meaning because it is placed in the context of a film that is otherwise in no way postmodern. Charlene as a character is part of and outside the world of this film, someone who, as a created fiction, means and does things that are different from the things the created fictions around her mean and do. We need to rethink Mike Leigh's realism to allow space for what Michael Fried calls the features of the representation that ought to be perceived as curious or problematic, features that have been "made invisible" by our disinclination to look for them. In *Vera Drake*, Detective Inspector Webster asks, "It's a bit of a coincidence, isn't it?" in the wake of a crucial moment of coincidence. That invocation of coincidence is not coincidental. Leigh's films are aware of themselves as art, and not only as life.

Charlene's exceptionality becomes realized in the final scene, when, without warning or explanation, she turns up pregnant. To some degree this fits her into a line of mysteriously pregnant women in Leigh's cinema, from *Hard Labour* through *Secrets and Lies* and beyond. But in each of those other cases, the pregnancy is a problem: to be gotten rid of, to be pursued to its end, to be debated and queried. We may never find out who Hortense Cumberbatch's father is, but the entire film rotates around one woman's desire to discover the identity of her father and another woman's desire to hide his identity. In Charlene's case, she simply is pregnant, and no one makes the slightest allusion to her biological condition—deeply ironic, given the fact that the two other people in the final scene cannot stop talking about biological conditions. Betty and Joy discuss the details of the wedding and the bride-to-be's hair, and Betty obliviously asks her daughter, who by all indications is not a bride-to-be, "Won't she look gorgeous, Charlene?" After Betty inquires whether there will be a professional photographer (an intimation of Maurice in *Secrets and Lies*), the momentarily voluble Joy mentions that she is quite nervous about the impending event and that she didn't want to eat anything that morning, for fear she might be sick. Betty, again completely insensitive to her audience, mentions that she vomited on the morning of her wedding, because "I was carrying Charlene at the time." Betty only acknowledges her daughter to request that she sit properly in the seat. Charlene announces that she's going home and then leaves, as Betty and Joy head to a back room to proceed with the

Figure 4. Character and context: three women in a room, in *The Short and Curlies*.

ministrations, chattering about roots, and a "spot" that Joy feels is on the way, which they decide can be disguised by makeup.

This summary of the facts of the scene demonstrates just how much is lost when we talk about people and events in Mike Leigh's films, to the exclusion of characters, shots, and sounds, since the cinematic composition of this denouement complicates what is already a subtly complex scene of familial discord. Leigh narrates the scene with typical economy, using only three shots. The first and third shots are long shots, framed from the back of the salon, the space into which Betty and Joy disappear at the end. The main room of the salon is a not-very-wide corridor, typical of the many shops to be found in the terraced architecture of High Streets in Britain. This is the fifth time over the course of the film that we have been in this salon, but only now are we made aware of its confining, rectangular shape—all the earlier views have been medium shots or close-ups, which gave us little sense of the room as a whole. We are at last getting the resonance of this space, of how it orients and affects its inhabitants.

Leigh has said that he and his cinematographer often ask each other, as they frame a shot, "Is this a man in a room, or is this a room with a man in it?" (Leigh, *Naked,* xxviii). In other words, they consider the tension between character and context, or, in pictorial terms, between picture and ground. These closing images of the salon give the impression of a room with a man in it, or rather (quite importantly) a room with three women in it, rather than three women in a room. We might say, to use the language of continuity editing, that Leigh is only now deploying the establishing shot of the interior of the salon—rather tardily, at the end of the film, after the salon has already been established as an important space for action and dialogue. One effect of this reversal of continuity convention is to accentuate the issue of context, and therefore to underscore yet again Betty's inability to perceive the contextual connection between Charlene and Joy, whom we see together here for the first time; Betty treats her daughter like an annoying customer and her customer like a beloved daughter. Another effect is to emphasize not only the room or the general context but verticality itself, as the narrow trajectory of the salon creates the impression of an alleyway—a verticality that works against the horizontal frame of cinema. The alleyway, either literal or figurative, is a crucial visual motif for Leigh, especially as the opening shot in several features he made after *The Short and Curlies* (most notably *High Hopes, Naked,* and *All or Nothing*) as well as one he made before (*Four Days in July*). This fondness for the narrow vertical, which Leigh discusses in this book's interview as a format he has wanted to adopt for the entire length of a film, illustrates that the cinematic frame is itself a centaur, vertical and horizontal at the same time—a dissonance even more apparent as Leigh was returning to the theatrical screen in 1988.

The three women are visible in the vertical shot, but even the closest and tallest, Betty, is easily contained within the frame—in other words, we are not allowed access to the details of expression and presumed interiority that a close-up or even medium shot affords. When we cut from the first narrow shot, at the moment that Betty asks, "Won't she look gorgeous, Charlene?" we go to a close-up of Charlene's unhappy face, as she replies, "Yeah," with an utter lack of enthusiasm. This close-up holds for forty-five seconds, as Joy and Betty natter on about nervousness and feeling sick and the virtues of conditioner; Charlene's only contribution is the announcement "I'm gonna go home"—an announcement that

Betty barely registers. The shot's only visible onscreen "action," if we can call it that, occurs toward its end, when Charlene's eyes follow Joy and Betty as they walk to the hair-washing room, which remains invisible throughout the scene. What begins as a straightforward close-up gradually turns into an unbroken shot, the camera holding on Charlene even as the traditionally important stuff—physical movement and dialogue, the sights and sounds of narrative cinema—takes place offscreen.

Why do we continue to look at Charlene, who has been the cipher in this quartet? That is a question with many answers, none complete. One answer is that the close-up allows Leigh to jostle our preconceptions of minor and major characters, since this minor character, as defined by her lack of screen time in the film, is accorded the role of a major character—that is, someone who gets the last, lingering close-up in the story. Another answer, or at least side effect, is that this moment accentuates the split between sight and sound, since we get no visual referent for 95 percent of the auditory information of the shot; this is the second time this split has been associated with Charlene, since the

Figure 5. Between major and minor,
between sight and sound: Charlene
in *The Short and Curlies.*

same sundering occurs in the TV-watching scene (where we hear but don't see what the characters hear and see). I will pursue that split between sight and sound more fully when we get to *Topsy-Turvy,* a film whose central agon is the split between sight and sound. A third answer, or consequence, is the dramatic emphasis on a woman who is becoming more and more horizontal (due to her delicate state), sandwiched between two shots that accentuate the vertical, further elaborating the degree of theoretical abstraction in a film that we presumed earlier to be just a soufflé based on body ailments and dirty jokes.

A fourth answer, or consequence, is that we are made to contemplate the face of a real-life centaur, a pregnant woman, and all the centaurical implications of the scene. There is so much of Charlene here, more of her physically than there has ever been in the film, and yet so little of her at the same time: we have access to her body, but not her mind. We may not have thought we needed access to Charlene's mind, since she seemed a bit player, merely a straight woman to Betty's comic monologues of corporeal unease. Now we care, because a plot event—the conception of her child—is the kind of thing, as our experience in consuming fictions tells us, that we are supposed to care about. So we want to know what's going on "in there"; and we get the textbook shot for finding out what's going on "in there," the close-up. But that close-up tells us nothing either about the plot event (where, why, and with whom it happened) or about the character connected to that plot; we glimpse only that Charlene is unhappy with Betty, the other half of her assigned pair, but she has been manifestly unhappy with Betty all along. This shot is in so many ways a shot of absence more than a shot of presence, and indeed we might think of Leigh's cinema in general as a cinema of absence—not through an asceticism or distance (as with, say, Ingmar Bergman and Michelangelo Antonioni) but in the way that psychological or narrative information is so often withdrawn at critical moments, in the way that things are not done, either by the characters in the film or the makers of the film. It is clear that Charlene has done something significant—she has gotten pregnant—but it is also clear, from her advanced state, that she has also not done, and will not do, something significant—she will not have an abortion. If a pregnant woman is a centaur of presence, then a woman who has had an abortion is a centaur of absence, two symbiotic beings that have been split apart. That is a brutal way of putting it, but Leigh's cinema (most obviously in *Vera Drake*) is brutal in its illustration that being pregnant and having an abortion are both messes, and that to be a person, or to become a person, or not to become a person is to be a mess. That may look like a realist bromide: "Life is messy." But for Leigh every mess is different.

Possibility is presence and absence coexisting. The third and final shot of this scene, the one whose composition repeats that of the first shot of the scene, shows Joy disappearing, in the foreground, to have her hair done for the last time before her wedding, and then Charlene disappearing, in the background, through the door and out into the street. It is a shot of two women absenting themselves, a shot that lingers on an "empty" frame of the depopulated main room of the salon, as we hear Betty and Joy resuming their infinite chitchat off-camera, one more schism between image and sound. We get not resolution but possibilities: the possibility of the marriage of Clive and Joy, and the possibility of Charlene's child, two events that remain in the realm of possibility for us because they are not narrated. This nonconclusion illustrates just how important pregnancy is in Leigh's cinematic vocabulary, and especially pregnancy in the absence of parturition. Pregnant women in Leigh's films are always actual pregnant women, complex characters firmly situated in time and place, living in a world of consequences; but they are also representations and speculations. They are simultaneously real and abstract, just as all his films are simultaneously real and abstract, simultaneously mimetic and conceptual. The lexicon I have identified, of side-by-sides and unbroken shots and centaurs, will allow us to see how the real and the abstract converse with each other at the level of form and content, of the actual and imagined.

Biography and Career Outline

Mike Leigh was born in 1943 in Salford, a borough of Greater Manchester.[5] He was the son and elder child of middle-class Jews who lived in a working-class area; his paternal grandfather, Mayer Liebermann, was a Russian immigrant who set up shop in England as a portrait miniaturist, framing and applying color to old family photographs. (This fact alone illustrates Leigh's long connection with the pictorial and not only the imitative.) Leigh's father, who Anglicized the family name in 1939, was a doctor, and Leigh's mother was a midwife—a shared vocation that the director underscored as part of his biography in the closing credits of *Vera Drake*. As a child, he developed talents in cartooning and drama; those artistic successes culminated in his winning a scholarship to the Royal Academy of Dramatic Arts (RADA). To take up the scholarship, he moved in 1960 to London, which has been his home ever since. As a student, Leigh chafed at what he deemed RADA's hidebound methods of training; after leaving RADA without a diploma, he spent the next few years pursuing his craft on his own, as well as enrolling in courses at Camberwell Art School and what is now the London International Film School. Influenced in mood by the work of Samuel Beckett and Harold Pinter and in practice by the experimental spirit of the sixties, he began to create, with actors, a series of plays that evolved completely from scratch. Some of these early experiments were more conceptual in nature than might be assumed—one uncompleted project imagined an island populated by fourteen girls named Doreen (Clements, *Improvised,* 13). In 1970, Leigh received financial backing, largely from Albert Finney's Memorial Films, to adapt *Bleak Moments*, his play at the Open Space, into his first movie. *Bleak Moments* was released in 1971 to fine reviews, including the announcement, from a young Roger Ebert, that Leigh's debut was "a masterpiece, plain and simple" (Coveney 87). The economic and cultural climate of British cinema in the 1970s, however, meant that, to Leigh's great frustration, he would not get the chance to make another theatrical film for seventeen years. During that interregnum, he told stories for the stage and for television.

Between 1965 and 1993, Leigh wrote and directed twenty-five original plays, including two short plays for television and one radio play; from 1993 to 2010, he stopped working regularly for the stage. (He made a return in the fall of 2005 with *Two Thousand Years*—the first story he has told that puts the Jewish experience in Britain front and center, and his first production for the National Theatre.) In 1971, Leigh met the actress Alison Steadman, who has since appeared in many of his films and plays; they married in 1973, had two sons, and split up in 1996. Between 1973 and 1985, Leigh made eight full-length films and five short films for television, all but one for the BBC, and all of which bore the authorial signature "devised and directed by Mike Leigh"; during this period, his film work was little known outside of Britain. Since his return to the movie theater in 1988, with *High Hopes,* Leigh's career has much more closely resembled that of a major European auteur, especially in the wake of the two major awards that *Naked* garnered at the Cannes Film Festival in 1993—a coup that earned him an Order of the British Empire. He is one of only eleven directors, and one of only four living directors, to have won both the Palme d'Or at Cannes (for *Secrets and Lies*) and the Golden Lion at Venice (for *Vera Drake*). That all-time list includes such names as Luis Buñuel, Akira Kurosawa, Luchino Visconti, and Michelangelo Antonioni. Mike Leigh and Robert Altman are the only English-language directors to have pulled off the double.

That highly compressed overview shows just how many stories Leigh has told in his life; it is impossible to discuss all nineteen of his feature-length films (let alone the plays) within one tidy monograph. Given this unenviable situation, I have chosen to emphasize the last two decades of his career.[6] The most obvious reason for this emphasis is that the films he has made since 1993, starting with *Naked,* dominate the cultural conversation about Leigh; given that this conversation needs to be completely reexamined, it is appropriate to concentrate on the more recent projects. Leigh himself is ambivalent about how to discuss his serpentine career, insisting that there are important continuities over his forty years of filmmaking, in terms of process, aims, and commitment to context, alongside important discontinuities, in terms of scope, audience, and cinematic sophistication. An earlier, much longer version of this essay included a section on his first two films, *Bleak Moments* (1971) and *Hard Labour* (1973), which illustrate Leigh's early exploration of film language, of the relationship between sight and sound, and of centaur figures such as the pregnant woman. Even more difficult to excise was a section on *High Hopes* (1988) and *Life Is Sweet* (1990), the first movies to gain Leigh a significant audience outside the United Kingdom; *High Hopes,* the first Mike Leigh film I ever saw, is a particular favorite of mine. The first eleven feature films of his career will be represented, in the following pages, primarily by *Meantime* and *Four Days in July*—films whose images, ideas, and themes not only crystallize the experiments of his early work but also lay out critical questions of character and plot and offer important instances of the side-by-side, the unbroken shot, and the centaur. Many of the other nine films made prior to *Naked* make cameo appearances throughout the essay; I urge my readers to seek them out to discover the full breadth and depth of this director's work.

Character and Plot:
Meantime and *Four Days in July*

Meantime (1983) and *Four Days in July* (1985) are, more explicitly than many Mike Leigh films, "about" something. *Meantime* is "about" unemployment; *Four Days in July* is "about" Northern Ireland. One might think that *Secrets and Lies* is "about" adoption, or that *Vera Drake* is "about" abortion. But adoption and abortion in the two later films are narrative discoveries rather than narrative premises. Unemployment and Northern Ireland, in the two earlier films, are not discoveries but inescapable atmospheric conditions about which everyone in each of these two films is thinking, and about which we are asked to think from the beginning—not least because the titles announce the central problems of the films.

Meantime and *Four Days* can also be said to be about two other things. *Meantime* is about character, and *Four Days* is about plot. We have seen that pairing before, in reverse order, in *The Five Minute Films*; *The Birth of the Goalie of the 2001 F.A. Cup Final* is about plot, and *Old Chums* is about character. The schism between character and plot, at later points in Leigh's career, operates not between films but within a film: in *Vera Drake,* where the heroine goes from being an individuated character in the first half to an element within a plot in the second half, and in *Topsy-Turvy,* whose two central characters personify the divide, as Sullivan cares about character (human emotion and probability, in his phrase) and Gilbert cares about plot ("the world of topsy-turvydom"). The central tension within *Topsy-Turvy* demonstrates one of the many ways in which that film, far from being "a Mike Leigh film" or "not a Mike Leigh film," as has been contested, may very well be *the* Mike Leigh film: a centaur film, split into character and plot, where the side-by-side and the unbroken shot lead us back through the history of side-by-sides and unbroken shots. Indeed, *Topsy-Turvy* and *Four Days in July*, both of which present Leigh far removed from home territory—a Victorian period piece, and his only film set outside of England—share a number of features. They alone among Leigh's films both begin and end with a long take. Furthermore, the first shot in each case depicts a grid of horizontal and vertical vectors, announcing the film's subject as the stage management of a theater; in the case of *Four Days* a theater of war, and in the case of *Topsy-Turvy* a theater of play. And the final shot in each case is a tour de force that foregrounds women, or a woman, caught in an act of comparison, engaged in a complex and perhaps irresolvable side-by-side.

To return to the pair at hand, let me clarify what "about" means, particularly in terms of character and plot. I mean that the subject matter of *Meantime* and *Four Days* involves not only the people and events of each film but also the ontological conditions, respectively, of character and plot. Plot is in some ways the crucial element of both *Meantime* and *Four Days*, since the characters' difficulties in each case arise from either an absence or surfeit of plot; each film posits an extreme narrative situation—characters in search of a plot, characters overwhelmed by plot—in which the story of the film unfolds. Unlike, say, Jean-Luc Godard's *Weekend* (1967)—a film that moves dialectically between diegesis and theory—*Meantime* and *Four Days* stay within a realist framework of people and events. They are plainly "Mike Leigh films" in the patience of their pace and in the way that the characters sit around discussing their daily lives. The films are theoretical in the way that they consider how character and plot, as constructs, govern our lives; they are not about character revelation or plot turn. Indeed, a great many of the characters in *Meantime* remain distant from us as characters; we don't get "inside" them, the way we might get inside characters in a Henry James novel. And there is hardly any more plot, in a conventional sense, in *Four Days* than there is *Meantime*; we don't experience plot as the motor of a machine, the way we do in an Agatha Christie novel. *Meantime* is about the condition of being in a world without plot, especially if we think of plot as the forces that shape us, and that are shaped by us in turn—if we think of society as a narrative. The society of *Meantime* is stripped bare of narrative shape and direction. By contrast, *Four Days in July* is about the condition of being in a world where plot dominates every aspect of life, where a master narrative shapes society and all its members; again, it is not that individual lives experience plot twists but that all these lives are deeply emplotted. The world of *Four Days* rests on two interrelated emplotting schemes, war and religion, both of which rely on master narratives to sustain themselves. *Meantime* is about a crisis occasioned by the absence of storytelling, and about living outside of history; *Four Days* is about a crisis occasioned by an addiction to storytelling, and about history swallowing you up whole.

| | |

Meantime focuses on a family paralyzed by unemployment amidst Britain's worst economic slump since World War II. This family is the Pollocks: the ineffectual father, Frank (Jeff Robert); the sour mother, Mavis (Pam Ferris); the smart but embittered elder son, Mark (Phil Daniels); and the apparently vacant younger son, Colin (Tim Roth). The Pollocks, who live together in a flat on a large housing estate, are adrift, not only without jobs but without even the illusion that jobs will ever exist for them again. *Meantime* is the closest that Leigh has come to the drama-less drama of Samuel Beckett and the continuous and unfulfilled waiting that is the subject of Beckett's most famous play. Other Leigh films also operate with only the smallest shards of story; but even the desiccated world of his first feature, *Bleak Moments* (1971), offers the illusion of a romantic relationship as a way of maintaining our investment in the "arc" of the characters (to use the conventional language of scriptwriting). In *Meantime* there are no love stories and not even the kind of work stories that animate Leigh's second feature, *Hard Labour* (1973); instead, we get the plotlessness of unemployment, the blunted narrative momentum of lives bereft of the rhythms of activity, rest, promotion, demotion, possibility, and surprise. The only potential drama involves Colin, who is hired by his aunt Barbara (Marion Bailey) to do some decorating work at her house; after getting lost on the way to his assignment, he discovers that Mark (who thinks Colin is being exploited) has reached the aunt's house before him, and he leaves when no one is watching. Barbara and her prim husband John (Alfred Molina) represent another in a series of financially successful but childless couples (such as Edward and Veronica in *Hard Labour* and the Butchers in *Grown-Ups*) that are contrasted with a central, childbearing couple. The crucial and groundbreaking variation here comes from the fact that parallel families are connected by siblings (Mavis and Barbara), a pattern that will inflect the narrative structure of future films like *High Hopes, Secrets and Lies, Vera Drake*, and, more obliquely, *Happy-Go-Lucky*. The parallel-siblings scenario forces the audience to consider two people raised with identical backgrounds of class, geography, and religion—the defining categories of British society—and who therefore have no external reasons for being different. We must tap into the characters, the individuals, to start to piece together who and why they are, rather than relying on systems of society to explain their actions and motivations.

The other principals in *Meantime* are the aimless skinhead Coxy (Gary Oldman), whose bravado impresses no one but Colin, and the shy Hayley (Tilly Vosburgh), on whom Colin has an unrequited crush. Coxy's last moment in the film shows him rolling around in a metal trash can, banging away at the inside, while Colin walks by, after the humiliation of his nonjob at his aunt's—a portrait of two men doing nothing, all day, every day, in the darkest moment of Margaret Thatcher's economic revolution. The title of the film resonates with the situation's motifs— the word "mean" suggesting the humble, or lower class, or miserly, or unimportant. But "meantime" chiefly denotes the yawning temporal blank into which the Pollocks and everyone around them has fallen. "Meantime" indicates a period between recognizable points, between beginning and end; in this film, what might be a brief interruption has turned into the full suspension of past and future; these characters live in a perpetual present, a plotless vacuum divorced from before and after.

Four Days in July, Leigh's last television film, is set and filmed entirely in Belfast, and it also operates through two parallel couples. The tart, intelligent Collette (Bríd Brennan) and the laconic, amiable Eugene (Des McAleer) are Catholic, and they are about to become parents. The reserved, slightly awkward Lorraine (Paula Hamilton) and the laconic, combative Billy (Charles Lawson) are Protestant, and they too are about to become parents. But in terms of narrative structure, Leigh's parallel stories here work quite differently from the way they do in *Meantime.* The Catholic couple and the Protestant couple do not intersect as a result of family connection, neighborhood proximity, or work environment. In fact, Collette and Eugene and Lorraine and Billy do not meet until the very end of the film—even though the film has juxtaposed them all along. If *Meantime* initiated the parallel-sibling model that would prove a persistent Mike Leigh trope, *Four Days* enacts parallel by fiat. That is, the movie goes back and forth between these couples only because the filmmaker has selected them as the subjects of his drama—there is no "organic" reason, nothing internal to the world of the characters of the film, that justifies their being united in a story. "It's all up to the man upstairs," a friend of Collette's announces, as they discuss her due date. In this situation, the man upstairs is Mike Leigh. No film of his had so plainly shown the hand of God, the maker and artificer wielding the mechanics of plot. Collette and Eugene and Lorraine and Billy are linked not because of who they are, as distinct human beings with distinct behavioral patterns and distinct activities. Rather, they are linked because of the categories to which they belong—Catholic or Protestant, or pregnant. If the parallel-sibling model of *Meantime* foregrounds individual character by exploring how people of similar backgrounds turn out to be different from each other, then the parallel by fiat of *Four Days* threatens to make the characters' individuality irrelevant. Leigh has joked that *Four Days* is his only "foreign language" film (Coveney 176), and indeed the film's syntax is radically different from that of its predecessors. But the deterministic plotting, which may look like a contrivance, is in fact organic, "true" to its context—because Belfast in 1985 was the most deterministically plotted place in Britain.

If the London of *Meantime* is plotless, the Belfast of *Four Days* has more plot than anyone could want. By unwritten rule, all films made and set in Northern Ireland during the 1970s and 1980s used the "troubles" as their dramatic engine; to set a film in Northern Ireland in this period was to immediately invoke a history, a geography, a context of constantly looming confrontation—all the constitutive elements of plot. This is Mike Leigh's war movie: Belfast was essentially run by martial law in 1985, and it was heavily policed by the Ulster Defence Regiment (UDR), in which Billy is an officer. And Leigh could have not have chosen any days more volatile than July 10, 11, 12, and 13, the culminating dates of what is known as the "marching season," when Protestants loyal to the crown march through various neighborhoods to celebrate William of Orange's victory, in 1690, in the Battle of the Boyne. That conflict, symbolically as much as practically, signaled the Protestant ascendancy and the diminution of Catholic power in Ireland, particularly in Ulster, the northeastern quadrant of the island. The phenomenon of the parades, which the film shows us in bits and pieces, further emphasizes *Four Days'* hypertrophy of plot or the communal at the expense of character or the individual, since parades advertise the social groups to which one belongs rather than idiosyncratic qualities of personal psychology and behavior. The parades' insistence on reinscribing a familiar story (the Battle of the Boyne) with familiar songs (such as "The Sash My Father Wore") makes history, event, and inheritance—all registers of plot—the focus of attention. Leigh further stokes the engine of plot possibilities by having July 13 fall on a Friday, thereby adding another aspect of plot—accident, or forces out of individual control—to the mix. If the family members in *Meantime* have too much time on their hands and nowhere to go, they also have no discernible external influences that shape their destinies. *Four Days in July*, by contrast, is in thrall to rigid predestination: Collette and Lorraine's babies are born on July 12, the day on which the Battle of the Boyne is celebrated, in the same hospital. This particularity of time, recognized as a set number of days, with a specific number of rituals, with a clear beginning and end, exactly reverses the vagueness of time advertised in the title of *Meantime*.

With all that, *Four Days in July* violates the strictures of Northern Ireland films, since most of its events amount to the quotidian and anecdotal. The narrative ignores the basic ingredients of the Northern Ireland cinematic genre: secret meetings, violent bloodshed, betrayal, and doomed romance.[7] Rather, *Four Days* is full of normal people doing normal things, like talking and walking and sleeping and drinking. Most of the film takes place on July 11, which Eugene and Collette spend sitting around the house. Brendan (Shane Connaughton), their friend and neighbor, comes over to fix the toilet; Dixie (Stephen Rea) stops by to clean the windows; he and Brendan trade stories and riddles. Eugene decides whether to have a ham sandwich or a cheese sandwich. Meanwhile, Billy and Lorraine attend one of the bonfires that traditionally accompany the eve of the twelfth, and he and his friends go home and discuss the antics of their youth. The biggest event of the eleventh involves Collette's attempt to bring a pram back to her house. It is precisely the juxtaposition of "Mike Leigh characters" doing "Mike Leigh things," in neighborhoods decorated with the icons of murderous tribalism, that makes *Four Days in July* such a peculiar project. The narrative design of *Four Days in July* is a centaur, composed out of two entirely different genetic patterns—the Mike Leigh movie and the Northern Ireland movie. And Northern Ireland is a centaur country, put together partly from Britain and partly from Ireland, a combustible collision of two different bodies. For that reason, among many others, it is entirely appropriate that Leigh should have brought his method and preoccupations to the province. We need to understand the supposed eccentrics and exceptions of Leigh's cinema, films like *Four Days in July* and *Topsy-Turvy,* as in fact its central texts, because their extreme conditions, their foreignness and incompatibilities, allow him to investigate the centaur in its natural habitat.

We will now move from overall structure to aesthetic details. The opening moves of both *Meantime* and *Four Days* articulate the issues I have been outlining by unsettling the relationship between space and experience. As *Meantime* fades in, we see a scribble of branches; the camera slowly pans left to follow a person in the distance, clad in red, who is jogging on the other side of a pond from the camera. This shot seems to fit the criteria of the unbroken shot, since the action (such as it is) unfolds slowly, more slowly than seems warranted by the information that the camera is recording. The follow-pan's insistence on the primacy of one object in the field of vision works in tension with the unbroken shot's typical neutrality. We then discover that we are in a large park, and the sense of disorientation becomes stronger when the red jogger, still in long shot, reaches a landing, where two indistinct people in light-colored clothes have gathered. The jogger runs past the landing, and the camera stops panning, thereby "losing" what has been its subject. The indistinct new people now appear to be the subject of the shot. As we wait, two people in dark-colored clothing, whom we had barely registered as background figures (the most minor of minor characters), join the two people in light-colored clothing. It turns out that the two people on the landing are Barbara and John, and the two people in dark clothing are their nephews, Mark and Colin Pollock. So the opening misdirection of the jogger, whom we never see again but whom we are tricked into considering the first character in the film, unsettles our perception of who "matters." Later in the film, we will return to a version of the green world, with glimpses of a canal and a grassy space; but these are further acts of misdirection, since *Meantime* is trapped in the gray world, grounded on a vast housing estate where people get lost, visually and socially. The final image of the opening shot is composed of two horizontal bars—that is, of the pond below and the trees above. The dominant horizontality emphasizes a broad panorama in which people disappear, their individualizing verticality barely discernible.

Four Days in July begins, by contrast, with a dominant verticality that chops the horizon into bits and pieces. We are looking down an alley, a perspective that funnels our view down to a point; the cross streets are no more than lines of perpendicular light. (This initial burrowing into the depth of the image will also inaugurate *Naked* and *All or Nothing*.) Closest to the camera is a group of three children, running and biking away from us; as they approach the first cross street, we see an adult on a bicycle, and then another, crossing the alley in the far distance. The children pause at the intersection for a few moments, and in this interval two dogs jog across from right to left. Despite the brick and pavement that tell us that we are in the city, the combination of children at play, the gentle rhythms of the bicycle, and dogs scampering suggests another version of *Meantime*'s opening green world, where people can

Figure 6. Vertical, horizontal, and the grid of emplotment at the start of *Four Days in July*.

imagine themselves outside the constricting instructions of civilization. That idyll is shattered by the most violent act we will see in *Four Days in July*. While the children wait, two armored trucks of the UDR cut down the closest cross street, slowly slicing their way through the vertical frame from left to right. The children do not register this as anything more than background activity, as we initially registered the figures that turned out to be Mark and Colin at the start of *Meantime*. Rather, they simply wait, and then continue their frolic down the alley; there is as yet no soundtrack music, so we lack the cues to tell us what to think about this. The unbroken shot lasts for forty seconds, as the children continue their jaunt down the alley and the two dogs wander back into the frame. Toward the end of the shot, once the children have moved deep into the space of the alley, we again see two UDR trucks, this time moving from right to left, slowly slicing across the next cross street down from the first; these may be the same two trucks, moving methodically through a small section of the verticals and horizontals of Belfast.

The implications of what we have just witnessed are fundamental to the subject matter of *Four Days in July*. Vertical framing is referred to as "portrait" for a reason—it emphasizes the standing human figure, allowing all the particulars of a person, the synthesis of the corporeal and the psychological, to govern what the frame is about. The horizontal orientation of the television and movie frame, or "landscape," diminishes the individual human figure, either by hacking it into bits and pieces (in a close-up or medium shot) or by making it only one informational element among several (as in the long shot that opens *Meantime*). We might translate this argument between vertical and horizontal as an emphasis on character as opposed to an emphasis on plot. The opening vertical of *Four Days,* aided by the figures of the three children, suggests that this film will make the individual human its center; but the forces of plot and plottedness—in the guise of those two trucks—immediately puncture that illusion. It turns out that we are looking not at the shape of portraiture but at the section of a grid. The second shot of the film confirms that reorientation, as we see two UDR trucks, in a wider shot, zigzag their way from one small street to another, at the same slow pace we saw earlier; the camera pans right to follow them down a longer street, and as the shot ends, the terraced houses connote a slight sense of the vertical. But the meanings of that vertical have changed radically. With two shots, Leigh has showed us the grid that is Belfast, a chessboard of spaces that is constantly monitored—an arena of emplottedness, governed by a rectilinear system that privileges territory over people. Are the two UDR trucks in the second shot the same two UDR trucks we saw in the first shot? There is no way of being certain, because these UDR trucks are designed to look exactly alike. The streets of Belfast are dehumanized by men in trucks, and the men in trucks are in turn dehumanized, subsumed into the anonymity of their plot devices, traversing and reinscribing a schematized space.

So Leigh begins both *Meantime* and *Four Days* with acts of misdirection, calculated to unsettle assumptions of character and plot. That misdirection continues in the very next sequence of *Four Days*, which follows the opening credits and the title informing us that it is Tuesday, July 10. Three members of the UDR, including Billy, pull over a ramshackle red van—standard procedure in a city where vehicles are routinely treated as potential agents of plot. The driver of the van turns out to be Mr. McCoy, a rabid Unionist who objects to being treated as a potential threat by the military force, since its members are, like him, "Ulster men." He launches into a tirade about politics and history, an ill-informed and unintentionally funny screed that roams from misconceptions about the settling of the province (whereby Fenian bastards, "those so-called Irishmen," are the latecomers) to the myth of the Irish language (that "Gaelic mumbo-jumbo") to the number of U.S. presidents that Ulster has produced. The next scene finds us back at the UDR base as the soldiers lie down on their beds, prefiguring the film's final scene in the maternity ward. Billy here delivers his own screed, complaining that "the Brits" in the regiment (the English imports) are like Americans in Vietnam, scared by the unfamiliar surroundings and unable to "tell one gook from another"; if the UDR were granted a forty-eight-hour news blackout, they could go in and root out all the problems. The long-term problem, as Billy sees it, lies in the Catholic injunction to "go forth and multiply," which inevitably means that there will be "more of them than us"; this pessimistic view of procreation manifestly opposes the throughline of the film—namely, Billy's pregnant wife Lorraine and her partner in plot, Collette. Billy concludes his complaint with the dark prediction that "they'll have a referendum across the water" that will "sell us down the river" and put them at the mercy of Catholic Nationalists.

In the first thirteen minutes of *Four Days in July,* then, we get massive amounts of speechifying and exposition. Leigh's films typically offer little in the way of establishing information, and their characters do not typically convey back-story information through dialogue. Indeed, Leigh films not only avoid this kind of material at the start, they also leave us in the dark by the end—as with the identity of Hortense Cumberbatch's father in *Secrets and Lies,* or the reasons for the rift between W. S. Gilbert and his mother in *Topsy-Turvy.* But the opening exposition in *Four Days in July* has nothing to do with character and everything to do with plot; not the particular plot circumstances of these specific people but the broader plot of Northern Ireland itself. McCoy, who hogs the initial screen time, will never reappear in *Four Days in July*; we might compare him with Wayne, the out-of-towner who offers a false lead at the start of *High Hopes* and who likewise disappears from that film. Plot, or being emplotted, is all that McCoy knows, and his speech, along with Billy's, alerts us to the asphyxiating power of narratives about the past and prophecies about the future.

The characters of *Meantime* grasp for plot wherever they can, even as the film fails to follow plot's requirements. For the Pollocks, unlike the citizens of Belfast, the connection to plot is always spurious, vicarious, or invented. Mark bets on horse races, Mavis plays bingo, Frank comments on the science fiction and sex that he sees on television. In each case, the relationship to plot (to adventure and possibility) has to be manufactured. Mark manifests this impulse in a more sustained manner than anyone else, by creating sardonic fictions; he tells his aunt that he could burgle her house, and he tells the clerk at the unemployment bureau that he has been hired by the government as a snitch—a spy to monitor the movements of dole-office workers. The opening shot of the film signaled the importance of offscreen space, and plot remains offscreen throughout. Even if we shift from plot as excitement or change to plot as the orderly arrangement of chronology, cause and effect, *Meantime* breaks down. Take, for example, a scene thirty minutes into the film, where Mark and his father sit on the couch, discussing the contents of a lurid tabloid newspaper (a publication that exists to sell plot to the plotless). Their conversation about sex and marriage could just as easily be dropped in ten minutes earlier or forty minutes later without changing any of the dynamics of the film. The same is true for a short scene, a single high-angle shot of Mark walking through Trafalgar Square; we don't know where he's been, we don't know where he's going, and nothing happens as a result of this walk. Leigh's movies are often composed of such moments, but there is usually the slight breeze of momentum, or the feeling that we are learning more about the characters in the absence of obvious drama. *Meantime* illustrates what it is like to live in a plotless world by refusing to follow the basic requirements of storytelling.

If *Four Days in July* offers two set pieces, in McCoy's declamation and Billy's diagnosis, that fix the characters of that film into a matrix of plot, *Meantime* features two set pieces that reinforce the weightlessness of choice in this world. The first of these is an unbroken shot, which for an astounding minute and a half presents us nothing but a washing machine. The shot begins by showing us Mavis banging on the rounded glass door of the appliance, complaining that it won't open; as Frank walks into the shot to help, the camera tilts down so that we are at ground, or washing-machine, level. The rest of the shot enacts one of Leigh's splits between sight and sound, as we see various Pollocks from chest down, bickering about the cost and operation of the machine; only the sight of Mavis twice leaning down, briefly, to pick up the laundry shows us any of the faces producing this chatter. The second set piece occurs half an hour later into the film, when an eccentric housing-estate manager (Peter Wight) comes to investigate the Pollocks' report of a broken window. He speaks in what seem to be Buddhist parables—about grains of sand and anthills—and gets into a low-key argument with Barbara about economics and power. The humor of the scene comes not only from the way in which the characters in the room talk at cross-purposes (like Clive and Joy in *The Short and Curlies*) but from the way the scene works purely as an interlude; we never see the estate manager again, we never find out if the window gets fixed, and none of the discussions bear any kind of narrative fruit. Both scenes isolate an element of cinema—a single shot, a dialogue sequence—and drain it of the signifying properties that we expect a shot, a sequence, or narrative cinema to convey. It is not that the scenes are meaningless, but they have to be divorced from plot, and its explanatory logic, to have meaning.

If plot is a fiction for the characters of *Meantime,* it is an overbearing fact in *Four Days in July.* Billy squats to check the underside of his car before he gets into it—not because he is pretending to be a spy but because he really might discover a bomb. If Mark carries around fictions of plot in his mind, Eugene in *Four Days* literally carries around plot in his body. He is disabled and forced to make his way around the narrow terraced house on crutches because of a series of plot incidents, three run-ins where he was an unfortunate bystander in the plot of Northern Ireland: a deflected bullet in 1979, a bomb in 1976, another bullet when leaving Mass in 1973. Eugene is a noncombatant in the perpetual conflicts of the province, but even those who try to absent themselves from plot are immured within it. Brendan and Dixie, the amiable plumber and window washer, chitchat about their shared personal experience as makers of homemade hooch in a matter-of-fact manner; but these experiences are a result of their having shared a cell in Long Kesh, Northern Ireland's most notorious prison, which also goes by the name of the Maze—another emblem of the grid. Billy and his friend, after a celebratory bonfire, jovially recall a beloved anecdote about the time when, drunk and fed up with army rations, they attacked and butchered a cow in a field. If we think of these anecdotes as *Four Days'* version of the mini-narratives that I have cited (the portrait sitters, cab customers, and abortion clients), then we can see the "normal" plotless Mike Leigh situations of sitting around and talking in the context of this film as creating the cracks where plot rushes in. Even colloquial parenthetical references to "the man upstairs," or Collette's observation about Dixie's arrival—"look, someone's waved a magic wand; there's a window cleaner at my house"—make the rhetoric of destiny, of authorship and magic, the inevitable discourse of this society.

Both films incorporate scraps of culture, but from very different perspectives. Mike Leigh's films usually do not require us to tap into a storehouse of knowledge about art—literary, visual, or acoustic—to understand what the characters are saying or what the sounds and images are evoking. And his films do not aggressively quote or "reference" other films. So the suggestion of Hopper in the café scene from *Secrets and Lies*, for example, can be guessed or missed by the viewer, with no effect on the viability of the scene. Consequently, the explicit allusions that we do get are particularly important—not because they distill the secret meanings of the film but because they indicate how we are to understand the dimensions of that film world. *Meantime* provides a concise illustration of these guidelines. Mark mockingly refers to Colin as a "Muppet" throughout, a nickname he changes somewhat affectionately to "Kojak" when Colin shaves off his hair at the end of the film; Coxy, pretending to jump off a balcony, calls himself "Spiderman"; Frank critiques Mark's attempts at humor by comparing him to the British television comedian Ernie Wise. That's about it—a small pool of allusions, indeed. The critical connecting element is that they are all contemporary, all common terms of late seventies and early eighties culture. A broader strain of influential contemporary culture in the film is punk music, through Coxy and other skinheads, and through the song that Mark plays loudly, which evokes the ethos of the Sex Pistols. Taken as a whole, this pool of allusions is not only small but extremely shallow. I do not mean "shallow" in a pejorative sense, where "deep" would mean sophisticated or learned; I mean "shallow" in the sense that there is no past or history to these allusions, just as there is no past or history to this culture. In an amnesiac society without plot, all culture is temporary.

The most important cultural allusions of *Four Days in July* are just as popular as those in *Meantime*. The two songs that we hear characters sing, toward the end of July 11, the long day at the center of the film, are just as much pieces of demotic culture as Muppets or Kojak or Sid Vicious. But unlike *Meantime*'s roster, these songs represent tradition, a musical inheritance that has been popular for, and handed down by, generations. Billy and his mates, after recounting the story of the butchered cow, sing "The Sash My Father Wore," a Unionist standard that we also hear played by marching bands. Here is the chorus of the song, which explicitly celebrates this central holiday of Northern Ireland:

It is old but it is beautiful, its colours they are fine.
It was worn at Derry, Aughrim, Enniskillen, and the Boyne.
Sure, my father wore it as a youth in the bygone days of yore,
And it's on the Twelfth I love to wear the sash my father wore.

Virtually every lyric speaks to the emplotted conditions of the characters of *Four Days*: the recitation of battles, the fetishizing of uniforms, the sentimentalizing of heroes, the veneration of national history, the commemoration of commemoration itself, and, most critically for the particulars of this film, the culturally prescribed bond between parent and child. As soon as Billy and company finish, we cut to Collette and Eugene lying in bed, trying to fall asleep. "I've got one, Eugene," she says; after a pause, she launches, tongue firmly in cheek, into a much less boisterous version of "The Sash My Father Wore." Eugene mutters feigned disgust and then joins in. He understands the humor of her jest; the inappropriateness of this song, for a couple that has a picture of the Pope on the staircase, demonstrates their ability to satirize and incorporate dominant Protestant culture. Eugene then asks her for a lullaby; she in turn instructs him to close his eyes and asks where he'd most like to be. "A desert island," he says. He is already on an island, of course (as another character notes earlier in the film), but it is not deserted: rather, it is overrun with people, all telling the same stories.

Collette pauses and then offers a musical rebuff to "The Sash My Father Wore," both a Catholic counterpart and a critique of ideology itself. This is the first verse of that song, "The Patriot Game":

> Come all ye young rebels, and list while I sing,
> For the love of one's country's a terrible thing.
> It banishes fear with the speed of a flame,
> And it makes us all part of the patriot game.

If Leigh could be said to stack the deck, in a film engineered as a parallel story of analogous couples, aspirations, and family situations, it is in the sequential presentation of "The Sash My Father Wore" and "The Patriot Game." Consider the key terms of this first verse: it is a song about people and not a thing (the sash), focused on hopeful youth and not embittered, unforgiving age, cognizant of the perils of loyalty, and alert to culture and history and society as games, designed with preassigned roles and predictable results. In dredging up these songs from her memory, Collette is reproducing the cultural lessons of her youth, the songs she heard so many times that they have become part of her inheritance. Unlike the Muppets and Ernie Wise, however, these were the cultural lessons of her mother's youth as well; Collette's individuality, as a person and a character, may be illusory, given that the cultural information she carries with her does not distinguish her from the vast majority of the people around her and before her. Just as Mark in *Meantime* recognizes the desperate situation of plotlessness, here Collette recognizes the desperate situation of being emplotted. But recognition, whatever its consolations, does not change the material conditions of the world.

Unlike any of Mike Leigh's feature films before or since, *Four Days in July* brings its central pregnancies to term. Such are the requirements of the world of plot, where pregnancy, with all its qualities of suspended possibility, has to be pushed to resolution. If the juxtaposed singing scenes were not evidence enough of the fated nature of the couples' entwinement, we get confirmation the next morning, when Collette and Lorraine wake up to find out that their waters have broken—on the anniversary of the Battle of the Boyne, the very epicenter of Northern Ireland's narrative. The destinies of the couples finally cross in the waiting room of the hospital, where Eugene, Billy, and a third man wait things out while the women (whom we see intercut only in close-ups) have their babies. We know the stories of Eugene and Billy, but the stranger, a Mr. Roper, is an unknown who cantankerously complains about the plants, the radiator, the cars in the parking lot, and the noise of the parades marching past. When Eugene interprets this last cavil as evidence of Roper's sympathies, he murmurs, in assent, "pack of eejits." But Roper takes this as an opportunity for further fulmination, saying that there are worse "eejits" out there, who are "murdering and shooting people in their own country." Roper, as an agent of wrath, bookends McCoy, since each appears for one scene, expresses displeasure, and departs. The correspondence becomes closer still after Roper, when asked if he had thought about attending the birth at his wife's side, snorts in dismay and launches a new sortie about the blight of children. His lament about the attendant obligations of parenthood—raising, clothing, feeding—and the inevitable disgrace that full-grown offspring bring concludes with the claim that "you're better off never bein' born at all." Roper's diatribe about plot events reveal him as a man too obsessed with the future to orient himself to the present, just as McCoy revealed himself as a man too obsessed with the past to orient himself to the present. (The film is one ghost short of *A Christmas Carol*.) In some ways, vivid minor characters are Leigh's stock in trade; but in this context they function almost allegorically, as reminders, at either end of the film, of the ways in which an emplotted world uses the past to create the future, at the expense of the everyday.

The scheme of the movie requires that on the morning of Friday the thirteenth, the day of superstition and coincidence, we discover Collette and Lorraine in adjoining beds in the maternity ward. Collette is awake and holding her baby, while a nurse is feeding the child of Lorraine, who is still asleep. Collette and the unnamed nurse chatter about Lorraine's baby, how lovely he is, and how "you never know." Their patter then follows this trajectory: he could turn into "a wee monster"; Hitler's mother didn't know the way her newborn was going to turn out; environment is the ultimate determinant of who we are; babies "are all the same" when they start; and this little one "could be another wee Hitler." Like so much in *Four Days in July,* this dialogue is completely plausible as "real" conversation; but the fact that these two characters are talking about the unknowability of character and about the way environment (or plot, in the context of Northern Ireland) shapes our ends, in a film that has brought Collette and Lorraine together not "naturally" but through the requirements of plot, reveals this as one of Leigh's signal moments of self-reflexivity. The "wee Hitler" remark causes Lorraine to stir and ask if her baby's been crying; the nurse quickly responds that they've been talking "about babies" and not "about your baby," but in the world of this film, the general and the particular are always in danger of confusion.

The nurse leaves, and the two leading women in the film have the opportunity to converse for the first and only time. After exchanging stories of delivery pain and duration, Collette gets down to the crucial question and asks Lorraine what she's naming "her wee boy." "Billy," Lorraine replies, without immediately explaining her choice; Billy's two mates are named "Big Billy" and "Little Billy," so the repetition of the name reaches absurdity, while fitting in perfectly with the way in which the plot-driven society deindividualizes its citizens. Lorraine feels obliged to return the question, and Collette replies, "Máiréad," after her mother, Margaret. Lorraine asks why she doesn't just call the girl Margaret, and Collette explains that Máiréad is the Irish for Margaret. We see Lorraine register this information, which immediately tells her that Collette is likely to be a Catholic and a Nationalist, given her preference for a Gaelic name over an Anglo-Saxon one. After an awkward pause, Collette asks if Lorraine's "wee boy" is named after anyone, and Lorraine proudly says, "After his daddy." Leigh cuts to a close-up of the face of Bríd Brennan, who plays Collette. She conveys a wonderfully subtle look that could be interpreted as mere watching or, just as easily, as fatal realization. Lorraine's decision *is* fatal; Billy might seem an innocuous name, but when

Collette learns that son and father share the name, the meaning of Billy is inescapable. The reason for Billy's popularity among the Protestant characters is of course the direct line it traces to the ancestral Billy, William of Orange, the bringer of plot. Collette and Lorraine, with their oppositional heritage but their shared French names, have both emplotted their children, giving them assigned roles that chart who they will be before they have a chance to create themselves. If this is a moment of realization for Collette, then she must be devastated to understand that her act of sentimentality, in naming her daughter after her mother, makes her no different from the emplotting Billies around her; she has unwittingly fallen for the patriot game as well.

"Daddy," the final spoken word in the film, is a sentimentalizing term that seems to evoke the special, individual bond between two people; but in this context it demonstrates how personal nostalgia is emplotted society's most successful disguise. And the last image is a side-by-side, unbroken centaur shot, over a minute long, of the two women in their

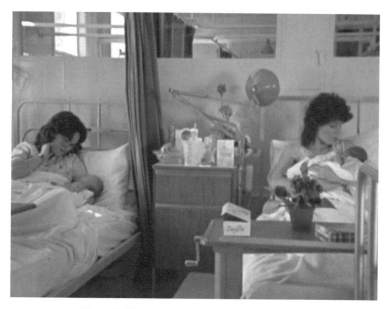

Figure 7. The side-by-side centaur
in the unbroken shot: Collette and Lorraine
at the end of *Four Days in July*.

beds, a simple arrangement that is among Leigh's most complex pictures. The shot contemplates the women and their babies for fifteen seconds, the only sounds the occasional gurgling of Máiréad and Billy, whose fates are now sealed, before the closing music and credits leak in. Mike Leigh has constructed an entire film so that he can get to this image, which, like Collette's face when she hears the word "daddy," can be read simultaneously as neutral and impassive or as bursting with revelations and ideas. And indeed there is more going on here than the film itself can contain, since it is only when this image gets in conversation with Hortense and Cynthia at the café, and Gilbert and Sullivan in the study, that the reach of its possibilities begins to unfold.

Meantime, by contrast, runs past its moment of closure. After Colin makes it back to the housing estate from his aunt's house, he is rebuffed when he tries to visit Hayley; he shows up at home wearing a hooded coat that he refuses to take off. His parents demand to know what happened, and Mark defends his brother by expelling them from the room. Colin and Mark sit down on the floor, and a very long side-by-side unbroken shot holds them together. Mark gently interrogates his brother about his return trip, about whether he's had dinner, and why he won't remove his coat. Mark announces that he's going to leave home, because all the tension is "doin' my brain in"; Colin looks surprised and slightly hurt. But he may realize, as we certainly realize, that this is an empty threat, since there is no reason to go anywhere else, given the ubiquitous absence of plot. The brothers are silent for the final twenty-five seconds of the shot, each smoking a cigarette and looking off into space. The side-by-side unbroken shot of siblings, a version of which also rounds off *Life Is Sweet* and *Secrets and Lies,* occupies a particular place in Leigh's cinema. The shot of Colin and Mark suggests the shadow of a mutual understanding between the brothers, but it does not suggest the kind of rapprochement that is apparent between Nicola and Natalie in *Life Is Sweet,* or between Hortense and Roxanne in *Secrets and Lies.* But neither does this shot articulate the stark centaurical mismatch of Collette and Lorraine, or of Gilbert and Sullivan. Appropriately for *Meantime,* the shot occupies an indeterminate space between, neither synthetic nor oppositional.

Even more appropriately, the shot does not offer a valedictory moment, as it does in *Four Days in July,* because we move on to the next morning. Colin has gone to sleep with his coat on and his head covered;

Figure 8. The side-by-side unbroken shot,
neither synthetic nor oppositional:
Colin and Mark at the end of *Meantime*.

when Mark pushes the hood off the next morning, he sees that Colin has shaved off his hair. He has done this to emulate the skinhead Coxy—at least, that's what Mark assumes—perhaps to invest himself with the kind of illusion of drama, of story, that Coxy thinks his confrontational appearance affords. Mark rubs Colin's head affectionately, teases him by calling him Kojak, and leaves the room; the camera holds on Colin's face, as opaque as ever, as the sounds of Pollocks bickering sift in from the other room, leaking into the credits as we cut to black. We are back in the ephemeral—a leave-taking as arbitrary as the film's commencement. If *Four Days* manifestly ends, *Meantime* simply stops, enclosed by a present tense with no fixed boundaries.

Art and Narrative: *Naked* and *Secrets and Lies*

Two films changed the picture of Mike Leigh. These films received the imprimatur of artistic importance by each winning two major prizes at

Cannes, transforming their director from a regional to a global name. Part of the picture-change, then, came from the fact that *Naked* (1993) and *Secrets and Lies* (1996) seemed to complete Leigh's translation from a televisual to an art-house context. It may not be coincidental that we see a flowering of extramural people and provenances in *Naked* and *Secrets and Lies*—its characters come from all over the United Kingdom and Ireland, and they travel to such exotic locations as Zimbabwe, Saudi Arabia, Australia, and the United States. Broader still, there was the perception of a quickly apprehensible "universality" to the ostensible themes or genres of the two films. *Naked,* which focuses on three days in the life of the lanky, smart, and dangerously volatile Johnny (David Thewlis) as he wanders around the big city, tapped into any number of millennial anxieties: the decline of the West, the collapse of belief systems, the fracturing of community, the increasingly fraught relationship between mind and body. The film also fit into recognizable narrative genres—the road movie, the angry-young-man story, the existentialist portrait of despair—and spoke to concerns beyond England's shores. Likewise, *Secrets and Lies* could be seen as not "just" a story about working- and middle-class Britons. The quest of Hortense Cumberbatch (Marianne Jean-Baptiste), a sensible black optometrist, to find out the identity of her birth mother, who turns out to be Cynthia Purley (Brenda Blethyn), an emotionally chaotic white factory worker, drew upon issues that transcended its local details: the mystery and intimacy of families, the matter of race, the tension between genetics and culture. And this film also fit a traditional cinematic category: the melodrama, or the woman's picture, skewing toward the emotional and the confessional in ways no one had quite seen before in Mike Leigh's films.

Each film produced its array of champions and naysayers—with *Naked* in particular attracting endorsements from high places. The most forceful of these enthusiasts may have been Susan Sontag, who in her 1996 essay "The Decay of Cinema" bemoaned the "astonishingly witless" fare that commercial cinema produced and suggested that cinephilia itself—the lifeblood of the art form as an intellectual and social practice—might be putrefying as well. The "great film," the "one-of-a-kind" achievement," had become an increasing rarity. Sontag named three recent "wonderful films" that managed to create "something special, necessary"; the first film on that list was *Naked* (Sontag 60).[8] She provided no further explanation for this choice, but the company that she cited elsewhere in the article—Dziga Vertov, Orson Welles, Jean-Luc Godard, Andrei Tarkovsky, and other approved giants—shows the modernist criteria under which Sontag was operating; no Leigh film before *Naked* would seem to have offered a sensibility commensurate with this all-star lineup. Indeed, the impulse to differentiate *Naked* from Leigh's earlier work has been a critical commonplace. A typical case is Manohla Dargis's 1994 *ArtForum* essay, which argued that Leigh had now "left behind the superficially gentle whimsies of his last two films, *High Hopes* and *Life Is Sweet,* and entered the lower depths" (Dargis, "Johnny," 55).

Leigh's biographer, Michael Coveney, while slightly hesitant to endorse the main line that argued for *Naked* as Leigh's "breakthrough film," nonetheless agrees that "there is something about *Naked*'s scale, ambition, and power that sets it apart." Hence the validation implied by one of the gold standards of cultural importance: a think piece in the *New York Review of Books.* Ian Buruma's article reintroduced, or more likely introduced, Leigh to this segment of the intelligentsia. While Buruma was more concerned with incorporating *Naked* into Leigh's larger aesthetic project than in differentiating it from its predecessors, this piece would likely not have been commissioned in the wake of any of Leigh's preceding films. The shock of *Naked* was twofold. To those unfamiliar with Leigh, the brutal and unreconciled complexities of the protagonists left no easy consolations; to those familiar with Leigh, the relentless focus on a violent individual, virtually stripped of context, seemed a surprising departure indeed. Leigh had suddenly made something "cinematic" or "filmic"—that is, dark, sweeping, larger-than-life, with visible camera work.

The praise for *Secrets and Lies,* by contrast, did not invoke terms like "cinematic" or "filmic." The strongest huzzahs came from the uninitiated, or the popular press, while the loyalists expressed disappointment or peppered their recommendations with qualifications. *Secrets and Lies* may have won the bigger prize at Cannes—the Palme d'Or, compared to *Naked*'s Best Director—but Leigh's longstanding fans hesitated to commit. Jonathan Rosenbaum approvingly quoted another critic's complaint, which accused *Naked* of "bombastic nihilism" and *Secrets and Lies* of "soft-heartedness," and agreed with the overall perception that these two films marked a change from all that had come before. Like Ray Carney, he saw Leigh not in ascension but in decline. The characters of *Secrets and Lies* "lack complexity," compared with those of *Meantime, Grown-Ups,* or *High Hopes,* a compromise resulting from Leigh's apparent decision to showcase "his gifts to a wider audience." A less ambivalent attack came from Richard Porton, who lauded the "darker preoccupations" of the earlier films and attacked the "depressingly upbeat tenor" of the recent film, which he damned by twice invoking the bogeyman of Bill Clinton, that middlebrow peddler of "New Age pieties" (Porton, "*Secrets and Lies,*" 52–53). And yet—something redeemed the film for Rosenbaum, who saw it three times and found it "as gripping the third time as the first": the acting, and the "relative largesse" shown to the dysfunctional family. Not "filmic" or "cinematic" qualities, then. Somehow the "willful sunniness" of the movie was preferable to the "facile and premature fatalism of *Naked.*"

So that's the picture. There are some problems with the picture, ranging from the claim that the two films are fundamentally different from their predecessors to the claim that they are fundamentally different from each other to the claim that they represent, collectively, some distinct rise or decline in quality. Let us look at two signature moments, two specific shots that are perhaps the most distinctive visual moments in each film and that do articulate significant differences between the projects. The differences I will address are the same kinds of differences we have been noticing in Leigh's cinema: differences of form, which yield questions about form and content. While these two shots have certainly been discussed within the context of each film, they have not, as far as I am aware, been explicitly considered together. By and large, as so frequently with Leigh, the conversation about these two films has lingered at the level of story, or has focused on broad issues of genre or affect—things like nihilism and melodrama rather than the structure of cinema.

The shot from *Naked* occurs during the second of the film's three narrative parts. A brief summary: Johnny, whom we see engaged in rough sex (perhaps rape) with a woman in a Manchester alley at the very start of the film, has fled his home town for London. In the first part of the film, he turns up at the apartment of his ex-girlfriend, Louise Clancy (Lesley Sharp), where he meets and has sex with her insecure roommate, Sophie

(Katrin Cartlidge). The constitutionally restless Johnny, distressed by the intimacy that both women now connote, runs from the apartment and heads for the streets. The second, and by far the longest, of the film's parts traces Johnny's wanderings as he meets strangers on the streets, in places of work, and in apartments; and the longest of these meetings involves the plodding, middle-aged security guard Brian (Peter Wight), whose job it is to protect an empty office building at night. Both men are avid readers of books, and particularly of the Bible, which Johnny is perusing on the ground outside the office building when Brian invites him in from the cold. After insulting the personal appearance and occupational duties of his rescuer, as he will do with so many interlocutors on this journey, Johnny engages Brian in a discussion about the nature of the past, the present, and the future. The protagonist scoffs at Brian's insistence that his future will redeem his tedious present, arguing for the continuity of time ("a constant process of coming into being and passing away") and the nonexistence of the present (since it is simply the meeting point of past and future, the invisible line where they abut). Their Socratic exchange goes into high gear as they move into a dark area of the building, illuminated only by a string of windows behind them. The camera pans left to follow their movement and stops when Johnny does; for a few seconds he is alone in the shot, and Brian is off-camera left. As

Figure 9. The real and the constructed: Brian and Johnny in *Naked.*

Johnny launches into an apocalyptic declaration, Brian walks back into the shot, and we get a very slow, barely discernible track in toward the men. Throughout the shot—which is well over two minutes long—the two men are backlit, reduced to silhouettes, and indeed only to torsos, as their lower bodies dissolve into the darkness. This moment might look more like art, and has been discussed as more like art, than many of Leigh's other unbroken shots because of the noir lighting—assisted by the bleach bypass process that turned the entire film gray and blue—and the drama of Johnny's rhetoric. We will get more precisely to the resonances of this moment, in terms of Leigh's vocabulary, in a moment.

Keep that picture in mind as we consider a shot from *Secrets and Lies*—the café shot that I have discussed in conjunction with *Topsy-Turvy*. The context of that shot helps to establish a fundamental structural difference between this film and *Naked*. Each film is divisible into three parts; but while *Naked*'s three parts are sequential, those of *Secrets and Lies* are parallel. In other words, the divisions are not a beginning, middle, and end of story time but three stories intercut with each other. If *Naked* traces the apparent aimlessness of a picaresque journey, within the venerable geometry of the three-act play, *Secrets and Lies* emerges from a familiar trope in Leigh—the parallel families of *Four Days in July* and the three interwoven couples of *High Hopes*. The first of *Secrets and Lies'* three parts, or at least the first to which we are introduced, consists of Hortense, whom we see grieving at her mother's funeral in the title sequence. The second part, to which we are introduced in the second sequence of the film, consists of the rotund portrait photographer Maurice Purley (Timothy Spall) and his tetchy wife, Monica (Phyllis Logan), who live in the childless middle-class circle of *Meantime*'s Barbara and John. The third part, to which we are introduced in the third sequence of the film, consists of Maurice's sister, Cynthia, and her daughter, Roxanne (Claire Rushbrook), who live together grumpily in a rented terraced house. In its first nine minutes, the films lays out its human landscape rather schematically, presenting each of the three narrative lines separately; by comparison, in *Four Days in July* we have to wait until the second of its four days before the Catholic couple is introduced. For all the ways that *Naked* blatantly trumpets theories of narrative—stories like science and religion that tell us who we are and why we do what we do—there is something equally exposed about the machinery of *Secrets and Lies.* Hortense, with her goal-driven desire to find out about her conception, is a full-fledged agent of plot; Cynthia, who does nothing with her day and night, is a plotless character waiting to be activated.

The café shot occurs when the first and third parts of this narrative collide, a collision that we have been anticipating since the beginning—by contrast with the meeting between Johnny and Brian, which, like virtually all meetings in *Naked,* arrives with no advance warning. Each of these shots seems to serve as the centerpiece of the film. That would make *Naked* a film about interpretation, aggression, and death, and *Secrets and Lies* a film about investigation, yielding, and birth. Such a division is too neat, but these two shots do help create a series of oppositions. In the first case, two men; in the second case, two women. In the first case, two people confronting each other face to face; in the second case, two people sitting side by side. In the first case, a deracinated nighttime setting that makes the characters' thoughts seem mysterious, vatic; in the second case, a mundane daytime setting that accentuates the awkward, "real" rhythms of the characters' conversation. Those three oppositions alone help fund many of the ongoing conversations about these two movies. The first is a male picture, populated by outcast individuals at war with each other but with no prospect of resolution. The second is a female picture, populated by an extended family waiting to be reintegrated, moving slowly toward synthesis. The first is dark, modernist, wide-ranging in its scope, difficult to watch; the second is bright, sentimental, tightly focused, as easy to watch as the most unambitious of entertainments. Those generalizations are spotted with truths, and their trajectories suggest a side-by-side of antitheticals, something along the lines of *Meantime* and *Four Days in July.* Most relevant to our formal interests is the way the shot from *Naked* disrupts the parallel orientation of the characters in a side-by-side, and the way the shot from *Secrets and Lies* offers the ne plus ultra of the trope. But beyond these broad strokes of opposition, there are critical correspondences and inversions that we need to address.

In both shots, the discussion pivots around a contested text, one that claims to connect the past, present, and future. *Naked*'s text is the Bible, which dominates the extended sequence with Brian and serves as an undercurrent throughout the film. At this moment, Johnny pounces on the security guard's hopeful regard for the future and offers an exegetical riff on the Book of Revelation (echoed by a precedent from the Book of Daniel) to illustrate what the future holds. The key passage for Johnny's sermon is a famous one:

> He forced everyone to receive a mark on his right hand, or on his forehead, so that no one shall be able to buy or sell, unless he has the mark, which is the name of the beast. Or the number of his name; and the number of the beast is six-six-six. (Revelation 13:16–18)

Johnny offers a contemporary explanation for the famous number: the bar code, which is to be found "on every bog-roll, on every packet of johnnies, on every poxy pork pie." This ubiquitous symbol, he explains, is "divided into two parts by three markers," and those three markers are always represented by the number six—a sign of the satanic nature of late capitalism. Extended evidence of this manifestation of the magic number, and its connection with the bar code, comes in the form of putative plans to "subcutaneously laser-tattoo that mark on to your right hand or onto your forehead," as already tested on American troops. And fulfillment of apocalyptic prophecy is to be found on the Day of Judgment, when seven angels will blow their trumpets and wormwood will fall from the sky; the Russian word for "wormwood," Johnny reveals to Brian, is "Chernobyl." As we hear Johnny's litany, we feel that he has delivered this speech before. The scene is self-consciously performative, as indeed is Johnny more generally, and as is the movie as a whole; while Brian lobs observations of his own in now and then, his job, like ours, is essentially to act as audience to a tour de force. The performative, one might say "artificial," element of the scene is literally underscored by the sound track, a driving harp that mirrors the lyrical intensity of Johnny's thought (and perhaps comments slyly on the angelic subject matter of his oration). Leigh has found a new way to affix the real to the constructed, fusing the real-time device of the unbroken shot and the plausibly unlit spaces of a building at night with the dramatic "staginess" we might expect in a theater and nondiegetic music that instructs us to pay attention.

The mood is altogether different in the café scene, where the lighting is flat and music is completely absent. Here the real-artificial dynamic is switched to Leigh's more typical formula: two people involved in chitchat who face not each other but the camera. *Secrets and Lies* will not be free of speeches; indeed, the climactic emotional moment of the film will come through Maurice's impromptu speech to his family, when he offers a compressed sermon on the dangers of "secrets and lies." But here Hortense and Cynthia stumble into intercourse, as the unacknowledged daughter tries to prod her mother into recognizing her. Cynthia suddenly remembers the circumstances of Hortense's conception and breaks down; even after her epiphany, however, she refuses to give the slightest shred of information, a refusal that will be unshaken for the rest of the film, even when all the other "secrets and lies" are rousted from their dark places. These two women remain separate throughout the scene, in part because of Cynthia's hoarding of information, and in part because of their side-by-side arrangement. But a significant part of the separation has to do with the specifics of the mise-en-scène. Hortense, who is black, is wearing a black blouse and a black jacket; Cynthia, who is white, is wearing a white blouse and a white jacket. So this eminently "believable" eight-minute shot—marked by stop-and-start dialogue, shy looks, awkward pauses, and all the ingredients of verisimilitude—transpires in what appears to be an allegorical color scheme. White and black serve significantly in the office shot from *Naked* as well, but almost at the level of abstraction, favoring neither figure as both are turned into shadows against a bright line, into images in front of a (movie) screen. The café setting is seemingly uninflected, with naturalistic banquettes receding perspectivally behind the two principals, grounding the scene in the diurnal—even a diurnal that is in many ways a concoction (as Leigh says at the start of this book). If Johnny and Brian find each other by accident and then start to play rehearsed parts in a drama, Hortense and Cynthia come to play parts—the black-on-black daughter grieving for her abandonment, the white-on-white mother trying to preserve the patina of innocence—but then find themselves in an improvisation.

And the drama involves in each case a text, a text about the nature of identity. The text in the café is not Scripture but a manuscript: the handwritten names, dates, and other elements of biography and lineage that establish the bond between these two women. This text, by contrast with Johnny's eschatological speculations, addresses the past and not the future; birth certificates tie a moment to the people that made it happen, receding backward into time with nothing to say about what lies ahead. Johnny punctuates each of his citations from Revelation, and their correspondence with a contemporary or imminent event, with a recurring declamatory assertion: "Fact!" The last version of these— "another fuckin' fact!"—proves wryly apt for the café scene, since it is precisely facts about fucking that are under examination here. If we take "fact" to be one of the subjects of Leigh's cinema, with all the complications the word implies, then the two scenes stage two different ways in which we judge things to be facts. Johnny's exegetical approach lingers on issues of correspondence and coincidence, focusing on the way that unlike systems—different languages, or ancient writings and astronomical phenomena—suddenly line up and make meaning of each other; it is no accident that he is a purveyor of puns, words that delight in two unlike meanings or ideas—two facts—being brought into collision with one another. The status of fact in the café scene is more ambiguous, and the question of who, between these women, gets to judge things as facts is up in the air. Cynthia denies the fact of this other woman, insisting that her manuscript must be disguising inaccuracies as facts; but when she recalls the past and is forced to acknowledge Hortense as fact, she withholds the fact (the fact of conception) that would help Hortense translate the words on the page into meaning, into history. Johnny's facts, and his nightmare scenario of bar-code identification, are radically impersonal; he presents his arguments as dispassionate, and the bleak world he imagines is stripped of any idiosyncratic distinguishing features. Hortense and Cynthia's facts are radically personal, important not as transhistorical proofs but as words and numbers, symbols and digits, whose codes matter only to them.

As a way of moving into two broad ways in which these later films converse, let us linger on Johnny's description of the bar code as an object "divided into two parts by three markers." Johnny is certainly prescient in at least this one instance, since "divided into two parts by three markers" is a reasonable structuralist analysis of *Secrets and Lies*. The three markers are those I have cited already—the three groups represented by three homes or emotional spaces of Hortense, Maurice and Monica, and Cynthia and Roxanne—and the two parts are neatly cleft by the café scene we have been considering. The galvanizing meeting takes place at the exact midpoint of the film, separating a half dominated by parallel, separated people and stories from a half dominated by people headed for a big pileup. The tripartite subdivision applies in a different way to *Naked*, since it shifts from Louise and Sophie's apartment to the streets of London and then back to the apartment. But the scene between Johnny and Brian does not occupy the center of the film, as the café scene does; its placement, about fifty minutes into the film, resists compositional neatness. This issue of the center and the margins, or of centrality opposed to happenstance, resonates in terms of the characterological center of each film. *Naked* has a dominant, central character, a focus of attention essentially unprecedented for Leigh; the subject of the film, however, is marginality, not only in terms of economic or social importance but in terms of events or situations that do not transform people but operate at the periphery of their lives. As David Thewlis observes on the DVD commentary, the film has only detailed "three days in the life of this character, not even exceptional days." The days may have been more exceptional for Sophie or Louise, but their status as characters secondary to Johnny serves to minimize the effect of the exceptional. *Secrets and Lies* has no central character, or perhaps it has two or three central characters, and we have seen how it scatters its attention from the start; but the subject of the film is centrality, or of scattered parts (of a family, of past and present) returning to some idea of a center, however temporary or illusory, through transformative events that these characters will never forget. Leigh's favorite device to signal exceptionality, or a day weighed far more heavily than the days before or after, is the party scene—and as with *High Hopes* earlier and *Vera Drake* later, the party serves as a device to bring the scattered and the central together.

These matters of the central and the scattered are aspects of the issue of minor and major. Leigh's interest in playing minor and major characters off each other, and using conventions of stereotype and plausibility to interrogate our assumptions about the essential and the inessential, gets played out explicitly at the level of narrative shape, of art making, in these two films. And I would argue that these two films are more self-conscious about artists and the nature of art than anything Leigh had made until this point. Leigh has always pursued theoretical or ontological questions about the art of cinema, or about devices and designs of all kinds. But these questions had been raised in the bridge between the characters and the audience, in the way a shot was framed or the way sequences were edited together, rather than within the diegesis of the film itself. There had been no artists, or artist-figures, in Leigh's films until now. This would change with *Topsy-Turvy*, of course, but a central contention of my argument is that *Topsy-Turvy* represents a grand synthesis and elaboration of Leigh's concerns rather than a deviation from them. *Naked* and *Secrets and Lies* are the most prominent antecedents, as explicit presentations of art and artistic self-consciousness—as demonstrated, in part, by shots like the ones that I have just been examining. The film-noir affect of the scene between Johnny and Brian, and the way that they debate Big Ideas, offers one version of artistic self-consciousness; the café scene between Hortense and Cynthia, the longest and most blatantly oppositional unbroken side-by-side centaur in Leigh's career, offers another version of artistic self-consciousness. In the following pages, I will consider the way the artist-figure in each film opens up central investigations of the structure of narrative, and especially minor and major narratives. (A longer consideration of art in these films would address genres of art, and arts that are deemed minor and major.)

Who are these artist figures, and how do they connect to problems of narrative? It is no great feat to identify Maurice as our candidate in *Secrets and Lies*, given his profession as a photographer, a profession that we see him practice in some detail, and a profession that drives a crucial social and class wedge between him and his sister; this is the artist as petit-bourgeois entrepreneur. We may be surprised to discover, in rewatching a film that is usually discussed as a story of a woman discovering her mother, or as a female story more broadly, that early on Maurice appears to be the protagonist; he, his wife, and his job occupy more than half of the first twenty minutes of the film, while we get only a brief scene, under three minutes in length, with Roxanne and the (perhaps) protagonist, Cynthia. Maurice's artistic counterpart in *Naked* is Johnny— an itinerant, wrathful provocateur miles away from Maurice's settled, mellow man of business. The two men have only a beard in common; and Johnny's artistic credentials seem much vaguer than Maurice's, given that Johnny's intellectual appetites are omnivorous and inclined toward matters of science and religion rather than the making of art as such. But Johnny certainly *looks* like an artist, or at least a certain stereotype of an artist: he wears black at all times, smokes like a chimney, rails at the world, fancies himself an outcast, and buzzes incessantly as the gadfly. His *cri d'artiste*, if we may deem it that, occurs during his first reunion with Louise, after she asks him if he was bored in Manchester. "I'm never bored," he exclaims, unlike everyone else, who (he says) thinks that nature, the living body, and the universe have been fully explained and that there is nothing left to learn. "So now," he tells Louise and his imagined larger audience, "you just want cheap thrills and like plenty of 'em, and it don't matter how tawdry or vacuous they are as long as it's new, as long as it's new, as long as it flashes and fuckin' bleeps in forty fuckin' different colors." Johnny is simultaneously the angry young man and the crotchety old coot, disgusted by the complacency of his world.

How does that make him an artist? We begin to see evidence of his affinity for art during his wanderings, when he shows up at the apartment of a woman whom Brian has been quietly ogling, for weeks or months, from across the street. Brian's attraction to her is fueled by the way she dances, distractedly and with loose clothing, in front of her window. Johnny asks her if she's the woman they've seen, explaining, "I said I'd come and say hello to Isadora Duncan." Once inside the flat, he notices a book she's reading, which she proclaims her favorite, and he declares its title and author: "*Jane Austen* by Emma." He claims that he doesn't read much, which we know to be a lie; when he sneaks away the next morning, after an aborted sexual encounter, he will steal four of her paperbacks, which we might well assume to be novels in a similar vein. Simply name-dropping Isadora Duncan and Jane Austen, as cultural references, may not sound like much—but these need to be put in the context of Leigh's career, where we rarely see people making casual allusion to works of literature or culture. Johnny's sense of ease around art and its manifestations will become even more explicit in his next encounter with a woman, someone he meets in a café the next day. She takes him back to her sublet, which belongs to two men, presumably gay, who are off in America. Always eager to riff on his surroundings, Johnny delights in the souvenir-size classical statuary on the mantelpiece, musing on "all these pseudo-Doric midgets with their novelty underpants" and punning that he's "not Homer-phobic" because he likes the *Iliad* and the *Odyssey*. When his hostess fails to get the joke, he reels off the basic ingredients of those epic narratives—the Wooden Horse, Helen of

Troy, the Cyclops—and pronounces it "good stuff." Undaunted by the incomprehension of his companion, he tosses in a final gag, this time playing off a plaster version of the *Discobolos,* pronouncing the subject to be "Pizza Deliveryman." Most importantly, Johnny is calmer, more in tune with his surroundings in this apartment, whatever its aura of kitsch, than anywhere else in the film—he tones down his patter and prepares to settle in for the evening. And for once, he will not be the one to decide to leave—rather, she will suddenly and rather inexplicably turn on him, demanding that he "fuck off." After trying his best to cajole her, Johnny exits in a rage, cursing her progeny—"I hope that all your fuckin' children are born blind, bow-legged, hare-lipped, homeless hunchbacks"—and mocking her attitude and clothing, which he bitingly terms her "ankle-length Emily Brontë winding sheet." Johnny may talk about chaos theory and the Bible all the time, but his expressed familiarity with the vocabularies of literature, visual art, and performance distinguish him from even the most articulate and perceptive characters in Leigh's films. That, in this scene, he should connect the childless Emily Brontë with hideous malformations of pregnancy hints at tenebrous links between creativity and infertility that have never been so explicit in Leigh's cinema—but which will come crashing together at the end of *Topsy-Turvy.*

Most blatantly, Johnny is a bearded man from Manchester who comes down to the big city to rattle people's received ideas about art—just like the bearded Mancunian Mike Leigh. I make that link somewhat facetiously and with no suggestion of psychobiography. But Johnny's activities, especially in the long middle of the film, do resemble one vital aspect of Leigh's working method. Actors often talk about feeling paranoid, or isolated, during stages of Leigh's process because they are off on their own, creating their own character, often with little to no contact with anyone else. Leigh separates actors playing characters who don't run into each other, or who don't run into each other until some delayed point in the evolving narrative, in order to imitate life, which is full of unplanned encounters; so much of life is accident and improvisation, or at least a significant chunk of life that Leigh wants to explore. The most publicized examples of artistic intervention are the ones I cited in the introduction: the galvanizing party scenes in *Secrets and Lies* and *Vera Drake,* where in rehearsal certain actors were shocked to discover the parallel lives, and the secrets, that Leigh had been developing all along. Whatever the eventual collision of the characters, they must first gestate individually. To that degree, then, Leigh's presence in *Naked* might also operate through Brian, someone who makes his rounds, checking on the actors/characters as they shape themselves, nestled in their own little cubbyholes of the story.

Those cubbyholes bring us precisely to the crucial connection between Johnny and Maurice: they summon the art of the *Five-Minute Films* by importing a collection of mini-narratives into the main narrative of the film. Johnny does this in the middle section of *Naked,* in the road movie within the movie, as his confrontations with Brian, the Austen reader, and the café girl (among others) offer a series of simultaneously connected and disconnected tales with people that we, and Johnny himself, will never meet again. Maurice's introduction of the mini-narratives is much more orderly, and it comes much earlier on in his film, in the guise of a montage of portrait sitters; indeed, a considerable portion of the first phase of *Secrets and Lies,* where Maurice is in some ways the dominant character, is occupied with shots of people sitting in front of his camera. It is worth stressing how different these mini-narratives are from the deployment of minor characters in earlier films. McCoy and the irate expectant father in *Four Days in July,* and the estate manager in *Meantime,* do raise questions about the aleatory, and the center and the periphery, and they jostle our sense of the shape of the film. But their job is to remain aleatory, to be unpredictable not only in what they say but in when or how they show up. In *Naked* and *Secrets and Lies* we have for the first time systems of mini-narrative, sequences organized by a uniting phenomenon—Johnny's wanderings, Maurice's job—that ask us to think collectively about people who have nothing in common, other than the one thing they have in common. It is perhaps too tempting, given our retrospective knowledge of the critical and transformative success of these two films, to argue that Leigh knew that he was shifting into a new narrative mode, that he was crafting stories that would attract a much larger and more diverse audience than he had had up to this point. But we cannot ignore that the affinity to genre—the angry-young-man movie, the melodrama—that we see in *Naked* and *Secrets and Lies* corresponds with a resistance to genre, or a resistance to narrative throughline, embodied by these flashes of people whose stories can't or won't or merely aren't allowed the time to latch onto the more streamlined film around them. The tension between throughline and mini-narratives, as later manifest in *All or Nothing* and *Vera Drake,* speaks to a desire to tell a recognizable story and to untell that story at the same time. The organized irruption of tributary narratives makes us aware of the conflict between the center and the margins, between major and minor narrative, more directly than had been apparent in Leigh's earlier features.

These two systems, however, are very different from each other. *Naked* offers an appropriately erratic wandering through the embedded narratives, of varying genres, time lengths, and dramatic intensity. We begin with Johnny's encounter with Archie and Maggie, two young, irritable, homeless Scots who have gotten separated from each other in London; Johnny is the even-keeled member of this triangle, as he wryly volunteers to help each find the other in turn, almost as if he has something invested in a relationship that is opaque to him. Hence his melancholy distraction when Archie and Maggie reunite and then proceed to kick and scream at each other, thereby erasing any illusion of romantic sympathy. One could argue that Johnny's unstated disappointment here—at the fact that people don't change, that crises don't really improve us—fuels the bitterness and insensitivity of his second encounter, with Brian, and his third, with the Austen reader. Such an argument would run against the very fact we have just observed (that people don't change), because it would signify a cause-and-effect in Johnny's behavior; and part of the difficulty of this protagonist is that it is hard to gauge how he will behave from moment to moment, to judge the effect of any cause. These mini-narratives, in other words, serve in large part to complicate the central character, liberating him from the love nest of Louise and Sophie's apartment—where he would have to play the same role of caustic lover again and again—and showing him to be not only predatory but responsive to his surroundings. This curiosity is expressed most succinctly in a question that he asks Archie, at a moment when the Scot seems particularly aggrieved and incoherent: "What's it like being you?" That question gets aired again with the Austen reader, before their sexual encounter turns unpleasant and then unfinished, when she crawls toward him and he asks, "How's it going inside there?" These flickers of tenderness are easily lost amid Johnny's sturm und drang, but they illustrate another connection between Johnny and Leigh.

What are those unbroken shots and side-by-sides doing but asking exactly these questions: What's it like being you? How's it going inside there? The longer the shot, the more awkward the side-by-side, the plainer it becomes that these questions cannot be answered, which just makes us want to ask them again. Johnny cannot help but pursue these messy queries, and there is a messiness about the structure of his mini-narratives. He meets Brian again after his encounter with the Austen reader, and through a shared breakfast he runs into the café girl; while he waits for the café girl to get off work, he has an extremely brief comic interlude with a chauffeur, who mistakes him for his client; once thrown out into the street by the café girl, he discovers a bill poster at his nighttime work and proceeds to harangue him at length, before getting kicked to the ground; finally, he is assaulted by a group of youths, for no apparent reason. That assault is filmed in an unbroken shot down a long alleyway—in other words, through a Leigh signature framing—as if to close off the long second part of the film with an autograph. The series has run the range from a minor character (Brian) who resists his minority by getting considerable screen time to a set of characters as minor as we will ever get in Leigh (the group of youths) viewed only in the distance and with virtually no distinguishing characteristics in the nocturnal silhouettes. This is a series that resists serialization, irregular in length, impact, and mood, sometimes doubling back on itself (in the cases of Brian and the café) and finally stranding us with an unexplained assault. *The Five-Minute Films* have been translated into something that barely has a connective shape, into stories that resist the codifying work of an organized collective.

Maurice's photo sessions, by contrast, seem quite shapely. They are unified not by the randomness of everyday life but by the order of special occasions—the occasions that require us to pose for a photographer so that we can remember some days above others, segregate them from the noise of the calendar. Maurice and Johnny do share a talent for cajoling and for forcing people to present some version of themselves; but if Johnny harangues strangers to try to make sense of the interior and the surface ("what's it like being you?"), Maurice teases strangers into presenting a surface for the camera, a surface that may or may not have anything to do with the interior. Aside from the fact that Maurice's job is to help his clients present packaged versions of their personality for mechanical reproduction, the photo sessions are themselves neatly packaged within the structure of *Secrets and Lies*. Of the twenty-one sittings that we see Maurice conduct in his studio, twenty take place in the first twenty minutes of the film; indeed, we discover him as much through his work as through his home life. These first twenty minutes are unusual in more ways than one. Critics have spoken of the photo sessions as an "inside, self-reflexive *jeu d'esprit*" (Jones 108) or a "Brechtian alienation or distancing device" (Watson 131), because so many of the fragments of people that we see are played by actors with whom we have become familiar earlier in Leigh: Alison Steadman, Liz Smith, Phil Davis, Ruth Sheen, and others. To those deeply immersed in Leigh's oeuvre, of course, there does seem to be something here of what Tom Gunning has called, in reference to the first decade of film, the cinema of attractions, typified by "the recurring look at the camera by actors" and illustrating "a fundamental conflict between this exhibitionistic tendency of early film and the creation of a fictional diegesis" (Gunning 57). Technically, the recurring look at the camera here is directed at a camera *within* the diegesis (Maurice's camera), but the fact that Peter Wight, who played Brian in *Naked,* should kick off this sequence of mini-narratives does suggest an extramural gambit that links these two films, that places narrative and performance as idea and theory in conversation with enacted narrative and performance.

But that argument doesn't fully respond to the way these narratives are situated in the story. At this early point in the film, we don't know much about the "major" characters, either; as I have noted, Cynthia and Roxanne get only three minutes of screen time in this phase. It is hard to be alienated or distanced from a story that hasn't really begun. In *Naked,* the mini-narratives unfold in the wake of a thirty-minute opening act, by which point the primacy not only of Johnny but of Louise and Sophie has been established; and Johnny's wanderings are interrupted by returns to Louise and Sophie and the flat, so that we feel the push and pull between primary and secondary stories. To some degree, Cynthia and Roxanne are not much more distinct for us in the first moments of this film than the onrush of babies, families, businessmen, boxers, and nurses whom we meet in quick bursts. But *Secrets and Lies* does something to counteract the ambiguity of minor and major, something unseen before in Leigh. Maurice and Monica, five minutes into the film, sit in their living room and deliver a shocking amount of exposition: most prominently, the fact that they haven't seen Roxanne in two and a half years, the fact that her twenty-first birthday is coming up in a couple months, and the fact that Cynthia and Roxanne have never been to this house. We might easily go an entire Mike Leigh film without finding out these kinds of details, and here they are, doled out to us in huge slabs. This is the real cinema-of-attractions moment; the unvarnished attempt to create a fictional diegesis is exactly what is most likely to distance us from the fictional diegesis, because it dislocates our sense of how a Mike Leigh film works. The first scene of the film has shown us a funeral, and the second scene has shown us a bride preparing for her wedding: death and marriage, the signal events of tragedy and comedy, the two cornerstones of plot, lead us into the film, and the subsequent exposition-heavy dialogue makes plot dominant from the start. Consider, by contrast, the mystery and relative silence of the first six minutes of *Naked*, where we watch Johnny engage in violent sex, head to London, and engage in chitchat with Sophie. There we get absolutely none of the biographical or psychological information that would tell us who these characters are, or why they're doing what they're doing. In *Secrets and Lies*, we get all this and more.

That opposition helps us align *Naked* and *Secrets and Lies* with antecedent pairs of antithetical films in Leigh's career. *Meantime* and *Four Days in July* offer a relevant dichotomy—the agon between character and plot, though pushed in a different direction now. In those films of a decade earlier, character and plot operate more conceptually, exaggerated or radically shrunk as conditions under which the people live and the events take place. *Naked* and *Secrets and Lies* foreground the character/plot divide as an issue for these particular characters and these particular narratives, rather than as global conditions like unemployment and war. *Naked* refuses to give us the back story of Johnny and Louise's relationship, or indeed anything about Manchester, a place that serves as a giant warehouse of back story in the film, full of data that might give us a firmer purchase on Johnny in particular; the information ban is interrupted only to provide elliptical information or misinformation (such as the condition of Johnny's mother). *Secrets and Lies*, as we have just noted, backs up the truck and hands out plot goodies by the handful. The five-minute experiments of *Old Chums* and *The Birth of the Goalie*, where Leigh pushed the two elements of narrative, character and plot, to their lowest and highest extremes found their fullest expression two decades later.

This ancestry highlights the importance not only of the simple presence of the mini-narratives within *Naked* and *Secrets and Lies* but of their very different structures and effects. Maurice's photo sessions begin on location, with the nervous bride whom he gracefully and professionally coaxes into smiling. We then get the exposition scene at Maurice and Monica's house, followed by Cynthia and Roxanne at home, and then Hortense at work and then at home, or at least her mother's house. Once the logic of parallel narrative has been established as the mechanism of the film, we arrive in Maurice's studio and receive the barrage of parallel narratives represented by the photo montage. As dissimilar, cinematically, as the rat-a-tat editing of the photo sessions may be to the eight-minute unbroken shot of the café scene, the device of parallel people linked only by the happenstance of time and space resonates throughout the meeting of Hortense and Cynthia. The fact of parenthood and the fact of those adoption papers would seem to fix a bond between them radically unlike whatever bonds might link those portrait sitters; but in both cases, the bonds are of plot rather than of character, of the things that operate outside rather than inside of us. Maurice and Hortense, connected by their professional understanding of the eye, are also connected as forces of plot, who help stage versions of people that may be unrelated to their character (through the portrait sessions) or who may bring plot crashing down on the unsuspecting (through the investigation of one's past). Indeed, Cynthia might be said to stand for the plotless, stuck in a tedious job, in a tedious home, with a tedious daughter. The meeting between Hortense and Cynthia is yet another iteration of the conflict between character and plot in Leigh's cinema, and the mini-narratives are yet another force that conspires to bring Cynthia back into the bustle of narrative.

Those mini-narratives themselves acquire a kind of plot, or a cohesion of story, as they go along. The penultimate sitters we see in *Secrets and Lies*—the last ones in this initial cluster, and the ones accorded significantly more screen time than the other clients in Maurice's studio—are a contentious newlywed Greek couple, whose narrative centers on two props: his glasses and her crucifix necklace. She insists he remove the spectacles, and he accedes only after objecting to the misrepresentation implied: "It's what I look like, okay?" He insists that she pull the crucifix out of her blouse, and she accedes only after objecting that this gift (presumably from a relative) "looks awful." The key word in both cases, as elsewhere in the film, is "look," and their argument has to do with the complicated intersection of character and plot; he thinks that the glasses help define who he really is, and she thinks that the cross misrepresents her taste, and that both are being asked to sacrifice character for plot, the genuine for the falsely commemorative. The argument about identity dovetails with the bar-code scene in *Naked* and the café scene later on in this film. The riposte to the Greeks will come in the person of the final portrait sitter, whose session rounds off the plot of the mini-narratives, turning it into a device of ironic contrast. This final sitter arrives deep into the film, after Hortense and Cynthia's meeting—that is, after Cynthia has been repatriated into plot itself. The sitter, unlike the Greek couple, wants "to look as bad as possible"; this is because her face has been disfigured by a nasty scar, caused by a car accident, and she is suing for damages. If plot, in the guise of accident and the unexpected, has just transformed Cynthia's life, it has also transformed this woman's, but with very different consequences. Her profession, as a beauty consultant, mirrors Maurice's in that it privileges illusions of character over interiority; but in her case, plot and character have come into ugly collision, while Maurice is able to keep separating the two.

The mini-narratives start with a bride dolled up for her future and end with a makeup artist brandishing the wounds of her past, a story of the promise of plot turned into disaster. It is fitting that when she leaves the studio, the final sitter is harassed by what appears to be a homeless man in the park and who turns out to be Stuart Christian, the previous proprietor of Maurice's photo business. His drunken, rambling accounts of a life in Australia that never panned out, of a plot that failed to materialize, seem to belong to a film like *Four Days in July,* one that features a number of marginal characters who pop in at unexpected moments. In *Secrets and Lies,* where minor characters live in the parallel and segregated world of the mini-narratives, his intrusion is as unsettling to the structure of the film as it is, within the diegesis, to

Monica and Jane, Maurice's assistant. And yet his story fits directly into the film's concerns; Stuart Christian's surname, like all allegorical titles, emphasizes his plot role over his individuation as character, echoed in Christian's failed pilgrim's progress to the Antipodes. He is Cynthia's doppelganger, in a sense, wrecked rather than rehabilitated by plot. He has come back to England to find his mother dead, a condition he shares with both Hortense and Cynthia, who in her first appearance in the film laments the death that, many years ago, forced her to stay home and take care of everyone, to sequester herself from the narrative of the world. Once Christian has staggered out of the shop, the final, streamlined forty minutes of *Secrets and Lies* take over, a torrent of plot that seems to redeem all in its path. Leigh gives us Christian as a counternarrative, the outcast who, like Malvolio and other victims of plot and plotting, is obliterated by the demands of drama.

No film of Leigh's, before or since, has appeared to scream "no" more forcefully or persistently, from beginning to end, than *Naked.* Yet the final word spoken in the film is "yes." It is spoken by a woman who has been out of sight for the entirety of the story, a woman whose brief appearance signals the last of the mini-narratives. This woman is Sandra (Claire Skinner), the roommate of Louise and Sophie who has been away the whole time in Zimbabwe, a nurse whose medical knickknacks dominate the apartment, attracting Johnny's attention from the start. Sandra offers a coda whose style jars with the rest of the narrative, since her hyper-organized manner clashes with the behavioral and moral sloppiness of everyone else in the flat, and because Claire Skinner's caffeinated performance, replete with tics and the comic habit of being unable to end any of her sentences, gives her the appearance of a stereotypically minor character. She returns to discover Jeremy Smart, a.k.a. Sebastian Hawkes (Greg Cruttwell), the predatory landlord who has raped Sophie and taken over the apartment—a man with whom Sandra appears to share an unexplained history. In the final stages of the film, after Jeremy has been scared into leaving, after Sophie has tearfully packed up her belongings, after Louise has gone to quit her job to prepare to return with Johnny to Manchester, Sandra and Johnny are the last ones left in the house. He is recovering from the attacks, and she is beginning to recover from the shock of discovering her home a shambles, when he chooses an inopportune time to make a sexual advance. "Enough!" she exclaims, addled by the chaos coming at her from all angles. "When . . . how . . . will . . . the world . . . ever . . ." she tries to ask, unable as always to conclude; Johnny helpfully supplies "end" as the coda to her thought, allowing her frustration to dovetail with his apocalyptic hangups. "Yes!" she agrees, before leaving the room to take a bath. That is the last thing anyone says in *Naked,* although it is not the end of the film. As with "Daddy" in *Four Days in July,* "Mother" in *Topsy-Turvy,* and "Drake" in *Vera Drake,* the final spoken word returns us through the film, coursing through its themes and preoccupations. In none of these instances does that final spoken word feel like a final word when it is spoken, since it is spoken in all four cases by someone other than the protagonist, and because it is frequently spoken before we get the final shot or scene of the film—in some cases considerably before the final shot or scene. We are left here with a concluding gesture of contradiction, or perhaps the centaur that the film has been about all along, the clash between yes and no, presence and absence, empathy and distance—the troublesome ambiguity of Johnny, a character who collapses the paradoxes Leigh has presented all along, eliding the side-by-side into a single person.[9]

If *Naked* is predicated on difference—Johnny's difference from the world around him, the film as different from Leigh's earlier films—*Secrets and Lies* may be predicated on familiarity, with all the inherent implications of the "familial." Eight distinct art forms appear, or are mentioned, in the first few minutes of the film, including: funerary sculpture; choral singing; photography; landscape painting; acting or performance; costume design; and puppetry. In each of these instances, the art form connects specifically to the personal or the domestic—art at its most familial, art in the settings and situations with which Leigh had been most associated. And the art form in this sequence that matters the most may be the art of stenciling—that is, the art of reproducing the same thing over and over, through the device of a preexisting shape. We see Monica in her house, stenciling a leaf design on an umbrella stand; that leaf design, shown in close-up, may seem to suggest aesthetics divorced from creativity.

The significance of this practice becomes clear later, when Maurice visits Cynthia for the first time in years and cautiously invites his sister to visit the home his wife has put together—a building that is a monument to applied art. The contrast in domesticity is sharpened by the fact that

Cynthia's house has no internal lavatory, and it is while Maurice is using the outside facility that the two of them engage, through a wooden door, in this conversation about Monica:

CYNTHIA: She's okay, then?
MAURICE: Yeah, she's fine. She's busy with the house.
CYNTHIA: What doin'? I thought it was supposed to be a new house, you said.
MAURICE: Stenciling.
CYNTHIA: What, drawin'?
MAURICE: No, stencils, on the wall. Decoratin.' You must have seen it in magazines. Very effective.

Cynthia's uncertainty about the condition of Maurice and Monica's house bespeaks not so much her naïveté about interior design, or about the larger preoccupations of middle-class women who do not have to work for a living, but a larger doubt about the relationship between the old and the new, or the traditional and the contemporary, or the personal and the impersonal. "Drawin'" leans on the individuality of the artist; "decoratin'" on the applicability of the art. The stencil gives us form without content, the rigid outline of something that allows for the illusion of independence—the color or density that we apply to our use of the shape—while nonetheless instilling uniformity. Stenciling allows us to graft someone else's design onto a surface of our own and then to remove the evidence of that graft, leaving the aesthetic value of the result largely in the eyes of the observer. To the uninitiated, it may look like art, the real thing; to the adept, it may look like a tacky imitation. Just like *Secrets and Lies,* as some argued.

Secrets and Lies reserves its most blatant act of stenciling for its penultimate shot, when Hortense and Roxanne, now trying to figure out what it means to be a family, peer into Cynthia's dilapidated shed. This unbroken side-by-side, over a minute long, of two sisters awkwardly reconciling in a backyard precisely recalls the unbroken side-by-side of two sisters awkwardly reconciling in a backyard at the end of *Life Is Sweet*; and the positioning (Hortense on the left, a Purley woman on the right) precisely recalls the arrangement of the café scene—so this is a stencil from another film laid atop a stencil from earlier in this very film. True to the art of stenciling, the color has been changed here. The black-versus-white

Figure 10. The side-by-side unbroken shot:
sisters Nicola and Natalie
at the end of *Life Is Sweet*.

clothing opposition of the café scene now becomes two women wearing black, a transformation that can be read in any number of symbolically convenient ways (for example: Hortense, the avatar of plot, conquering Cynthia, the avatar of character). And the subdivided rectilinear shapes of the shed, through which we watch them, themselves look like stencil

Figure 11. The side-by-side unbroken
shot, stenciled: sisters Hortense and Roxanne
at the end of *Secrets and Lies*.

forms, a grid now adopted not to show plot's tyranny (as did the grid of *Four Days in July*) but instead to connote plot's potential for liberation.

The movie follows this design with two final stenciling gestures. First, the view cuts to a high angle of the women in the garden, now joined by Cynthia—thereby duplicating the cut to a high angle after the sisterly side-by-side at the end of *Life Is Sweet*. Like that earlier film, *Secrets and Lies* transforms characters who seem irreversibly set in their ways into characters who accept the necessity, or at least the usefulness, of conventions—that is, of stenciled versions of the self and the world. Hortense presents a seemingly banal moral to her sister—"Best to tell the truth, innit? That way no one gets hurt"—by way of wrapping up their rapprochement, and we might wince. As a fixed code of behavior, this stenciled sentiment would seem inadequate to the complications of the world—as will be demonstrated by Vera Drake, whose interior and exterior lives explode when the truth is told. Second, in a move that allows *Secrets and Lies* to provide its own critique, we hear cheerful Cynthia dithering over her girls, pleased that they have gotten a happy ending: "Look at you, sitting there—like a couple o' garden gnomes." The happy ending does threaten to turn everyone into a garden gnome: a cuter, smaller, friendlier, less animate version of a real person. We might call this a "character." That may be both the difficulty, and the desired consolation, of narrative art.

Topsy-Turvy Girls, Career Boys: *Career Girls* and *Topsy-Turvy*

Late in the twentieth century, Mike Leigh made a film that doesn't look or sound much like a Mike Leigh film. Its visual style displays none of the hallmarks I have been tracing—the unbroken shots, the side-by-sides, the visual centaurs. The film's sound track is likewise surprising—a smooth jazz sheen with lounge-bar vocalizations, the kind of music that sets a permanent mood of limpid emotional accessibility and of the conventional pleasures of mainstream cinema. The film's dialogue features the lexicon of psychological self-examination, as characters spill their guts about vulnerability, parents, childhood, searching for a good partner—the kind of immediate exteriorizing of the internal that

Leigh's films historically have avoided with great care. The film's narration offers moments when we enter, for the first time in his career, the consciousness of its main characters—moments constructed, as such moments are traditionally constructed in the kinds of films Leigh avoids imitating, with close-ups of the characters staring thoughtfully into the distance, close-ups reminiscent of the formulaic interiority of Hollywood storytelling. The film's structure relies on flashbacks throughout its eighty-seven minutes—a clear departure for a director whose earlier work had always followed a strict forward chronology, a new stratagem that showed Leigh blatantly reorganizing the events of the real rather than appearing to stand in removed observation of them. And the film's conclusion presents a flurry of startling coincidences that seem to shatter verisimilitude, foregrounding the artifice of authorial machination over the empire of the plausible.

The most obvious candidate for a late-twentieth-century Mike Leigh film that doesn't look or sound much like a Mike Leigh film is *Topsy-Turvy* (1999), a Gilbert and Sullivan drama of the Victorian world, festooned with comic songs. But clearly the film I have been describing is not *Topsy-Turvy*. As I will show, *Topsy-Turvy*, despite its radically different subject and historical moment, manifestly explores many of the recurrent elements I have been identifying; its visual predilections, its bipartite structure, its opaque presentation of characters' consciousness, and its thematic preoccupations all correspond directly with fellow members of the Leigh corpus. Rather, the unlikely candidate—the film I have sketched above—is *Career Girls* (1997), a sometimes neglected work sandwiched between two of the director's greatest successes. When considered another way, reduced to certain bare elements of character and plot, *Career Girls* might look very much like a Mike Leigh film. What could be more typical than a story of young-to-middle-aged people adrift in the world, chitchatting on a weekend in which nothing transformative happens, and parting in a way that resolves absolutely nothing? This sounds like the script for *Meantime*, or most explicitly *Naked* (a film that is in some ways the doppelganger of *Career Girls*). So once more we have reached a point of uncertainty about what a Mike Leigh film is. Stylistically and structurally, *Topsy-Turvy* is the more typical example; indeed, it is in many ways a summa of his work. But a one-paragraph movie-guide listing that reduced *Career Girls* and *Topsy-Turvy* to personnel and events would make the first look like much more of the same and the second look like a bolt out of the blue, Leigh reinventing himself as an artist.[10]

That last phrase matters, of course, since *Topsy-Turvy* is all about people reinventing themselves as artists—or people consciously fooling themselves into thinking they are reinventing themselves as artists in order to go on doing much more of the same, without feeling they are just doing much more of the same. Its story of the career crisis that struck William Schwenk Gilbert and Arthur Seymour Sullivan in 1884, a crisis that resulted in the creation of *The Mikado,* looks invitingly allegorical, when we consider how different, in such superficial ways as setting, period, event, story, and narrative trajectory, *Topsy-Turvy* looks from anything in its rearview mirror. A film about an artist worried that he is engaged in repetition of early work; about an artist determined to stop doing the kind of "trivial soufflés" that amount to nothing; about an artist aiming to leave a lasting mark on the world by creating something big and serious and meaningful; about an artist who, by channeling a new way of thinking about his art, manages to reinvigorate his career. Could this be the story of Mike Leigh, using *Topsy-Turvy* to remake himself? One huge problem with that diagnosis lies in my use of the word "artist," since I have just used it as a stand-in for Arthur Sullivan; it is he who calls the collaborations with Gilbert "trivial soufflés" and who aspires to write at least one "grand opera" before he dies. As far as Gilbert is concerned, there is no such thing as a career crisis; entertainments flow, without anxiety, from his pen. The link between Sullivan and Leigh is one that the film may tease us into believing, over the first part of the film; but it is a link that becomes more and more difficult to sustain as the film goes on. We need to be careful with *Topsy-Turvy's* tempting suggestions, its seductive implications about the artists in the story and the artist of the story.

My first goal, as we proceed, will be to rescue *Career Girls* from the perception that it is a bagatelle, a "soufflé" perhaps, by comparison with the grand sweep of *Topsy-Turvy. Career Girls* is the least discussed of the films Mike Leigh has made since 1988, but it needs to be understood as a radical and disorienting landmark. My second goal will be to suggest the ways in which *Topsy-Turvy* is a masterpiece, one of the great films of the last quarter century. To demonstrate this with any hope of success would require an entire book, which the film eminently deserves. I will, in the latter stages of this section, try to suggest this by focusing on the final four scenes of the film.

| | |

Like *Naked, Career Girls* begins with a northerner heading south to London in search of someone from the past; like *Naked,* it follows that northerner on a few days' traumatic circuit of the big city; like *Naked,* it ends with that northerner retreating from the woman who was the reason for the journey south. The very different nature of those circuits becomes immediately apparent if we compare the mode of transportation and the camera work in each case. *Naked* jump-starts us into its world through a jittery, handheld shot that runs down a dark alley to discover Johnny apparently raping a woman, a woman we will never see again and whose history we will never learn; when he flees the scene and steals a car, visually we are back-seat passengers, watching the nighttime miles of the motorway flash past, accompanied by the restless harp music that will lead us through the film. When Johnny abandons the car in London and pauses, at daybreak, to figure out his next move, the camera tracks around him at a low angle, a drum beating three times dramatically as we watch a dangerous man about to launch himself in to a new world. This overture connotes anxiety, threat, intimacy, fear—and the sense that we may be in a very different kind of Mike Leigh movie.

By contrast, *Career Girls* allows us to glide gently into its world, placing us on a train as it moves rapidly but effortlessly through a dully pleasant landscape, permitting us to observe our northerner as she flips casually through a magazine. It is worth pausing to note that this is the first train of Leigh's filmic career, and to consider the consequences. Trains have, of course, long served as literal and figurative engines of plot in cinema. Consider, for example, Alfred Hitchcock's *The Lady Vanishes* (1938), a film that meanders for nearly half an hour at a Middle European hotel, awash in characters but sluggish in narrative momentum—until everyone boards a train, and plot kicks in with a vengeance. While the railways have been affianced visually with cinema ever since the Lumière brothers supposedly startled their public by showing a train pulling into a station, the railways have also served two very practical purposes in the areas of narrative drive and dramatic variation. The fact that trains (unlike cars or feet) have specific destinations, and specific destinations that span significant distances, creates a narrative arc that provides the viewer with a sense of comfort and security; given that we are going somewhere on a literal level, we might assume we are going somewhere on a storytelling level. And the obvious opportunities for strangers (to cite Hitchcock again) or even old acquaintances to run into each other on a train, to feed the engine of plot, makes this choice of transportation an ideal mechanism for the kinds of shifts in story and rhythm that unimaginative screenwriting manuals so eagerly endorse. The effect of the train as a cinematic device will be underscored at the very end of *Career Girls,* when this northerner, walking toward the train that will take her back out of the city, announces, "I don't like stations. I like trains, though."[11]

That sentiment emphasizes the peculiarity of this film within the context of Leigh's career. His movies have in many ways lived in stations—in the places where people are fixed or stuck, unable to escape, often thinking about the possibilities of going one direction or another but usually regarding them wistfully, or enviously, or simply with bemusement. (This is especially true of *Meantime* and *Four Days in July.*) One could argue that this northerner's *preference* for trains over stations might be perfectly in tune with the preferences of her predecessors; the fact that she actually gets to ride a train makes her a kind of foreigner in the gallery of Leigh characters. That foreignness is announced from the start, not only by the opening shot of calm and effortless movement but by the mellow musical strains to which I have alluded. That smooth jazz in the background sounds exactly like the kind of irenic fare that would actually be played on such a train—setting up a consonance between image and sound that has been atypical for Leigh, especially when compared with the contrapuntal music that characterizes the opening moments of *Naked.* The persons responsible for this score are neither Andrew Dickson nor Rachel Portman, Leigh's regulars to this point, but Tony Remy and Marianne Jean-Baptiste, the latter of whom played Hortense in *Secrets and Lies.* Jean-Baptiste thereby directly connects the end of one film with the beginning of the next, in more than one way. Hortense conducts the train of plot that drives *Secrets and Lies;* without the quest to discover the history of her adoption, that film would be as narratively static as *Meantime.* So we have two models of the past to consider here: Johnny's and Hortense's. In the case of *Naked,* that past remains always tantalizingly out of reach, as we are never told why Johnny assaulted the woman in the opening shot, what the story of Johnny and Louise's relationship is, how exactly Jeremy and Sandra know each other, and so forth—none of which should surprise us, in the context of Leigh's filmmaking. In the case of *Secrets and Lies,* negotiation with the past becomes the film's subject matter, as characters like Cynthia, Maurice, and Monica, trapped in the Leigh biosphere, where the past intrudes only by inference, are opposed to Hortense, who is on a mission to discover something specific, like a character from a regular movie. The shock of that film lies not in the mere unfoldings of secrets and lies but in seeing the victory of conventional storytelling over the storytelling of the unresolved.

Given this dichotomy, it seems fitting that Hortense's voice should introduce us to Annie, the northerner on the train, since Annie likewise has embarked on a trip into the past. And we have barely escaped the opening credits before the train of the plot comes hurtling down the track. Annie looks up from her magazine, stares softly into space, and, like characters in countless mainstream movies before, enters the flashback zone. We cut to a bulletin board, helpfully titled "Accommodation"; the

Figure 12. The corridor-space as the opening
shot of a separate film: Annie in *Career Girls.*

camera then tilts down to reveal the dermatitis-scarred face of a young redhead jotting down an address and follows her as she walks shakily down a hallway peopled with extras. Now, if we choose to consider *Career Girls* as in effect two films running simultaneously, then this image serves as the opening shot of the other film, and this image reminds us of the opening shots of several other Leigh films, from *Bleak Moments* to *Four Days in July* to *Naked*. The trope of the narrow street-space or corridor-space leading away from the viewer marks the flashback zone of *Career Girls* as part of a familiar narrative grid; what is unfamiliar is the deployment of that grid within the smooth-jazz confines of another film. Annie emphasizes the incompatibility of these two different ways of making cinema when we return, after the hallway shot, to the present, and see her smile in recognition of that past self—again, like a conventional character in a mainstream film. But what if we think of this smile not so much as the outward, visible manifestation of a hidden interior feeling—a device almost absent in Leigh until now—but as a reverse shot in traditional film grammar? In other words, we might think of her as looking at a film of her past, rather than recalling it—contemplating a different kind of movie from the one she is in. *Career Girls* uses a familiar tale of reunion and reminiscence as part of a dialectical clash between radically opposed specimens of cinema.

The dialectics become more apparent when we return to the flashback zone, as a handheld camera on a gray street moves toward a doorway, watches the younger Annie lurch in from the right, and swings upward to reveal a window on the floor above. It becomes apparent, as Annie speaks on one side of the door, and Hannah and Claire respond, half-hidden, on the other side, that this Annie is not only younger and less attractive; she also belongs to an entirely different school of acting. After the three women have moved upstairs, we are treated to a startling array of tics and mannerisms by Lynda Steadman and Katrin Cartlidge, who play Annie and Hannah, while Kate Byers, who plays Claire, performs something like the school of normalcy, sitting and watching and wryly smiling at times, like a spectator in front of a couple of comic actresses. What makes *Career Girls* different from earlier instances of apparent performative incongruity—such as the incongruity between Cynthia and Hortense in *Secrets and Lies*, or between Sandra and Johnny in *Naked*—is that the mannered and the realistic (for lack of better words) are used not to distinguish one character from another; in the case of *Career Girls,* the same characters alternate regularly between the mannered and the real. In other words, Annie and Hannah appear in this film as alternately stylized and plausible, in two distinct incarnations—thereby moving Leigh's interest in the oppositional from the larger arena of antithetical narrative foci (plotlessness in *Meantime* versus hypertrophy of plot in *Four Days in July*) to the space of single characters within one film. The conceit, within the plot of *Career Girls,* is that the stylized versions of Annie and Hannah evidence the inherently mannered psychology of the college-age student; but Claire's restraint, and the seemingly affectless extras we saw in the hallway shot, emphasize that the flashback zone does not manifest an exclusively mannered psychology. Instead, the flashback zone resembles "a Mike Leigh film," with both stylized and plausible characters, in a Mike Leigh fashion, with unresolved histories and plot lines, while the train-carriage zone screens a more conventional story in a more conventional way. One could say that the shifts between past and present serve as aliases, in this film, for an argument between the eccentric paths of *Naked* and the more direct destinations of *Secrets and Lies.*

There is a term that we can use to describe these shifts between past and present, between one kind of cinema and another kind of cinema, between one incomplete version of experience and another incomplete version of experience: a centaur. In other words, *Career Girls* enacts this recurring feature of Leigh's filmmaking not through a single image of two complementary halves of human bodies, or even through an image encompassing presence and absence, but through the very narrative structure of the film. Again, this is not just about the basic strategy of flashback, or crisscrossed moments of time; it is about the alternation between a cinema of theatricality and a cinema of omission. And this flamboyance, or theatricality, of the scenes from the past applies not simply to the acting styles. These scenes are flamboyant, or theatrical, in the ways in which they fill us in on the back story of these characters—showing their physical and psychological travails as students at a London polytechnic, from boyfriends and non-boyfriends to troublesome parents and musical predilections. The most dominant musical predilection of their earlier era is a shared reverence for The Cure, whose songs dominate the diegetic and nondiegetic background of many of the flashbacks. The Cure's gloomy post-punk romanticism underscores the Kabuki expressiveness of the flashback zone (in contrast with the Noh restraint of the present day) in *Career Girls*—the music's insistence on the delicious tragedy of one's misunderstood life encourages the exteriorizing, even if only vicariously, of things often kept tucked away in our secreted self. Emotions and motivations bubble up to the surface, whether through Hannah and her stream of cruel remarks, or through Annie and her radioactive self-consciousness, or through their friend Ricky (Mark Benton) and his clumsy attempts at seduction. The past, in *Career Girls*, is a place where the individual and the world spill into one another, blurring the line between the tangible and the emotional, between what we believe and what we want to believe.

In the flashback zone, Hannah and Annie (and, at times, Claire and Ricky) take turns addressing the book that they treat as an oracle, Emily Brontë's *Wuthering Heights*. They chant "Ms. Brontë, Ms. Brontë," as if invoking a muse, and then ask for some clairvoyant prognostication about amatory details: "Who will I have sex with next?" or "Will I find a feller soon?" or "Will I have a fuck soon?" Then, in a modern version of the I Ching, or *sortes Virgilianae,* the novel is opened at random, to see what carnal guidance might be given—sometimes with good news ("erecting himself" or "must come"); at other times, such as in the case of the unfortunate Rick, with calamity (a blank page). This mystical belief in meaningful coincidence, or fate, or the will of the gods, belongs firmly in the world of plot—where accidents are not accidents, where implausible events are routine, where things are ordered in ways beyond anyone's control—and it has therefore been typically banished from Mike Leigh's cinema. Leigh's films seem to be full of the random, of characters drifting in and out, of events that may or may not find resolution; that is, they are full of the promise of plot, but not necessarily its realization. Things don't happen for a reason; things happen. Is life, is story, a series of ungoverned accidents, or a series of accidents whose governance will be revealed in due time? This is exactly the argument in which Sullivan and Gilbert engage, as they squabble over what shape their new opera will take. Sullivan wants to create a work that lives "in the realms of human emotion and probability"—in other words, in the unpredictable feelings and events that shape (without purpose) everyday life, and that have shaped Leigh's oeuvre until this point; Gilbert prefers the "familiar world of topsy-turvydom" (in Sullivan's phrase), a landscape of magic and of switched babies miraculously reunited, of the gears and pistons of fanciful plot.

And this is where *Career Girls* gets strange. For all the talk of destiny and plot in the flashback zone, that half of the narrative resembles "a Mike Leigh film" in its ambling events, unfulfilled storylines, and emphases on the diurnal. Something completely different takes over in the present day, however. After fifty film minutes of the unremarkable—Hannah and Annie chat awkwardly, reminisce gingerly, and embark on a house-hunting tour—we leave the realm of human emotion and probability and head straight for the world of topsy-turvydom, as a series of three increasingly implausible coincidences unfolds. First, the smarmy real estate agent in the last apartment on the tour turns out to be Adrian Spinks (Joe Tucker), a man from college with whom Hannah slept and with whom Annie fell in love, in a relationship of uncertain duration. So far, so possible. And second, Claire, whom neither has seen since the college days, jogs by Hannah and Annie in the park, cocooned by a Walkman, unaware of the identities of the women she is running past. Hannah and Annie, conscious of the implausibility, marvel at this "one in a million" coincidence.

This level of narrative artificiality is difficult to digest in a Mike Leigh film; but we have not reached the climax of this peculiar sequence. We move from the unlikely but feasible (Adrian) to the highly suspect (Claire) to the apparently ridiculous, when Hannah and Annie, just before returning to the train station, decide to drop in on their old flat, which was located above a Chinese takeaway. When they find the spot, they discover Ricky sitting in a self-enclosed trance on the steps of the restaurant, hundreds of miles away from his home in Hartlepool; their long-lost companion has chosen to return to his spot of romantic humiliation, ten years after the fact, at the precise date and time of Hannah and Annie's return. This is the equivalent of the magic lozenge against which Sullivan fulminates, the preposterous device that enables the dramatist to engage in convenient absurdities and correspondences. The two halves of the film have leaked into each other, and the plausible present has merged into the mannered past.

This conversation between two halves of a whole—between past and present, implausibility and likelihood, role and individual—governs the structure and story of *Topsy-Turvy* as well. This movie could be de-scribed as one continuous flashback, a recollection of an era of anxious uncertainty for its two principals. In this sense, the cinema audience "remembers" the historical moment of *Topsy-Turvy* much as Hannah and Annie "watch" their past in *Career Girls. Topsy-Turvy* is not only about the past in the way that any historical drama is about the past; its lingering interest in the present of its time—the obsession with the telephone, the fountain pen, the electric doorbell, and all the brand-new gadgets of 1884, with the newness of that now—makes its story as much about the negotiation between time periods as the more blatantly reminiscent approach of *Career Girls*. Furthermore, as I have already suggested, the later film also features a centaur couple, a symbiotic pair that presents a wistful amalgamation of possibilities. This fantasy of splicing is given voice in a line from *Career Girls* that I cited in the introduction, when Hannah says to Annie, apropos of their respective faults and strengths, "Well, you see, if we could be a combination, we'd be the perfect woman, wouldn' we? Unfortunately, we can't." Again, the fact that "Hannah" and "Annie" are essentially the same name under-scores their interrelatedness, and the title of the film itself conveys not only a problematic term for professional women—it makes a centaur of adulthood and childhood, of the conforming, economic space of "ca-reer" and the eccentric, psychological space of "girls." The synthesis is an illusion—a point underscored nicely in *Topsy-Turvy* when Gilbert, pacing in Richard D'Oyly Carte's office, peers at an old poster for *HMS Pinafore* and exclaims, "'Sullivan and Gilbert'—who are they?" The unfamiliar reversal of those names makes clear how fragile the identity of the partnership is, how evanescent the synthesis of art.

Topsy-Turvy stages a split between the defining centaur of cinema—that is, between sight and sound. Although Gilbert (Jim Broadbent) is a maker of sounds, in that he creates dialogue and lyrics for his char-acters, the film clearly associates him with sight and the realm of the eye; he moves actors precisely around the stage during rehearsal, and in his office he maneuvers little colored blocks, representing characters, around a model of the set of *The Mikado.* Sullivan (Allan Corduner), by contrast, occupies himself solely with the work of the ear, a trickier organ to define. He objects, when he and Gilbert are still at loggerheads before their breakthrough, that his partner and Carte are treating him as "a barrel-organ," wherein one need only turn the handle and "'Hey Presto!'—out pops a tune." He asserts that writing music is an act of mystery, by contrast with the rather mechanical way in which Gilbert spits out visual spectacles of plot.

The moment in *Topsy-Turvy* that most clearly enunciates the centaur that governs the film occurs a little more than half an hour into the story, when the two artists meet to discuss their follow-up to *Princess Ida*. This is the first time that the two appear onscreen at the same time—their mutual introduction, in filmic terms, has been delayed for a very particular moment. Leigh uses two of his signature techniques here, the unbroken shot and the side-by-side, not only to present the conversational particulars that define this pair but also to articulate how and why this culture war matters. In a shot nearly three and a half minutes in length, we see Gilbert sitting at the left of the frame, ready with his new script, and Sullivan on the right, two sides of an equation that will not work out, joined by a sofa in Sullivan's study; a tray full of cups and saucers occupies the foreground. As always, this side-by-side device strains the bounds of verisimilitude, since people in the "real world" are much more likely to converse across from each other than alongside each other. But we could argue conversely that the traditional grammar of continuity editing, which records conversations through a series of alternating close-ups, and that therefore involves, on a practical level, shooting the same scene many times again, from different camera angles, uses a system of fakery to represent the real. In other words, this combination of the side-by-side and the unbroken shot is both fake and real, both implausible and faithful—or, as I would prefer it, it is neither fake nor real, neither implausible nor faithful, but a constructed investigation of what these ideas might mean at the time and place of the conversation depicted.

Clearly, the fake and the real are exactly what is at stake between Gilbert and Sullivan here. As I noted in the introduction, Gilbert would seem to have no objection to being allied with the fake, since, as he will declare when they meet again in front of D'Oyly Carte, "every theatrical performance is a contrivance, by its very nature." Furthermore, the conversation at this moment is also about sounds, fake and real—or, rather, decorative and substantive. After some ritual pleasantries and the introduction of yet another newfangled invention (lump sugar from

Lucerne), Sullivan admits that he can no longer produce the sounds that Gilbert requires of him. "I want a chance for my music to act in its proper sphere," he pleads, in effect asking for a divorce between image and sound, or at least between a certain kind of image and a certain kind of sound. By contrast, Gilbert's script, which he brandishes, revolves around a magic potion, whose effect is "to transform the character who takes it into whatever he or she is pretending to be."

We have seen and heard this all before, in a café near Covent Garden. It is worth reminding ourselves of the correspondences. W. S. Gilbert, the person on the left in *Topsy-Turvy,* belongs to the world of the eye, to the theatrical and cinematic space of the image. This cements a bond between Gilbert and Hortense, a bond that may seem unlikely, since Gilbert makes his living by operating in a world of imaginative fantasy, while Hortense makes her living by operating in a world of calibrated reality; Gilbert, furthermore, labors to ignore the hard facts that undergird Sullivan's desire to dissolve the partnership, while Hortense labors to expose the hard facts that Cynthia would like to ignore, the hard facts of the partnership she would rather not acknowledge before it has even begun. So, Gilbert and Hortense represent not identical twins but a side-by-side of their own, joined not by duplication but by chiasmus. We could flip this around for Sullivan and Cynthia, who in many ways might seem completely antithetical. But Cynthia's immersion in the world of sound goes beyond what I called, in the introduction, logorrhea and a plaintive voice. From the start of the film, we understand that Cynthia and Maurice have not seen each other in years and only communicate by telephone—which, according to Maurice, "is not the same thing." While Hortense initiates her contact with Cynthia through the telephone, it is Cynthia who at first wants to keep it on that level, by demanding that Hortense not make herself visible by showing up at Cynthia's house. Cynthia implausibly asks, after phoning Hortense, whether she is "on the phone"—that is, whether she has a home phone, an odd redundancy that serves to insist on Cynthia's association with the aural. More broadly, Hortense is a character who says very little, while Cynthia is a character who cannot stop talking, and her vocal fibrillations, from crying to laughing to nagging to cooing, define her presence in the film. If Cynthia, in this side-by-side, is someone who cannot believe her eyes, Hortense is someone who cannot believe her ears.

I am not arguing that *Topsy-Turvy* is a remake of *Secrets and Lies*. But I am arguing that the two films investigate, in similar ways, the problem of how we wish to know the world. At one point, we see Gilbert phoning the Savoy Theatre to inquire, through code, about the previous day's box-office receipts. The card that he uses for that code has two words on it: "favourites" and "hysterical"—in other words, the familiar and verifiable (favourites) and the strange and psychological (hysterical), or, one might say, the seen and the imagined.[12] *Career Girls* serves as both a false and true corollary here, since that epistemological tension is projected not through two specific characters but through two specific characters' navigation of the space between present and past, between the tactility of experience and the invisibility of memory. So multiple and various are the tendrils that connect these three films—*Secrets and Lies, Career Girls,* and *Topsy-Turvy*—that we could call them a trilogy, each founded on a central pair of characters, as opposed to clusters centered on a family or group (*Meantime, High Hopes, Life Is Sweet*) or an individual (*Naked, Vera Drake, Happy-Go-Lucky*). The defining characteristic of the central pair of characters in each film of this trilogy is a split; they are simultaneously united and separated, simultaneously centaurical and side-by-side. Before we examine the conclusion of *Topsy-Turvy,* let's consider how the split operates as a principle of the film, beyond (or perhaps as a result of) the presence of Gilbert and Sullivan. The four categories of split we will consider are: the conceptual, the structural, the narrative, and the visual.

Gilbert himself articulates the major conceptual split in the film—or, in his case, the major conceptual split in *The Mikado.* When Durward Lely, the actor playing Nanki-Poo, objects to his costume and to the lack of a corset, which he says he requires to "produce the required vocal vigor," Gilbert pooh-poohs him: "Come, come, Lely. This is not grand opera in Milan. It is merely low burlesque in a small theater on the banks of the River Thames." This might seem to undersell *The Mikado,* but the phrase "low burlesque" certainly resonates with a recurrent strain of humor, particularly humor that does not aspire to the condition of realism. (It is worth noting that both Gilbert and Leigh were/are skilled caricaturists.) Even within this scene in the dressing room, Gilbert's choice of genre seems a little odd, since Mr. Wilhelm, the costume designer, has defended his sartorial choices as "properly researched and authentic to the last thread." This also sounds like Leigh, who always emphasizes research and authenticity as key elements of his process, and not only in historical pieces like *Topsy-Turvy*. How are burlesque and the authentic compatible? This gets further muddied a mere seven minutes later in the film, when Gilbert is trying to get his three little maids to walk in the Japanese manner, in pursuit of authenticity. The eccentric dancing master John D'Auban objects to having his expertise called into question, declaring that he's arranged terpsichore "for pantomime, burlesque, and the ballet, for many a season, always to great acclaim." Gilbert is ready with a reply: "D'Auban, this is not low burlesque, this is an entirely original Japanese opera." He may as well call *The Mikado* a centaur: it is low and grand all at once, unified and harlequin. In this way, *The Mikado* resembles *Career Girls,* since it too is a peculiar mixture of the realistic and the absurd. *Career Girls* may be the more outlandish of the two, since it reflects no attempt to mesh the commonplace and the ridiculous, or even past and present; Gilbert may be more aware that he is concocting an oxymoron.

Topsy-Turvy's structural split occurs a few minutes before the mid-point of the film, and it is literally a cut, or a near-cut. As Gilbert paces in his study, worked up over the career split between him and Sullivan, a Japanese sword that he had purchased at an exhibition in Knights-bridge and hung on the wall suddenly falls, nearly hitting him. This quasi-accident jogs his memory, or his imagination (it is unclear what the chain of cause and effect is), and so *The Mikado* is born. This would appear to be a dubious piece of stage business—granting the existence of the legend that Gilbert indeed had such a dangerous epiphany. Does the fact that an implausible coincidence, or correspondence, actually happened make it any less implausible? This pales in comparison with the topsy-turvydom of *Career Girls*, but it will prove the thin end of the wedge for *All or Nothing* and *Vera Drake,* where crucial "real-life" coincidences—plot conveniences that are possible if not likely—change the directions of the films. The claim that such things could take place does not make them any less surprising in Leigh's cinema, given that virtually nothing like them occurs before *Career Girls* and *Topsy-Turvy.* The falling sword, however, is not the most unexpected part of this scene. As he mulls over the weapon and pulls it out of its sheath, Gilbert suddenly gets an idea—exposited through the thoughtful expression he wears, the camera tracking quickly into his face and the broad smile he levels on us. This is an unprecedented direct address, one that would seem to break Leigh's rules about an observational, as opposed to a participatory, camera. In effect, this is another version of the entrance to the flashback zone in *Career Girls,* where the thoughtful expression serves as a well-established transition to memory. Here it is not memory (the past) but imagination (the future) that is being accessed. How do we reconcile this fake gesture with Leigh's realism? The contextual answer is that we are about to enter the lovingly fake world of *The Mikado,* and that *Topsy-Turvy* has to bend its aesthetic principles in order to spring into that unreal place. Once again, we are made to feel the split, the uneasy boundary between two different modes of experience.

This leads us directly to the narrative split, or the two principal narrative splits, in the film. The first of these is the shot that follows on from Gilbert's close-up, a shot that shows us the stage of the Savoy and the chorus about to sing, to prepare us for Ko-Ko's entrance. When and where, exactly, does this scene take place? At first, we might think we are looking inside Gilbert's mind, as we are asked to look inside Annie's mind on the train. But the longer the scene goes on, the longer it seems to be an actual, rather than imagined, event. We have been watching a number of excerpts from *Princess Ida* and *The Sorcerer* to this point, so the stage show itself is not unsettling; it is the uncertainty about its location in time that is different. This split between present and future might seem less important than the split between present and past in *Career Girls;* after all, there is no psychological bridge we must cross between the two time periods, since we are watching people in the world (real people) on one side of the gap and people on display (fake people) on the other side of the gap. These are ontologically different environments. Stylistically, this actually mimics the clash of acting styles between the younger and older Hannah and Annie. But I want to push the strangeness of this maneuver, whatever the reality or fakeness of the two spaces, because it suggests that the framework of the film is much looser than we are accustomed to in Leigh; we really can't plot these moments out on a chronology, the way we have typically been able to do. That looseness also applies to what I consider a second narrative split: the excursions into a range of characters, especially the principal players in D'Oyly Carte's company. These excursions are far too detailed and unpredictably arrayed for us to think of them as mini-narratives; and yet the actors, for all their source of interest, must always be peripheral in a story that filters everything through Gilbert and Sullivan. Leigh manages to create a film that is both focalized and unfocused, about two men and about a company of thespians, and two large choruses as well. This other version of the split between the unified and the harlequin persists to the end of the film, when Gilbert and Sullivan are forced to cede the final words—both spoken and sung—to one of their employees.

Finally, the visual split offers a way of getting us to that end and its subtle complications. The film begins with such a split, as we fade in to see seven rows of purple seats on the ground level of the Savoy Theatre. As an usher moves across the screen from left to right, checking each chair, the camera—evidently perched on a crane—glides quietly down, into the lower-level seats, and then slides quietly up, revealing the illuminated and decorated balcony and the stairs cutting through the upper-level seats. The most patent split here is the graphic one, the crisscross formed by the horizontal and vertical lines of the seats, which are simultaneously separate and connected, multiply replicated similes for Gilbert and Sullivan themselves. The initial handling of the verticals and horizontals recalls the first shot of a film that would seem to be the furthest, in spirit and subject matter, from *Topsy-Turvy*: a film not about entertainment but about war, not about the gilded past but about the grimy present, not about the most cherished achievements of British culture but about the part of Britain that most Britons would like to forget. The film is *Four Days in July*, a film built literally and metaphorically on the phenomenon of the grid, of crisscross. The rules and limitations that drained the vitality out of Belfast are now magically transformed into the rules and limitations that breathe life into art—rules about musical composition and rhyme, limitations of genre that enable its practitioners to be free.

The conclusion, perhaps the epilogue, of *Topsy-Turvy* is comprised of four scenes that follow the triumphant first night of *The Mikado*, where Sullivan and Gilbert and the rest of the cast stand on the stage, receiving thunderous applause. The first of the final scenes shows Gilbert and his wife, Kitty (Lesley Manville), in bed, as he ruminates about the letdown that follows a successful production and she asks him about what his next work might be. Gilbert prods her for a suggestion, and she haltingly improvises a surrealist scenario involving dozens of doors and clocks, hundreds of nannies pushing empty perambulators, and the hero strangling the heroine with her own umbilical cord. The second scene also shows a couple in bed: Sullivan and his mistress, Fanny Ronalds (Eleanor David). In this case, their discussion begins in earnest (after Sullivan's declaration of his first-night emotions) not with *The Mikado* but with her announcement that she is pregnant and that she will make her "own arrangements" to have an abortion; only after this matter is resolved does she offer her thoughts on Sullivan's latest comic opera. The third scene transports us to the dressing room of Leonora Braham (Shirley Henderson), the alcoholic actress who plays Yum-Yum; she is holding a glass of sherry, staring into the mirror, and reciting the so-liloquy that precedes Yum-Yum's solo near the start of act 2, "The Sun, Whose Rays." The fourth scene—which might be, but does not need to be, read as a continuation of the third—shows Leonora/Yum-Yum on stage, singing "The Sun, Whose Rays" from beginning to end, as the camera cranes slowly back to show first the stage, then the orchestra, and then the audience of the Savoy Theatre.

The scene between Gilbert and Kitty is significantly the longest, unfolding over more than four minutes of screen time. The initial shot shows Gilbert sitting on the left, on the edge of Kitty's bed, while Kitty lies in the bed, on the right of the frame. One could describe this as a perpendicular arrangement, with Gilbert looking essentially toward us and Kitty looking toward Gilbert—although they are misaligned spatially, so that he is closer to the camera than she is, resulting in an awkward diagonal. Their dialogue here will proceed at cross-purposes, in terms of the visual representation of their bodies and the meanings of the words they use. The scene is comprised of twenty-seven shots, and it is edited through "conventional" means. In other words, we begin with an establishing shot that shows both characters from roughly the waist up, and then we cut in to closer two-shots or close-ups as the conversation progresses. Our expectation might be, when we see the first establishing shot, that the scene will unfold in one continuous take, in the manner of the scene I have discussed earlier between Gilbert and Sullivan in Sullivan's study, the extended side-by-side that stages their artistic incompatibility. Within the context of a Mike Leigh film, it might be surprising to see such a conventional rendering of the last appearances of Gilbert and Kitty in the film. Earlier, when Gilbert reads aloud some particularly fanciful excerpts from *The Mikado* to her, after Sullivan had expressed his enthusiasm for the project, she comments archly: "It certainly is rich in human emotion and probability." Gilbert's reply—"Hardly"—shows that he has failed to notice her sarcasm. Within the aesthetic context of the film, Kitty's critique of her husband's purchase on verisimilitude, and of Sullivan's concession to a script that violates his principles, seem to mark her as an arch-realist. So what do we make of this scene at the end, her big moment in the film, being presented through continuity editing—Hollywood's invisible illusion—rather than through the apparent realism of an unbroken shot? About as topsy-turvy as an arch-realist writing an Ionesco play—which is essentially the dramatic construct that she pitches to Gilbert here.

The second scene is more conventional, or unconventional. Sullivan and Fanny are on screen for a little over two minutes, and the scene begins with a side-by-side, Sullivan lying on the left side of the bed and Fanny on the right, framed at a slight angle from the footboard. In this case, Sullivan plays the role of the bedridden invalid, complaining about his "wretched kidneys," whereas in the preceding scene Gilbert had tried to cast Kitty in that role by insisting that she "must be tired," when she clearly is not. In stark contrast with that previous scene, this vignette of Sullivan and Fanny consists of only two shots, the first and longest of which involves a slow track toward the two of them, as she communicates the fact that "an old demon has come back to haunt us at a most unwelcome time." This design may seem unsurprising, echoing as it does such closing gestures as the side-by-side of Natalie and Nicola at the end of *Life Is Sweet,* where the twin sisters both resolve and fail to resolve their differences. What might seem surprising about it is that Sullivan and Fanny are allowed this valedictory construct, when the film has clearly shifted its balance, by the end, to Gilbert as the dominant personality; and the contained Victorian housewife Kitty has emerged as a more complex character by this point than the free-spirited Fanny. Why does this couple and not the other couple merit the Leigh treatment? The slow track does not in fact end the scene, since we cut after ninety-eight seconds to a medium close-up of Fanny kissing Sullivan, and a modest pan right to Fanny's face and then left to Sullivan's, as he thinks abstractly about all that has happened.

The economic disparity, on the level of editing, between the Gilbert scene and the Sullivan scene is further accented by Leonora's two scenes, each of which is represented through a single shot. The dressing-room moment seems to echo the Sullivan scene, as the camera tracks into Leonora's mirror while she recites her lines. It is worth noting that the track behaves somewhat differently here. The shot now begins with the track, whereas in the earlier shot the camera is still until Fanny begins to communicate her news; and the track on Leonora's reflected image moves much more quickly, even urgently, as if the camera were eager to capture something, or someone, as opposed to moving us gradually into the sphere of something, or someone. The scene here is not a side-by-side but a face-to-face, as Leonora speaks her lines—which tellingly touch on beauty, sitting and wondering, vanity, nature, and childhood—to herself, or to some imagined version of herself, or to the specter of her audience. Cross-purposes, which have been a literal and thematic issue of these closing scenes from the start, now manifest themselves not only between man and woman but within the self, or between a life and art. So this shot represents an actress offstage (in "real life") using invented words (the stuff of "art") to plumb some sense of identity.

The final shot of the film takes us away from this quiet study of the private to a show-stopping foray into the public. The complicated crane

Figure 13. Theater in film, film in theater:
Yum-Yum and Leonora at the end of *Topsy-Turvy*.

shot that closes *Topsy-Turvy* begins in medium close-up, with Leonora as Yum-Yum no longer staring directly at anything but looking dreamily off to the upper left, much as Sullivan does at the end of his scene. As in the preceding shot, we begin with the camera already moving; here it rotates about ninety degrees, turning from a right profile of the actress to a frontal shot and then moving back in a lovely sweeping movement to take in the whole stage, the conductor (who is not Sullivan) and his score, the orchestra, and the first rows of the audience; it finally moves upward to take in the entire scene, perched above this world, taking in the platform of art and the rows of spectators, the diegetic and nondiegetic alike. From an empty house in the first crane shot of the film to a full house in the final crane shot—from mere possibility to transubstantiation.

What are these scenes about? Let us start with two of Leigh's omnipresent interests: motherhood and pregnancy. The obvious subtext of the first scene, with Gilbert sitting somewhat primly on his wife's bed, is that these two childless people do not sleep together. Kitty's increasingly absurdist narrative of doors and clocks and stairs, and empty prams and birth and a strangling umbilical cord, blatantly illustrates her hardly displaced despair at not being a mother. Through an understated bit of acting on Jim Broadbent's part, it is unclear whether Gilbert understands this despair and chooses to ignore it, or whether his concern with giving birth to art completely blinds him to the less metaphorical anxiety about parturition that has consumed his wife. We can hardly miss the juxtaposition between Kitty, the infertile would-be mother, and Fanny, the would-be mother who wishes she were infertile. And, in turn, we are made aware anew of all the stories of pregnancy, abortion, and infertility that haunt such films as *Hard Labour, Grown-Ups, The Short and Curlies, High Hopes, Secrets and Lies,* and *Vera Drake,* to name only the most obvious cases. The film that most closely parallels *Topsy-Turvy* in this regard is, once again, *Four Days in July.* As we have seen, *Four Days in July* also closes with a paired portrait of childbirth, in that case enacted more directly with Collette and Lorraine holding their babies side-by-side in the maternity ward. In a coincidence that may be accidental but is no less important for it, we see Gilbert, during the premiere of *The Mikado,* roaming the streets of London to avoid facing "the foe," his term for the audience. At one point, he is accosted in an alley by a mad Irish woman, presumably a prostitute; Gilbert reacts with horror, pushing away this wretch, as he will repulse physical contact with his wife. The woman screams, as he runs off, "Who made the world?! Arsehole!!!" The actress playing the woman is Bríd Brennan, who, in her only other appearance in a Leigh film, played Collette in *Four Days in July*; this almost unrecognizable cameo deepens the conversation between these two films. The answer to her question—"Who made the world?"—would appear to be the female organs of reproduction, an answer that dovetails with the issues of creativity and potentiality that dominate the end of *Topsy-Turvy*.

And who is this Leonora Braham? We learn earlier in the film that she has a little boy, apparently born out of wedlock, who is both her delight and her curse, since his existence dulls her appeal to prospective husbands. So we have, in the final sequence of *Topsy-Turvy*: a woman who wants to be but cannot be a mother, a woman who can but does not want to be a mother, and a woman whose status as a mother is both a pleasure and a damnation. And what are the lines of Gilbert's that Leonora recites to herself, before the mirror? What are these silly words spoken by the empty-headed fourteen-year-old mock-Japanese schoolgirl Yum-Yum?

> Yes, I am indeed beautiful! Sometimes I sit and wonder, in my artless Japanese way, why it is that I am so much more attractive than anybody else in the whole world. Can this be vanity? No! Nature is lovely and rejoices in her loveliness. I am a child of Nature, and take after my mother.

"Mother" is the last spoken word in *Topsy-Turvy,* as "Daddy" was in *Four Days in July.* The problem of the maternal here resonates beyond the triptych of non-, quasi-, and semi-mothers. Perhaps the most mysterious character in the film is Gilbert's mother, from whom both he and his father are estranged—for reasons that do not begin to get explained. We last see this frail woman about halfway through the film, propped in her bed (an image obliquely recalled by the bed scenes at the end), amid her two spinster daughters, using an ear trumpet to hear a report on their accidental meeting with Gilbert and Kitty at the Japanese exposition that would prove to be the inspiration for *The Mikado.* Her two most memorable moments of conversation are a question about whether "Lucy" (Kitty's given name) is *"enceinte,"* or pregnant, and a final warning to her unmarried daughter Maude never to "bear a humorous baby"—a superfluous and cruel directive to a woman who has clearly passed the age of fertility. So Gilbert's own libretto, as reimagined by Leonora, takes us back to the riddle of his own fraught relationship with childbirth, even as he denies it when asked to confront it by his own wife. Pregnancy and motherhood are hardly omnipresent subjects throughout *Topsy-Turvy,* as they are in *Secrets and Lies* and *Vera Drake.* But they get suddenly tied together by the end of the film, putting the subjects that *have* been omnipresent—the difficulty of collaboration, the trauma of making something new, the complexity of invention—in a light that looks much more familiar in Leigh's career.

If the final spoken word of *Topsy-Turvy* reemphasizes the mother, the final sung words seem to avoid, or sidestep, the issue of parentage. After her first, private soliloquy in the dressing room, Leonora (now unambiguously as Yum-Yum) produces a second, public one on the stage of the Savoy Theatre. The private/public split has heretofore marked the film through the antagonism between Sullivan's fantasy of the artist who dwells in "probability" and "the realms of human emotion" (namely, the private area of feeling) and Gilbert's concern with his public, and the artist's reception (as illustrated by his initial appearance in the film, declaiming the *Times'* review of *Princess Ida* to his wife and servants). The schism between the two comes together in Leonora, whose side-by-side private-public performances raise issues about the illusory intimacy of film and the openly shared space of the theater, among other dichotomies. And what song is she singing in public? "The Sun, Whose Rays Are All Ablaze," Yum-Yum's solo near the start of the second act of *The Mikado.* This lovely hymn works as an oral side-by-side, since its two parts consist of first a paean to the sun and second a paean to the moon, and a declaration of the singer's similarity to both. Yum-Yum praises the spheres for their confidence and lack of false modesty, as they take turns in their celestial reign, and she triangulates them with herself by connecting her own ambitions—to rule the world, to be acclaimed by mankind—with those of the twin circles of light.

Yum-Yum's evocation of day and night—sun and moon—recalls the identification of sight (and the world of reason and evidence) and sound (and the world of mystery and speculation) that I earlier connected, respectively, with Gilbert and Sullivan, and their Mike Leigh forbears, Hortense Cumberbatch and Cynthia Purley. The curious thing here is that the sun, represented by Yum-Yum as an unabashedly boastful presence, resembles more closely the Sullivan we have just seen with Fanny; he begins their scene by declaring, "I'm proud of myself, triumphant, exhilarated." By contrast, Gilbert wallows in false modesty or anxiety about his next piece, acknowledging the opening-night ovation only through the decidedly downbeat observation that "there's something inherently disappointing about success." Indeed, he sounds much closer to Yum-Yum's moon, who, while lacking "diffidence" or "shyness," does operate by "borrow[ing] light" so that "through the night / Mankind may all acclaim her." Given Gilbert's notorious penchant for borrowing (from his earlier plays, from Japanese culture), which results in the nighttime acclaim of the Savoy that we have just witnessed—in contrast with Sullivan's supposed interest in Romantic self-discovery and not commercial approbation—Gilbert now seems more the lunar figure. So, if Yum-Yum's song is about her two progenitors, is it about Gilbert and Sullivan as we have seen them all along (sun and moon, the visual and the aural) or the Gilbert and Sullivan of the final scenes (sun and moon, boastful/fertile and borrowing/nonprocreative)? This switch between the two had already been signaled in the cut that precipitates the epilogue, when we jump from a wide shot of the two creators on the opening-night stage, receiving a standing ovation, to the first shot of the Gilbert/Kitty bedroom sequence. We go from Sullivan on the left of the frame and Gilbert on the right to Gilbert on the left and Kitty on the right, so that in the split second that it takes our eyes to adjust from one place to another, Gilbert seems to be beside himself. And that being beside himself, whether on the literal levels of framing or montage or the broader sense of being of two minds, connects Gilbert to Leonora, whom we will see, side by side, as private and public, as herself and as Yum-Yum. Gilbert's move toward the female and the putatively irrational, even as he reacts in horror to his wife's scenario of an irrational drama of perambulators and strangulations, enacts yet another topsy-turvy reversal in a film that has been about reversing and confusing categories and expectations.

The matter of the mother does lurk, however, within Yum-Yum's ode, if only by implication. While Gilbert's lyrics cite none of the sun or moon's classical names, their apposition here clearly recalls the Greco-Roman personalities of Apollo and Diana, or Apollo and Artemis. Diana and Artemis have many attributes, but perhaps the most prominent of these is virginity. And Yum-Yum, the fourth woman in these final four scenes, shares that attribute—unlike any of three women who have preceded her (Kitty, Fanny, Leonora), all of whom are identified by frustrated or denied or problematic motherhood. Peculiarly but appropriately, Diana and Artemis are also connected with childbirth—and there is no more fitting analogue to Leigh's figure of the pregnant woman as centaur, all possibility and no delivery, than the Diana/Artemis paradox that joins chastity to parturition. (The chaste arrangement of the Gilberts' sleeping situation would seem to emphasize this.) That Leonora, or Yum-Yum, should embody such a paradox is fitting for any actor, of course—especially an actor playing another actor, first alone and then in the process of acting, yet another centaurical concoction. Shirley Henderson is bearing twins at this point, carrying both fictions within her and yet not really carrying anything at all. During a rehearsal scene, we see Gilbert punctiliously instruct his actors on not only the correct rhythm of speech he requires but the precise relationship between dialogue and movement; these actors seem extensions of him and not independent creators, instruments rather than inventors. Yum-Yum and Leonora are different—or at least they are allowed to be different at this moment.

It is with Leonora that we need to conclude, the not-quite minor and not-quite major actor who literally takes center stage. *Topsy-Turvy* concludes with two scenes that have never happened, and probably could never happen, in "real life." Leonora's line reading of Yum-Yum's speech, in her dressing room, would completely disappoint Gilbert. She speaks the words as if they are her own—slowly, thoughtfully, self-consciously, but reflectively. If we are unfamiliar with *The Mikado,* we might easily assume that this is Leonora thinking aloud and not reciting memorized language. But those words are written to be enunciated not "artlessly," as we hear them enunciated here, despite Yum-Yum's use of that word, but theatrically, as the fake species of speaking that occurs before a solo in a Gilbert and Sullivan opera. The artificial is translated into the real, before our eyes and ears. And the final moment is also untrue to its source material. The gorgeously crafted crane shot that takes us from a close-up of Yum-Yum to a wide shot of the entire Savoy Theatre in no way imitates the experience of being in the Savoy Theatre in 1885, however properly researched and authentic to the last thread the mise-en-scène may be. The crane shot does imitate the experience of turning a completely theatrical moment into a completely cinematic one by giving us a movement and a perspective that only film can provide. So, just as the shot of Leonora in her dressing room shows us film acting—precise, delicate, intimate—through an observatory camera, the shot of Leonora on stage shows us theater acting—expansive, bold, communal—through a camera movement that is as "cinematic" as Leigh had yet attempted. These two shots are Leigh's greatest diptych, a side-by-side of two centaurs, of theater and film, his two media intertwined in two different ways. The Savoy was the world's first theater to be illuminated fully by electric light—creating its own sun and moon, and preparing the way for light to pass through a projector and onto a screen. This room is the epicenter of modernity, and we are only ten years away from the birth of cinema. In two shots, Leigh allows theater and film to see and hear what the other has to show and say.

Vera's Fingers: *All or Nothing* and *Vera Drake*

What is a human being? One could argue that this is the central question of Mike Leigh's films. It is a question first articulated through his process, in the way in which the actors slowly accumulate the bits and pieces of their characters through research, improvisation, and collaboration. The fact that the characters are developed by the people who will portray them—rather than being developed by a screenwriter—makes the actor and the role fundamentally intertwined. Leigh's films often deploy the physical particularities of the actors to make us think about the connection between the actor and the part—a connection made even tighter when we consider that his actors do not undergo noticeable changes in weight or physique to play their roles. We are particularly aware, when we watch David Thewlis in *Naked,* or Katrin Cartlidge in *Career Girls,* or Timothy Spall in *All or Nothing,* that we are simultaneously looking at an actor, a character constructed over time by that actor, and a physical body that the actor and the character share. When we consider how frequently we watch Leigh's characters doing workaday tasks, or having humdrum conversations, or behaving the way that "boring" people who aren't usually allowed into movies behave, we have another angle on the question of what a human being is—especially a filmed human being. If in many films the line between fully formed, complex people at the center (played by stars) and contributing, one-dimensional people at the periphery (played by minor actors) is firmly drawn, Leigh's films often make the arbitrary nature of that distinction palpable, since frequently the tiniest of roles evoke as many shades of possibility as the main parts. Leigh has said that all the actors in his films are character actors—actors whose variability blurs the line between the central and the peripheral.

This question—What is a human being?—also pertains to the recurring visual, thematic, and structural patterns that we have been tracing in Leigh's career. The device of the side-by-side asks us to consider how two specific people, or two versions of people, are related. The identity of one is wrapped up, genetically, in the identity of the other, as with parent and child, or brother and brother, or sister and sister; or the identity of one is wrapped up, by habit or need, in the identity of the other, as with librettist and composer, or friend and friend. How can we know one separately from the other? Aside from the specifics of any two people, the side-by-side more generally makes us think about where the contours of a single human being begin and where the contours of another one end. A centaur sometimes frames parts of the bodies of actors/characters in a single tableau: one person's head with another person's belly, one person's torso with another person's legs, one person's back with another person's front. At moments like these, the question of what a human being is becomes literalized—although the centaur does not always pose that question visually. The broader issue of synthesis, as with the paired Catholic and Protestant couples in *Four Days in July,* gives us another shade of this problem. What is a human being, or an entire group of human beings, if we can only understand that being or group as a counterweight to another being or group? The unbroken shot provides another epistemological approach, simply by asking us to look, and look, and look. When we look at an image for a longer duration than most films have trained us to look at an image, for more time than is required to understand simply what is happening on the level of plot, we start to wonder why we are looking at it. Is there something "more" to this? If most shots in most films give us information, Leigh's unbroken shots often require us to ask whether we are getting the right information, or what information means.

But this question—What is a human being?—has another prominent dimension in our culture: it is the fundamental question of the issue of abortion. The question can be asked at every stage of gestation, from conception to birth; the answer, at each stage, is bound up in a complex nest of biology, social values, and metaphysics. It is a question that operates at the center of *All or Nothing* (2002) and *Vera Drake* (2004), if more obviously in the second than in the first. By framing the following section through this question, I want to clear away the perception of *Vera Drake* in particular as a discrete film with its own subject—abortion—and reintegrate this work into a career-long concern. Pregnancy and abortion recur throughout Leigh's films, starting with *Hard Labour*, which in its depiction of class and circumstances serves as an early version of *Vera Drake*. Pregnancy is an issue, small or large, in *Grown-Ups, Meantime, Four Days in July, The Short and Curlies, High Hopes, Life Is Sweet, Secrets and Lies, Topsy-Turvy, Happy-Go-Lucky,* and *Another Year*; abortion is discussed explicitly in *Hard Labour, High Hopes, Naked,* and *Topsy-Turvy*; and a dead baby provides the most chilling moment in *The Kiss of Death.* Pregnancy enacts at least two of Leigh's devices: it literalizes the centaur by conjoining two beings into one, and it provides a vertical version of the side-by-side by framing two interdependent humans. More broadly, pregnancy serves as a figure of potentiality, of transition, of the "what if," of questions without immediate resolutions. Leigh's movies offer a landscape where transitions and possibilities coexist with the monotony of habit and repetition; pregnancy and abortion bring those contradictions into sharp focus. *All or Nothing* and *Vera Drake* address the question of the human self in ways that are structurally very similar, but with very different consequences.

Another, seemingly cold-blooded, way of thinking about the issue of abortion in the context of Leigh's work is to think about fractions of people, or what might be called "people on the cusp of viability." The most patent expression of these slivers of people, or slivers of character, is the device of the mini-narratives, a storytelling instrument with its roots in the *Five-Minute Films*, where Leigh exhibited fractions of life in different shapes and sizes. We have seen an expansive and eclectic version of the mini-narratives during Johnny's peregrinations in *Naked*, where fully formed characters like the night watchman Brian coexist with sketched-in people like Maggie and Archie and barely present entities like the young roughs who assault the hero. We have then seen Leigh reshape the mini-narratives into a more regulated and congruent series of shapes in *Secrets and Lies,* when a parade of people (or characters, or actors) present themselves for Maurice's camera, framed in similar ways and offered as brief points of contact rather than as potential participants in the drama. *All or Nothing* and *Vera Drake* synthesize these two approaches in a way that complicates the relationship between the mini-narratives and the larger superstructure of the films. The fractions of people that we encounter here are, respectively, the passengers in the back of Phil Bassett's cab and the unhappily pregnant women that Vera Drake visits. On a formal level, these groups of people closely resemble the *Secrets and Lies* model, since they are, like Maurice's subjects, clients; the connection has to do with labor of a certain kind, and the relationships are specifically transactional. The arc from *Secrets and Lies* to *Vera Drake* is a progressively complicated one, since the economic nature of the exchange gets fuzzy. Maurice has made a good middle-class business out of portraiture; Phil is far less competent as a cabbie, making barely enough money to help his family get by; and Vera does not realize that she is in a professional relationship at all, since she believes she is providing a free service, even as her clients in fact are paying a procuress. That developing uncertainty about what the transaction means and how it works will underpin Vera's insistence that she has not been doing what she is accused of doing. In this trio, it is the artist—Maurice—whose product has the most precise economic value of the three, despite art's notorious shiftiness when it comes to fixing its worth. The problem of what each of these activities means becomes increasingly acute, as we move from making photographs to sitting in a car to terminating pregnancies—that is, from creating to being to destroying.

The framework for these three kinds of encounters depends on what you do rather than who you are; the personalities and interior world of Maurice, Phil, and Vera may matter in some abstract way, but they are not directly relevant to the jobs they perform. Johnny's encounters in *Naked,* by contrast, emphasize not what you do but who you are, people defined not by occupation but by disoccupation. In other words, *Naked* offers a different fraction of the self. As a nonsystematic system, this might seem unlike what we get in the two more recent films. But the final mini-narrative in *All or Nothing* and *Vera Drake* sends each film spinning off in a different direction. The last passenger that we see in Phil's car appears around the halfway point of the film, and the conversation that Phil has with her causes him, in a state of catatonic depression, to switch off his mobile phone and radio receiver and head off to the coast; this desertion coincides precisely with the moment that his son Rory suffers a heart attack, and the effects of these synchronized events threaten to destroy Phil's life with the mother of his children. Vera's final client provides an undoing that is far more traumatic in its consequences than Phil's; a teenage girl nearly dies as a result of the procedure, and Vera's life soon disintegrates. In *Vera Drake,* the membrane between the characters contained by the mini-narratives and the characters who roam in the main story is tender and frail, and the film turns inside out when that membrane breaks.

Phil's cab passengers resemble Maurice's portrait sitters in the way that we see so many of them in mere glimpses. By contrast, Vera's clients resemble Johnny's acquaintances in that we linger with them, the fractional characters gradually filling in before our eyes. Indeed, the correspondences between Vera and Johnny are significant—perhaps surprising, given that they would appear to be the two most dissimilar people in Leigh's cinema. One distinction they share is incontrovertible ownership of the stage; no other films to this point in his career, with the possible exception of Leigh's first film, *Bleak Moments,* so clearly puts one character front and center. Johnny probes his minor counterparts by asking, "How's it going inside there?"—trying to push his way abruptly into their closed psychological spaces. Vera literalizes this approach, moving from the metaphysical to the physical, using a syringe to purge her clients of what's "inside there." The peculiarity of Vera's task, and of her approach to her task, is that she tries to treat her clients as if they were Maurice's sitters—chitchatting, or soothing any anxieties with vague reassurances and explanations. She is, in effect, caught between Johnny and Maurice, between the personal and impersonal, herself an unresolved centaur of openness and secrets, life-affirming and death-dealing, a fuzzy amalgam of personhood that the question of abortion raises but can never fully answer.

The fact that *All or Nothing* and *Vera Drake* offer parallel series of clients represents merely one of several striking likenesses between the two movies. For all the correspondences, or calibrated oppositions, I have been tracing between adjacent works in Leigh's career, no contiguous pair can match this one for similarity of content and structure. Both films follow a four-step pattern: a two-part premise, followed by a critical plot development, tied up by an intimate visual moment. The first part of the premise is a middle-aged working-class man and woman living in the same house as their son and daughter, who are in their late teens or early twenties. The second part is a parallel family; this second family will be confronted with the complication of an unwanted pregnancy. The critical plot development occurs as a caesura, about halfway through the story: a medical emergency that changes the course of the film—a medical emergency that is associated with unlikely coincidence. And the intimate visual moment transpires at a crucial emotional and narrative point in the later stages of the film; a very long unbroken shot, a slow track, shows the principal man and principal woman in profile, looking at each other, gradually moving their heads together, a gesture that seems to transform their relationship. That cinematic recipe describes both *All or Nothing* and *Vera Drake*. Some of the ingredients will be familiar: the parallel-narrative structure of *Four Days in July* and the caesura of *Secrets and Lies* and *Topsy-Turvy*. But we now also have a number of new defining characteristics; these two films not only mirror each other—and mirrors will prove vital within the stories—but they introduce new elements into Leigh's vocabulary. These defining characteristics are: the balanced personnel of the central family, the seismic use of coincidence, and the substitution of the side-by-side signature shot with a face-to-face. Each of these characteristics, in different ways, will offer new questions to pursue.

At this point, it will help to fill in the names and specifics of these scenarios. The central man and woman of *All or Nothing* are Phil (Timothy Spall), the cab driver, and Penny (Lesley Manville), who works in a supermarket; their children are Rachel (Alison Garland), who works in a nursing home, and Rory (James Corden), who sits around all day doing nothing. This is the first structurally "balanced" family in Leigh's cinema: a mother, father, daughter, and son, all living under the same roof. Given Leigh's interest in family dynamics, it is perhaps surprising that it took him so long to explore this particular arrangement of characters. One of the ironies of this theoretically balanced domestic formula is that this is, at the start of the film, as unhappy a family as Leigh has presented since *Meantime*. Indeed, the echoes with *Meantime* are plentiful, including the use of a decrepit housing estate as the governing space of the film, and the broader picture of people young and old living plotless lives.

This quadrilateral—mother, father, daughter, son—operates alongside two corresponding families on the estate, who share story time for the first half of the film. One of these families is comprised of the single mother Maureen (Ruth Sheen), who works at the same supermarket as Penny, and her daughter Donna (Helen Coker), who works at a coffee shop. Maureen is jocular and determined to be optimistic—but she and her child argue much more frequently than they converse. The other family is the most dysfunctional of the three, since the father, Ron (Paul Jesson), another cabbie, and mother, Carol (Marion Bailey), are perpetually drunk or recovering from drunkenness, and their unemployed daughter Samantha (Sally Hawkins) plainly despises them. The dramatis personae illustrate the challenge Leigh has built for himself in this narrative: three roughly similar groups, undifferentiated by the class issues that served to triangulate the drama in *Secrets and Lies,* each stuck in slightly different ways, but not in ways so different as to create storytelling momentum. In effect, there are two groups of mini-narratives, or at least narratives with shared characteristics, in *All or Nothing*: the cab passengers and these three "main" families, who live in identical-looking flats on the estate, pigeonholed architecturally as the passengers are pigeonholed thematically. Even *Meantime,* for all its disavowal of plot, uses the tension between the indigent sister and the suburban sister to stake out its dramatic territory. None of the three families in *All or Nothing* seems to have a last name—at least, for most of the film's two hours. What is a human being? Someone distinguishable from other human beings, if merely through the artifice of a name passed down from generation to generation? If so, all of these characters' purchase on independent humanness would be tenuous.

The surname that we eventually do get appears to be in dispute, and Leigh directly links that dispute with the problem of abortion. I have not called Phil and Penny husband and wife, because they cannot seem to agree on whether they are legally bound or not. We find out, ninety minutes into the film, that Rory's surname, and Phil's, is Bassett, when Phil finally arrives at the hospital to see his son. This information only leaks out because a nurse requires Phil to name the patient as proof that he is his father. But the "Bassetts," as such, may or may not exist.

It may have come as something as a surprise to us, about forty-five minutes earlier in the film, when Penny tells Carol, at a karaoke bar, that she's not married—since all the domestic scenes until this point have implied that this family has been together for twenty years or so, and storytelling conventions suggest that such an arrangement must be based on matrimony.[13] Given this new information, we can plausibly believe that Penny and Phil decided to stay together because she got pregnant with her first child (seemingly, Rachel) rather than due to any impending plans to make things official. In their situation, of course, other couples might have opted for an abortion—a scenario explicitly illustrated by the scene that we see intercut with the karaoke scene.[14] Back on the estate, the two-months-pregnant Donna is fighting with her violent boyfriend Jason, who is enraged by her condition, and by the fact that she hasn't yet decided whether "to get rid of it." While Phil and Penny are as flaccid as Jason and Donna are fiery, their parallel situations underscore a recurring problem and illustrate the fate that might have befallen Rachel, and perhaps Rory as well. That situation is underscored further the next day, when Maureen discovers that Donna is pregnant and confesses that she knew Donna's father for only "about five minutes."

So at least three of *All or Nothing*'s young-adult characters, and possibly all of them, were conceived under circumstances that might have led to abortion—circumstances such as a teenage mother, the unlikelihood of a future marriage, and working-class poverty. And abortion, as an aspect of plot, occurs directly through the drama of Donna and her dilemma. More broadly, as Leigh observes in his commentary on the DVD, *All or Nothing* "is a film about waste, about potential . . . about young people's lives going to waste . . . all going nowhere." These young people are all the offspring of bad marriages or no marriages, and they seem ready to reproduce (literally) the misfortunes of their parents. Leigh's terms—"waste," "potential," "nowhere"—could as easily apply to the results of abortion as to the results of pregnancies carried to unhappy term.

Phil's version of the story—of whether there is such a thing as the Bassetts, whether these are vaguely affiliated individuals or an official organization of persons—occurs in conversation with a cab passenger, specifically the last and most expansive mini-narrative of the film. The mini-narratives have presented an array of fractional people until this point, each glimpsed long enough to categorize: two Asian men speaking Punjabi, three boys in school uniforms, a widower bringing flowers to his wife's grave, a young woman scraping together enough money for her fare, two people headed to a party, three drug-addled people heading back from a party, a belligerent, and a drunk. These fractions are the flip side of the three families. We see the passengers for a few seconds, but they are quickly distinguishable from each other; by contrast, we live with the film's central characters but feel them to be very much alike, all defined by the same words or images or activities. Both of these characterizations change when Phil picks up a French woman, Cécile (Kathryn Hunter), who expresses a surly anxiety about tunnels. Just as the parallel editing of the karaoke scene and the abortion conversation highlights questions of identity, family, and the decisions that make or unmake us, Phil's ride with Cécile is intercut with the developing situation of Rory's heart attack and the rush to get him to the hospital. When Cécile asks if he is married, Phil responds that he is; more precisely, he says, "yeah," which is about as committal as he ever gets. Indeed, Phil's identity, such as it is, is the most vexing aspect of watching *All or Nothing*, since Timothy Spall portrays him as a blank, an opaque presence who might be haunted by something vague. The fact that Maurice in *Secrets and Lies*, whom we saw in conjunction with the sequence of mini-narratives most like those in *All or Nothing*, was also played by Spall accentuates the dissimilarities between the characters—the sensitive, can-do photographer replaced by the zoned-out, helpless cabbie. (The consanguinity, in the body of the actor, of these opposed roles plays into the first version of the question of the human that I raised at the start of this section.) But Maurice and Phil, for all their differences as people, do share a medium for communicating with their clients—or, rather, they both use indirection to make contact. In *Secrets and Lies*, the medium was the lens of the photographer's camera, an instrument for refracting light that allows the professional to concentrate on an image of his subject. In *All or Nothing*, the medium is the rearview mirror, which Phil uses to observe his passengers, an instrument for reflecting light that allows the professional to concentrate on an image of his subject. Each man negotiates with his clients—those fractions of life that drift into his office—by framing them, by considering them as characters, as constructs. We will see, in a moment, how disastrous the absence of such an instrument will prove for Vera Drake.[15]

Phil's extended conversation with Cécile, which constitutes the only real intercourse we see him have with any of the passengers, serves the narrative purpose of clarifying the driver's dissociation from his family, since scenes of Rory's heart attack and frantic rescue calls are intercut with the cab ride through the Blackwall Tunnel and into the West End of London. Cécile, who procures antiques for high-end customers, seems to represent a continental, urbane, haughty antithesis to Phil. But, as is appropriate in this moment of high-density parallelism, it turns out that they have something in common: difficult relationships with their only sons, and a general agreement that life is predicated on isolation and solitude; in Phil's words, "You're born alone, you die alone," and in Cécile's, "You are right—it is fucking lonely." This simultaneously consoling and dispiriting encounter, which confirms connection by confirming separation, seems to cause Phil to snap, as much as cause and effect could be said to operate at all in his case. Perhaps it is merely the fact that his worldview and her worldview coincide on this point, and that he needs to mull over the work of coincidence. He turns off his receiver and his phone and drives off to Kent, just at the moment that Penny hears about Rory and tries desperately to get into contact with Phil, so that she can get a ride to the hospital. I stress the coincidental because that is what comes into play here, in a way that might seem completely out of place in "a Mike Leigh film."[16] As we have seen, coincidence suddenly emerged from exile in *Career Girls* and *Topsy-Turvy*. In those films, coincidence and plot materialize almost in quotation marks, in ways that alert us to their mechanics and artificiality. It is one thing to pack so much coincidence into a film, as *Career Girls* does in its final half hour, as to make it a prominent and propulsive element—a series of encounters so clearly programmed as to make them a curious conceit evident to characters and audience alike. And it is a similar thing to make coincidence the very stuff of W. S. Gilbert's stories and the sticking point in the collaborative rift between him and Arthur Sullivan. In each of these cases, coincidence is metacoincidence, a conversation about the infrastructure of drama, the cinema object and an x-ray of that object all at once.

What is most curious about the central coincidence in *All or Nothing* is that its plot consequences are relatively minor, since Penny does manage to get a ride to the hospital, and Phil does eventually meander back to civilization. The consequences are even less noticeable on the level of irony, which is one of coincidence's major ambitions. Phil's walkabout and Rory's heart attack do not constitute any kind of interlocked reversal or reflexive comment, in contrast with the central coincidence in *Vera Drake*. Indeed, there is something distinctively arbitrary about this coincidence, since it shifts the movie neither on the level of character (an epiphany) nor on the level of plot (a narrative turn). The coincidence will prey on Penny, who berates Phil for disappearing. And the coincidence will seem to confirm Phil's plot-based, or externally driven, view of the world, where things happen completely out of our control; like a Greco-Roman or a medieval, he sees life as prey to fickle gods and fortune. As he finally sits by his son's hospital bed, Phil opines, "You never know what's gonna happen, do you? . . . He might win the lottery tomorrow. It's kismet, innit?" The lottery and kismet: the tools of topsy-turvydom. And this is the curious heart of Leigh's experiment in *All or Nothing*. He returns to the scene of *Meantime*, a film with zero to little plot, and jolts it with an apparently arbitrary plot development (Rory's heart attack) and an arbitrary, ill-timed decision (Phil's unexplained journey to the coast, which results neither in epiphany nor in narrative turn). There is the faintest whiff of topsy-turvydom in the reconciliation that takes place among the Bassetts and the prospects of a happier family life, as they exchange pleasantries around the recovering Rory. But the bolt of coincidence in the middle of the film remains unnecessary and unexplained, since the closing act of reconciliation is essentially independent of it.

Let us leave the Bassetts to their mysteries for the moment and consider the apparently analogous, though in fact radically different circumstances, of the Drakes. Each of the Drakes, far from being alienated from their labor, seems to find fulfillment of a kind through work, and those separate endeavors provide the foundations for their unity: Vera the housecleaner (Imelda Staunton); her husband Stan, the mechanic (Phil Davis); their son Sid, the tailor (Daniel Mays); and their daughter Ethel, the light-bulb-factory employee (Alex Kelly) all carve out separate spheres of society in the London of 1950, and their enterprises almost stand in miniature for a hopeful Britain recovering from the first half of the twentieth century. This quadrilateral family may not be much better off financially than their counterparts fifty years later, but the harmony of genders in the household is buttressed by a harmony of amiable, indeed quietly delighted, coexistence. If the Bassetts appear to blend in with their neighbors, thereby emphasizing their nondistinctiveness as a group of persons, the Drakes are conspicuously whole by comparison with the broken-down families around them. The film's first scene shows Vera helping out the physically debilitated George, who lives with the equally afflicted Ivy. On the way downstairs from her visit to George and Ivy, Vera runs into Reg (Eddie Marsan), a young man living on his own, bereft of parents. There are no parallels to the Drakes in their milieu, since other young people are sundered from their parents and other middle-aged or elderly people are sundered from their children.

The second part of the premise that links the films again serves to underline the very different applications of that premise. I have described this second part as a family alongside the central family, one that is confronted with the complication of an unwanted pregnancy. In *All or Nothing*, Maureen and Donna live literally alongside Phil and Penny, in an apartment further down the dingy row of estate flats. In *Vera Drake*, "alongside" denotes not architectural structures but storytelling ones. Susan (Sally Hawkins), the daughter of one of Vera's upper-class employers, a Mrs. Wells, is date-raped and impregnated by a fellow member of the well-to-do. This parallel between classes, rather than within classes, is one of Leigh's oldest devices, beginning with *Hard Labour*—a film with which *Vera Drake* has many clear affinities. If the narrative muddle of *All or Nothing*, implied by the title, lies partly in the difficulty of making fine distinctions, *Vera Drake* lays out its personnel in a far more familiar pattern. To complete the tripartite structure, we shift from the Drake family to the Wells family to Stan's brother Frank (Adrian Scarborough), whose arriviste wife Joyce (Heather Craney) cherishes her detached home and modern comforts. Like the stenciling Monica of *Secrets and Lies*, Joyce wants a child, and she gets pregnant in time for the climactic dinner when coincidence pays a call. The three parallel women in *Vera Drake* linked to pregnancy—Vera, Susan, and Joyce—offer an orderly pattern of constraints and choices, an array of attitudes inflected by class, money, and ambition, as opposed to the disorderly, meandering plot of the first half of *All or Nothing*, where patterns of this kind are much more elusive.

What names mean, and what pregnancy means, are the dominant concerns of this film. By names, I mean first and surnames, lexical markers of individual identity and of group identity. All but one of the six abortions we witness in *Vera Drake* occur outside the bounds of wedlock—that is, the pregnant women are either unwed or are bearing the fruit of adultery. The one "legitimate" abortion Vera provides is for a beleaguered woman already weighed down with seven children, a woman for whom family has become not a refuge but a crushing burden. "Vera" and "Drake," together, denote a rare woman in this world—one who combines pregnancy with happy marriage. Pregnancy and abortion, among their many other consequences, are about last names—and the heft of belonging, of inheritance, of the completion that last names, and especially shared last names, entail. Surnames are precisely applied, with titles, in the film, as Reg deferentially refers to Vera as "Mrs. Drake" when they first meet, and she in turn refers to her principal employers as "Mrs. Wells" and "Mrs. Fowler." The very name of the film advertises the partnership between a first and last name in a way that no other Mike Leigh title does. And the title, when it appears, emphasizes conjoined duality even more explicitly. The film begins with credits on a black background, and after the names of the leading actors and the director, we see, in capital letters on the right side of the screen: "VERA DRAKE." The left side remains black for a few seconds, until we fade in to an image of Vera in a courtyard; as Vera Drake fades in, "VERA DRAKE" fades out. This indexical juxtaposition enacts the most important side-by-side of the movie. The left side of the screen shows us a person, and the first part of the film will be about people; the right side of the screen shows us language connected to that person, and the second part of the film will be about language. This title image splits them into two, as the film will split them into two at the moment of coincidence; the rent will not be reparable.

To get to that split in the story, we need to consider the mini-narratives of *Vera Drake*. As with Phil's cab passengers, these fractional people cover a swath of types: a nervous young woman who doesn't want her boyfriend to know; a beleaguered mother of seven; a blithe lady with a drink in her hand who claims to have done this before; a terrified Caribbean immigrant; an adulteress who worries that she may die undiscovered because "no one would know" and who calls herself "a terrible person." But if the succession of people in Phil's back seat never really requires him to change his expression, Vera's group gets progressively more daunting. The mini-narratives, in the *Five-Minute Films* or in *Secrets and Lies,* are nonserial; there is no propelling narrative that carries over and through them. One could scramble the order of people, or almost all the people, without apparent difference. But Leigh constructs a clear arc for Vera. She is upbeat and in command with the nervous woman and the mother. Then she seems, to our eyes at least, somewhat diminished by being looked down upon, if ever so slightly, by the blithe lady and her friend. Then the Caribbean immigrant protests the brevity of the procedure, is dismayed when she discovers that she will not be getting a follow-up visit, and looks stricken when Vera heads for the door—a look that Vera registers and is unable to soothe. For the first and only time in this series, we stay with the patient after Vera is gone, and we see the woman begin to cry; the physical and emotional pain that Vera leaves in her wake has been kept offscreen until now. She will finally witness it in the presence of the adulteress, who wails and doubles over in fear and shame before the procedure begins, a spectacle that Vera watches helplessly.

Interwoven throughout all these, and climaxing between these last two troubled clients, is the other abortion story in the film—that of Susan Wells. As we learn, she cannot confess her condition to her forbidding mother, and so she manages, through the instruction of a friend, to secure an appointment with an internist, and then a psychiatrist, and then a gynecologist, to rid her of her difficulty—all for a sum fifty times higher than what Vera's clients are paying to her supposed friend, and black marketeer, Lily (Ruth Sheen). Although the seismic coincidence is yet to come, these parallel events underscore just how out of balance and frayable this world is, and not only because of injustices of wealth or station. Vera's good cheer, which seemed so welcome to her patients and to us in the first few cases, looks increasingly limited as a resource by the time we get to the last two women. The critics who have lauded Vera as an angel—a rousing corrective to pro-life theocracy—and those who have condemned her as an angel—an implausibly good person who beggars belief—have both failed to watch the film at this critical juncture. Someone who can see such suffering and then return to her happy whistling, and who can keep getting personal discounts on rationed items like sweets and sugar from Lily, without asking how and why, is someone who willingly distances herself from the consequences of her actions and from the world as it is. Such a being is not angelic but human. For all the precise realism of postwar life depicted in the first half of *Vera Drake,* for Vera this is as much a fantasy land as the Japan of *The Mikado*; everything turns out magically right, even as everything could so easily turn catastrophically wrong.

Here is one more important aspect of these mini-narratives, before we get a Sunday party that causes family life to go topsy-turvy—a trope vital to both *Secrets and Lies* and *High Hopes.* (A slightly less traumatic party will mark the midpoint of *Another Year.*) We have noted how Maurice and Phil use indirection, and specifically refracting or reflecting surfaces (the lens of a camera, the rearview mirror of a car), as a way of doing their jobs. Vera's technique, by contrast, is to speak to her clients directly and openly and engage them in direct conversation during the procedure; she has no mediating instruments. That directness proves, on a biological level, to be her undoing, when the sixth client we see, Pamela Barnes, nearly dies as a result of the syringe, the blunt and un-subtle instrument that Vera has used on her. The instrument that might have rescued Vera is a speculum—an instrument that would allow her to see what she is doing, an instrument whose name means "mirror" in Latin. The theme of the mirror, or the glass, therefore runs through all three sets of mini-narratives: the photography studio, the taxi cab, and the abortion rooms. This is appropriate, given that the mini-narratives provide reflections of each other, fractions of people glimpsed in pieces. The connection is even stronger in *Vera Drake*, because the idea of the mirror is connected explicitly first with pregnancy and then with family, in two separate unbroken shots. The first instance occurs early in the film, as Joyce, intent on conceiving a child, forces herself on a somnolent Frank, and Leigh records the sexual consequences by slowly tracking into the dresser mirror in their bedroom. The second unbroken shot occurs on the night before the party, as Vera and Stan sit in bed and Stan recounts a story from the war, a story about death and chaos in France—again narrated through a slow track in. Stan speaks of an "old girl" who was staggering past him, muttering in French; he asks Vera to guess what the woman was holding, and after his wife asks the answer, he replies, "A pair of old mirrors." He then comments on the darker fates of his own parents, and we discover that Vera's mother never told her who her father was and that Stan's mother died when he was twelve. The two mirror shots, two unbroken shots of two brothers in bed, mirror each other in their framing, and they mirror issues of parentage and loss. We realize now that the title credit was itself a mirror, since we saw Vera Drake on either side of the midpoint of the screen; and we shall soon see how powerfully both mirrors, and the dialogue between master narrative and mini-narrative, can transform their subject matter.

Virtually all of the commentary on *Vera Drake* has emphasized the bipartite nature of the film, as the perhaps naïve world of the Drakes, which plays out for the first hour or so, comes to a sudden halt when the police come to Vera's home to arrest her for inducing a miscarriage, on the very Sunday when the Drakes are celebrating Ethel's engagement to the unassuming Reg, and when Frank announces that Joyce is pregnant. The schema of *All or Nothing* is reversed, as this beautifully integrated family begins to fall apart. To apply the metaphor I suggested in introducing this new feature of Leigh's storytelling, the film we thought we were going to watch has been aborted, and unsettlingly so. Many complained about this narrative abortion (without using that term), decrying the loss of the carefully rendered details of daily life in 1950s London and of the finely wrought domesticity for which Leigh is so well known. The second part of the film, by this reckoning, turns into a plodding police procedural, with no real suspense or drama; Susan disappears completely, and Joyce turns into a judgmental shrew. Worse still, Vera Drake, the animating character who energized the film from its opening frame, turns into an enervated blank, meekly led from scene to scene, in effect becoming *All or Nothing*'s Phil Bassett. I would suggest that these critics have not looked at the opening credits, which warned us that the first half of this world could only exist so long as a second half could be kept at bay. What has happened, to phrase it in terms of the title, is that the "Vera" half of the film has given way to the "Drake" half of the film. The surname no longer denotes the comforts of family; rather, it becomes a word that places us into a matrix, that allows us to organize people's places in society. The personal has given way to the public, and we are left to address the battleground between the two—a battleground that features, among its most prominent skirmishes, the battle over abortion. The women who governed the world of the first part of the film (Vera and her clients, legal and illegal) give way to men who govern the second half of the film (doctors, policemen, lawyers, and judges). Leigh's figure of the centaur, of two entities conjoined, springs apart into two entities opposed: women and men, the family and the state, the private and the communal. That split has been present in the protagonist's centaurical name all along: "Vera," the "true woman," the Victorian angel of the house who has in fact lied to her family for decades; and "Drake," the male bird, and the name of one of England's greatest military aggressors.

We have seen this splitting of the film into two halves before—in *Secrets and Lies* and *Topsy-Turvy.* And we have seen the centaur as a dramatic construct before—in *Four Days in July* and *Career Girls* and especially *Topsy-Turvy.* But doctors and policemen and lawyers and judges? These are truly bewildering developments. There is not a single doctor in Leigh's cinema until *All or Nothing.* The closest we get is two nurses—the maternity-ward chatterbox in *Four Days in July* and Sandra in *Naked*—but we see neither engaged in medical procedures. And there is not a single significant policeman or lawyer or judge in Leigh's cinema until *Vera Drake.* Considering that doctors, policemen, and lawyers are perhaps the three most commonly represented professions in recent cinematic and televisual drama, that omission seems remarkable. The presence of all these creatures, in multiple incarnations, marks one of *Vera Drake*'s starkest departures from precedent. Susan Wells alone sees three different doctors, and a fourth saves Pamela Barnes's life. Four policemen show up at the Drakes' home, we encounter others at the station, and we get an affiliated industry—prison guards—at the end of the film. We see two different judges and three different lawyers at three different judicial proceedings in the closing stages of the story. The sudden, multiple intrusion of these character types into the world of "a Mike Leigh film" may be as alarming to us as it is to Vera herself. Doctors and policemen and lawyers and judges are the four prime agents of plot (or perhaps we should say symptoms of plot), since they appear whenever plot—especially death and crime—has happened or is about to happen. And we might consider the second half of *Vera Drake* to be plot's revenge on character, after being kept at bay so frequently over thirty years. By *plot* I mean not so much "events," since by conventional reckoning the latter half of *Vera Drake* is less eventful than the first;

rather, I mean *plot* in the way we considered it in *Four Days in July*, as a system of external, organizing forces that shape the lives of individuals, whether they will them to or not. (*Four Days in July*, of course, gave us soldiers—amplified policemen—but soldiers who never have to do high-stakes soldiering, as opposed to the high-stakes doctoring, policing, and lawyering that we see on display in *Vera Drake*.) And nothing activates those forces more than death. No one dies in a Mike Leigh film, until *Vera Drake*. This claim is contestable, depending precisely on what we mean by "one." Is an aborted blastocyst, embryo, or fetus a "one"? Even when abortion comes up as a subject in Leigh's earlier films, it is either as a past event (*High Hopes, Naked*) or a future one (*Topsy-Turvy*), or it is discussed as happening offscreen (*Hard Labour*). At least six deaths occur in *Vera Drake*. Or do no deaths occur in *Vera Drake*? The very language for discussing this question seems impossible to pin down. The entire range of plot-governing men that are unleashed on Vera may not in fact be able to determine what plot event, if any, has happened.[17]

The principal policeman that we get seems well-briefed not only on Mike Leigh's films but on the central epistemological questions of this particular film. Detective Inspector Earnest Webster (Peter Wight) travels with his own nuclear family—Detective Sergeant Vickers, a male underling who insists on proper procedure and grilling of witnesses, and WPC Best, a female underling who looks concerned and calms the nerves of those witnesses. Webster and his dependents arrive at the hospital where Pamela Barnes is recovering, and they proceed to question her mother, Jessica. When Vera performed her procedure on Pamela, she mentioned that Jessica's face looked familiar; Jessica, in turn, recalled with some dismay that they worked together at the Sunlight Laundry before the war. When Webster questions Jessica about the perpetrator of the crime, she at first refuses to answer, only reluctantly giving up Vera's name, explaining that they last saw each other in 1931. The suspicious Webster then declares, "It's a bit of a coincidence, isn't it? Somebody you haven't seen for years just suddenly turns up on your doorstep?" But is this really a coincidence? Given the tightly networked and closely circumscribed working-class society that we have seen, such an event seems well within the range of the likely. Indeed, it is more surprising that Vera and Jessica had not seen each other for twenty years. The main function of Webster's suspicion seems to be to raise coincidence as an issue, to speculate on how facts turn into plots. He is himself about to perpetrate the most plot-infested coincidence in thirty years of Mike Leigh movies by foisting the surprise of Vera's arrest onto the surprise of Joyce's pregnancy onto the celebration of Ethel and Reg's engagement—a concatenation worthy of W. S. Gilbert, or the final scenes of *Career Girls,* now in the service not of comic resolution but of tragic downfall. Webster's dismissal of the face value of evidence bespeaks a conspiracy theorist, a hunter of plot. But we shall see that one particular plot interests him more than any other, one system that society uses to govern itself and control its citizens. The name of that plot, or system, is language.

The first thing that Vera says to Webster, after his arrival, is, "I know why you're here." This statement is even more likely to catch his attention than Jessica Barnes's purported coincidence about the Sunlight Laundry, because Earnest Webster is a world-class skeptic. For someone to say that she "knows" something, before any evidence is laid out, is to ask for trouble. Trouble for Webster involves not heated questioning, at least not in the case of Vera Drake. Trouble looks something like this:

VERA: I know why you're here.
WEBSTER: Beg your pardon?
VERA: I know why you're here.
WEBSTER: Why are we here?
VERA: 'Cause of what I do.
WEBSTER: Because of what you do.
VERA: Yes.
WEBSTER: What is it that you do, Mrs. Drake?
VERA: I help young girls out.
WEBSTER: You help young girls out.
VERA: That's right.
WEBSTER: How do you help them out?
VERA: We're having a party today.

Vera's non-sequitur—"We're having a party today"—interrupts this moment from a Harold Pinter play, the speaker's words getting tossed back to her, returned carefully *as* words, as objects to be explored. Here he is again, after Vera has recovered her composure.

WEBSTER: How do you help them out?
VERA: When they can't manage.
WEBSTER: When they can't manage.
VERA: That's right.
WEBSTER: You mean, when they're pregnant.
VERA: [nods]
WEBSTER: So, how do you help them out?
VERA: I help them start their bleeding again.
WEBSTER: You help them to get rid of the baby.
VERA: I've spoiled their day for them now, haven't I?
WEBSTER: You perform an abortion. [pause] Is that right, Mrs. Drake? You perform abortions, don't you?
VERA: That's not what I do, dear. That's what you call it, but. . . . They need help. Who else they gonna turn to? They got no one—I help 'em out.
WEBSTER: Did you help Pamela Barnes in this way?

This is not quite like any kind of questioning we are used to seeing a film policeman conduct. Webster's tone is firm but gentle throughout, allowing Vera's phrases to hang between them. Eventually, he touches on the words that she will not touch—"pregnant," "baby," and "abortion"—and allows her to respond. His style, fittingly, is maiuetic—that is, characteristic of a Socratic midwife, slowly guiding Vera's confession out of her, occasionally applying pressure ("pregnant," "baby," "abortion") when necessary. They reach an impasse when Vera acknowledges that the conversation they are having is about language, as much as, if not more than, the crime: "That's what you call it." At this point, he gives a final tug—"Did you help Pamela Barnes in this way?"—to conclude the operation, to make clear exactly why he is here. Has Earnest Webster delivered a child or performed an abortion in this act of midwifery? That is a question the film poses, without presuming to answer for us. But Vera has clearly been emptied of something that was inside her, and she will remain empty for the rest of the film.

The ensuing interview at the police station again aims to convert experience into words, a conversion in which Vera is unable to take part. Webster begins by using her kind of language: "You help women who are in trouble." Here, he appears to be opting for her circumlocutions ("in trouble") over his clinical terminology ("pregnant"). But he retains control of the conversation by replacing her word, "girls," which has a maternal tinge, with "women," which forces her into being not a mother but a citizen. Such distinctions are lost on Vera at this point, since she has already abandoned her mind and her body, completing the chiasmus with Phil Bassett, who recovers his mind and body in the second half of *All or Nothing*. The last flicker of engagement occurs when Webster takes a guess about her past: "Mrs. Drake, did it happen to you, when you were a girl?" He coaxingly balances her most familiar and comforting designation ("Mrs. Drake") with her preferred word ("girl") and manages to get her to arrest herself, as she is wiping her nose. Her frozen look reveals nothing and everything—either a silent admission or shock at his misapprehension of her motives. From this point, language will become ossified, translated from oral to written; a signed confession is manufactured from scraps of words she manages to contribute. Detective Sergeant Vickers, whose job it is to put that confession down on paper, asks her to return to an earlier moment, when she was asked how long she has been helping women in trouble. When Webster had finally suggested "about twenty years," her reply was: "Maybe, yes . . . no . . . I don't know." Vickers tries to get her to agree to begin the statement with the declaration, "I have been helping girls out for twenty years." In what seems to be an effort to soften the terms, or more explicitly to allow for Vera's avoidance of the specific, Webster leans back solicitously and asks Vickers to amend the end of the sentence to "for *about* twenty years," as if to reflect more accurately what the suspect said. This has the whiff of concession, and of compassion, allowing Vera to remain vague, to cling to the imprecise that she seems to think will help her avoid confronting the specificity of her situation; it's Webster's equivalent of Vera's "you'll be right as rain," the particulars-avoiding bromide that she offers her abortion clients before leaving. But "about twenty years" is not really her phrase at all; it is Webster's phrase, constructed to seem like Vera's idiom. The emplotting Webster successfully co-opts Vera into language by creating the illusion that she is writing her own story.

That phrase—"for about twenty years"—heralds the final movement of the film, when people and events will be categorized not only by words but by words' even more rigorous colleagues: numbers. When a policeman reads out the official indictment against Vera, the click-clack of unambiguous facts leaves her without recourse, confronted by six separate numerical accusations, one perhaps for each of the clients we have seen: "You are charged that you, Vera Rose Drake, on the seventeenth day of November 1950, at 37 Flixton Street, North 1, with an intent to procure a miscarriage did unlawfully and feloniously use an instrument on Pamela Mary Barnes—contrary to section 58 of the Offenses against the Person Act, 1861." Numbers, with their narrow disregard for the subtleties of existence, will continue to mount against her, from the individually numbered exhibits at the trial, to various dates for appearance in court, to her home address, to the length of her prison term. Numbers are the familiar patois of police dramas; but they are alien music in a Mike Leigh film. Leigh's films have so often resisted single definitions, preferring the open meanings of the side-by-side and the centaur. It is no accident that his most emplotted film, the one where character is most confined by codes and regulations, is the one whose title counts off numbers: *Four Days in July*; or that the film that preceded *Vera Drake,* where so little is defined, and causes and effects seem only tenuously acquainted with one another, should feature the number that is no number: nothing. The prosecution of Vera Drake will be a deliberately desiccated narrative: people are turned into names, and things are turned into words and numbers. As serious and melancholy as the proceedings are, one cannot help also reading them as a parody of realism, or a parody of the kind of thing some people seem to think constitutes realism. The film takes the courtroom, that most reliable of dramatic spaces, and turns it into a lifeless museum of facts, of external evidence, of the observable and confirmable, the kind of thing that realism supposedly favors. It is both a parody of realism and a gutting of melodrama, reducing narrative to its dull nuts and bolts, its mere mathematics.

Who or what is the human being described, in that official indictment, as "Vera Rose Drake"? Her middle name materializes for the first time in the film, and we hear the phrase "Vera Rose Drake" on five more occasions, as she staggers through procedures, arraignments, and trials. A middle name serves to clarify the human being in question, making fine separations between this particular Vera Drake and other potential Vera Drakes. But "Rose" is not a name used by anyone who knows her personally; it is a relic from her birth certificate. We have met a Rose by another name in Leigh's cinema. That other Rose, who also finds that middle name used against her, is Cynthia Rose Purley. This is the person that Hortense says she is looking for, when she first calls, and this is the person cited on Hortense's birth certificate. Cynthia likewise finds herself trapped by numbers and laws and documents—specifically, in the café by her daughter. The cruel element of topsy-turvydom is that the unaborted child, Hortense, uses numbers and words to rescue Cynthia from herself, while the "girl" (Pamela Mary Barnes) who undergoes an abortion is used as a collection of words and numbers to prosecute Vera. Cynthia, born a few years after Vera's calamity, eventually manages to reconcile the identity on paper with the identity in person, the precise with the vague; for Vera, these are irreconcilable.

The tension between "Vera Drake" and "Vera Rose Drake" is most visible in Vera's fingers. When she first arrives at the station, before being interrogated, she is asked by WPC Best, the policewoman, if she has any jewelry. Vera says no and then is reminded about her wedding ring. She tries to avoid traumatic separation by adopting the local language of numbers, saying that she hasn't taken the ring off "for twenty-seven years." But this number, because its significance is merely personal and not evidentiary, does not matter. Vera slowly slides off the ring and then winces, gripping the finger with her handkerchief after it is gone, as if to staunch a wound; this procedure—the application of pressure and resultant pain—parallels the removal of the personal from the body entailed by Vera's abortions. Her ring finger might represent the human being as a collection of memories and associations, as the accumulated symbols (like rings) to which we choose to give meaning, and the self that we freely designate. It is not quite so neat as that, because the wedding ring is a token of the emplotment of marriage. Vera's fingers will matter again after she has signed the statement, and immediately after the indictment that calls her Vera Rose. We see WPC Best carefully applying Vera's fingers to ink, and applying the inked fingers to paper, to record the identifying marks known as fingerprints. As with the ring, there is a paradox at work here. Fingerprints are a familiar instrument of emplotment, the somatic equivalent of numbers, a legal device to fix the meaning of an individual; but those prints irrefutably denote us, in the way that a ring cannot. Which version of the finger—as bearer of ring, or as bearer of swirling lines—truly offers a synecdoche of human beings, or of this human being? Vera's fingers mean something else as well.

They are murder weapons, since they were used to grate carbolic soap, pour disinfectant and water into a bowl, insert a syringe into pregnant women, and squeeze a toxic mixture into their vaginas. Her fingers are one of Leigh's most complex centaurs, an unstable combination of the chosen and the genetic, the intimate and the impersonal, the nurturing and the destructive.

It is as Vera is getting printed that Webster walks in and announces that Stan is waiting to see her, and that her husband still doesn't know why she is here. Webster leans in conspiratorially and asks, "Why don't you tell him yourself?" Once again, this appears to be an effort at rapprochement, an attempt to give the private some purchase on the public, while simultaneously serving as another inducement for Vera to use language, to convert experience into words. Vera agrees, thereby setting up what I described at the start of this section as the fourth element that unites *All or Nothing* and *Vera Drake*: an unbroken shot that shows the principal man and principal woman in profile, looking at each other, gradually moving their heads together, a shot that seems to transform their relationship.

The version that Leigh concocts in *All or Nothing* is clearly designed as that film's signature image, a glacial forward track that over the course of nearly four and a half minutes moves in from a full shot of Penny and Phil to a tight close-up of their faces. It is the night of Rory's attack, after Rachel and the parents have returned home, and Penny has angrily punctured Phil's sudden and grandiose plans to save enough money to take the family to Disney World. Phil, devastated, finally expresses some of the things he has kept locked up for years, declaring that their relationship is on the verge of collapse: "It's like something's died." The "like," of course, is critical, since nothing really dies until we get to *Vera Drake*. When Rachel, speaking on the stairs with her mother, takes her father's side, a chastened Penny returns to discover Phil sitting and waiting for her. With a bare minimum of dialogue—"I feel cut off . . . Yeah, me and all . . . You used to make me laugh . . . D'you wanna go to bed?"—they literally move toward reconciliation, first with a hug and then with a kiss that ends with them touching nose-to-nose and forehead-to-forehead, for the final minute of the shot. The dramatic situation and the long take would make us expect a side-by-side arrangement, as we have seen so many times in the past. But Leigh abjures that convention, perhaps because the side-by-side, so frequently an adjacency of opposites or mismatched pairs, might not make sense with two characters who are not really opposite at all. Given the enfolded inwardness of both Phil and Penny, it is difficult to gauge what a side-by-side might offer, in terms of ideas or beliefs or even emotions. It therefore seems fitting that this couple that, even in a moment of reunion, cannot find the words to acknowledge what they want should turn away from us; and even more fitting that Leigh should end the shot with that most unorthodox of gestures (for him), the fade-out, an editing device that hides from us what the rest of the shot might depict. Phil and Penny are somehow unphotographable, two people who even when restored to the family live much more inside themselves than outside themselves—a trait inherited even more powerfully by the illegible Rachel. The movie, I would argue, is about looking at people who will not look back, who refuse direct address, just as Phil sees his passengers through a mirror. This, too, is the human—and it stretches the capabilities of cinema almost to the breaking point.

The face-to-face design is repeated in *Vera Drake,* just as the film is about to launch into a seemingly endless cycle of repetitions—facts of the case repeated, close-ups of a devastated Vera repeated, awkward scenes of family life repeated. In contrast with *All or Nothing,* by the time the face-to-face arrives in *Vera Drake* we have already seen what was later deemed, and seems to have been deemed during production, the film's signature moment. That moment occurs as the police arrive at the party, and it frames Vera in the left foreground, in close-up, with Ethel, Joyce, and Frank ringed around her, slightly out of focus, in medium shot. As Vera realizes what is about to happen, the self gradually fades from her face, and the film switches from one kind of story to another kind of story. The shot is not even thirty seconds long, and it does not quite fit the rules of the side-by-side. It feels, however, like an unbroken shot. And we do have four characters looking directly toward the camera, in a kind of doubled side-by-side; the contrast between Vera and family (Ethel, Joyce, and Frank) does articulate a central tension between the individual and the communal. So there may seem to be less at stake, on the visual/conceptual level, when we get to the interrogation room and Stan and Vera face each other; Vera has already confessed, already been changed, in that earlier moment. There are two key aspects of this face-

Figure 14. The face-to-face and the
unphotographable: Penny and Phil
in *All or Nothing*.

to-face—a shot over two minutes long that tracks in for its first half—that complicate its effects. One of these is that as Stan and Vera's faces get closer and closer, we anticipate the direct contact that we saw with Penny and Phil. But instead their heads slide past each other, and she leans in to whisper her confessional circumlocutions into Stan's ear. Her face, or

Figure 15. The face-to-face and the
unspeakable: Stan and Vera in *Vera Drake*.

the defining features of her face, are tucked behind his head, so that we get the momentary suggestion of a centaur, as if they were two conjoined bodies—distinctly different from Penny and Phil, who remain separate even as they touch. This image of combination and symbiosis arrives at the moment when they are about to be most separated, physically and psychologically, as she is sent to jail and he tries to reorient himself to a wife different from the one he thought he knew. The other complication is that Webster is lurking in the background of the shot, positioned centrally between the husband and the wife, facing us and leaning on a chair; a temporary and perhaps salutary consequence, for Stan and Vera and the audience, of their heads sliding past each another, is that Webster disappears temporarily—only to reappear when they move their heads back again. One of the cardinal conditions of the side-by-side, of which I am considering the face-to-face an irregular offspring, is a lack of self-consciousness about being watched. All the prominent side-by-sides until now have occurred with no one else in the room, or the garden—freeing up the artifice of the arrangement by implying that nothing, not even a camera, is observing these people. This shot in the interrogation room may be the most discomfiting moment in *Vera Drake*, because we are so conscious of Webster as our double, and so conscious of the bliss of solitude, however illusory or fleeting, that Stan and Vera might imagine when he is blocked from view. They are not only people now. They are characters.

The last word of the film is "Drake." It is spoken by another voice of the law, a prison guard, as Vera inches her way up a jailhouse staircase. "Mind where you're going, Drake," the guard instructs—an unnecessary directive, since she's doing everything possible to avoid making contact with everyone around her. "Daddy," the final word of *Four Days in July*, serves to illustrate that all the asphyxiating beliefs and conditions that have governed the film, and seemed at last possibly amendable, are about to be disastrously reaffirmed. "Drake," by contrast, confirms that an entirely new set of principles has been established. Vera has never been called "Drake" in her life. The surname that she gained from her husband, a name into which she poured meaning by creating a family and a social identity, by giving that name context, has been stripped back down to a monosyllabic, regulatory designation, as neutral as a number. "Vera," "Mrs.," and even "Rose" belong to her; but not the flat, unadorned "Drake." One answer to our initial question—What is a human being?—would be: a creature with a first name and a last name. This answer might allow Vera to think of the creatures she has destroyed as not human. But such an answer would make Vera herself not human at this moment. Vera has been turned into a word, a word that has never been applied to her before, just as films always threaten to turn people into characters and, more dangerous still, life into art. Leigh's cinema, whatever the loving acclaim that has been bestowed on it, has never been afraid to follow through on that threat.

Five Lessons, Four Seasons:
Happy-Go-Lucky and *Another Year*

The protagonist of *Happy-Go-Lucky* is a woman who does not know how to drive. The protagonist of *Another Year* is also a woman who does not know how to drive. In the first instance, the protagonist is thirty-year-old Poppy (Sally Hawkins), an effusive, constantly delighted primary school teacher who decides to take lessons, in the wake of the theft of her bicycle. In the second instance, the protagonist is the fiftyish Mary (Lesley Manville), a neurotic, constantly anxious secretary who decides to buy a car, in the belief that it will grant her freedom, and possibly a new life. "Not knowing how to drive," in Mary's case, means that she is a terrible driver, who buys a terrible car, which brings her terrible luck. Mary's terrible luck recalls her counterpart protagonist, who thinks of herself as both happy and lucky—as the title of Poppy's film suggests. One critic, writing after *Another Year*'s premiere at Cannes, suggested that Mary is a "tragic photo negative" of the "genuinely sunny Poppy" (Noller)—a claim that aptly points to Mary's dogged determination to be both happy and lucky, to somehow switch films and enter the more temperate climate of the earlier movie. These two stories, along with *Vera Drake,* constitute a kind of trilogy centered on a manifestly happy or unhappy woman; Vera in the first half of her story is relentlessly happy, and in the second half she is relentlessly unhappy. As different in tone, subject, and even style as these three films are, their shared interest in depicting a central figure marks at least a temporary shift in Leigh's narrative modus operandi—which has almost always concentrated on a central pair (*Career Girls, Topsy-Turvy*) or, even more typically, a family or cluster of families. The one obvious exception is *Naked,* and it will be useful for us to consider Johnny alongside these women. Despite the patent differences in temperament, deeds, and background among the films, and in their explorations of the argument between center and periphery, between the one and the many, *Naked* offers a way of thinking about Poppy and Mary—not least the fact that one of the first things that we see Johnny do is get in a car and drive to London.

In this brief look at Leigh's two most recent films, I will consider two primary cinematic elements. The first of these will be narrative structure—particularly, the tension between a narrative throughline and narrative byways, another version not only of Johnny's one-versus-many centrality but also of the continuously changing role of mini-narratives, or nested narratives, in Leigh's cinema. The second of these will be the unbroken shot—particularly, the final shot in each film, which I will consider as part of a change in the way Leigh has used the long take, especially since the final shot of *Naked.* But first, a few words about happiness and luck. *Happy-Go-Lucky,* as a title, is another kind of centaur, bringing together a condition of character and affect (happiness) and a condition of plot and circumstance (luck). If Poppy's happiness and Mary's unhappiness are fixed aspects of their characters, the issue of luck raises the prospect of the unfixed, of those things (like coincidences) that happen for reasons out of the characters' control—or for no reason at all. In *Happy-Go-Lucky,* Poppy's friend Zoe (Alexis Zegerman) says that "people make their own luck"; in *Another Year,* Mary's friend Gerri (Ruth Sheen) calls herself "lucky" and Mary says that she "deserves it." Both of these characterizations—luck as something you shape, or luck as something you earn—are predicated on a basic misunderstanding, or avoidance, of the nature of luck: luck, by definition, is indiscriminate, inattentive to particulars of character, causing plot shrapnel to explode in ways irrelevant to the construction of the self. We might say that the world of *Meantime* is luckless—in that nothing resembling coincidence or the unexpected penetrates its environment—while the world of *Four Days in July* is entirely predicated on luck, both in the structural "luck" of its two mothers-to-be giving birth at the same time in the same room, and in the degree to which its world constantly puts the hazards of luck at play, as represented by the three violent incidents that Eugene's body has had the (bad) luck to experience. We might ask again the presiding question of the previous section: What is a human being? Some centaurical combination of internal barometer (happiness) and external circumstances (luck), perhaps. Or does that describe not so much a human being as a fictional character—a being defined by a specific, persistent navigation between internal attributes and authorial design?

If we rotate luck 180 degrees and consider the obverse of the fortunate—that is, the random—we have a way into the initial narrative design of *Happy-Go-Lucky*. There is an apparent randomness to the unfolding of the film, simply one incident after another (Poppy goes to a bookshop, Poppy goes clubbing, Poppy goes trampolining, Poppy learns flamenco), rather than narrative drive—that is, the kind of thing that requires a certain luck (such as the arrival of policemen to arrest Vera on day of her big party) to put a jolt into the proceedings. There are two strands in the film that tug significantly against this episodic pattern. One strand is a boy-meets-girl story, occasioned in the film's second half by Poppy meeting the tall, handsome social worker Tim—a nice piece of luck. It is worth noting that boy-meets-girl, or girl-meets-boy, one of the foundational instruments of narrative cinema, has been absent from Leigh's films since *The Short and Curlies* (a film multiply relevant to *Happy-Go-Lucky*). Romantic encounters of this nature either take place before the film has begun (in the case of families), or they fail to follow a comic path toward marriage (or at least a fixed relationship, as suggested at the end of *Happy-Go-Lucky*). So Poppy is potentially pulled out of the world of unrelated incident by what, in stories involving charming young ladies, is the most conventional of forces; what makes this contextually unconventional is that it has been virtually unknown in Leigh, just as those highly conventional plot-device characters, police and doctors, were virtually unknown in Leigh's films until *Vera Drake*.

But the far more important tug, for the film as a whole, is represented by the five driving lessons that Poppy takes with her instructor, the irascible and humorless Scott (Eddie Marsan). In a DVD extra, Marsan says that he believed during the long preparatory process, in segregation from the other actors, that Leigh was constructing a dark, brooding film—given the rage and bitterness of his character. When Marsan, as Scott, first began improvisations with Sally Hawkins, he discovered that his character was the "antithesis" of the lightness and generosity represented by Hawkins—and that he was working in a very different story from the one he had imagined. Marsan's comments point to two crucial aspects of the driving lessons. First, the idea of antithesis, of two opposed forces brought together, is another way of naming a centaur—a relationship underscored by the fact that these two antithetical characters sit side-by-side for considerable portions of the film. Many of the side-by-side centaurs that we have noted in Leigh's films involve two people of the same gender. The Poppy-Scott centaur, by contrast, calls to mind the antithetical conjunction of Clive and Joy in *The Short and Curlies,* the figure of humor and the figure of humorlessness; Scott's monomania is centered not on jokes or the body but on dark plots of conspiracy theory and antisocial screed. Poppy and Scott starkly suggest Thalia and Melpomene, the muses of comedy and tragedy, driving a red car around the streets of London. The second crucial aspect of the driving lessons connects with Marsan's sense that he had been making another movie all along—because in effect *Happy-Go-Lucky* does become another movie over the course of those lessons. The five events are structured through repetition, routine, and system: the repetition and routine of weekly lessons at noon on Saturdays, but also the repetitions, routines, and systems entailed by learning how to operate a motor vehicle. In the unsystematic life and narrative of Poppy, these lessons—which gradually build from amusing tension to out-and-out conflict—offer the rubric of plot, of system, that the rest of the film lacks, until the arrival of girl-meets-boy. It is as if the mini-narratives of the earlier films—those events governed by such systematic processes as studio photographs or taxi rides—have become not tributaries of the main narrative, offshoots of the possible, but the momentum of narrative itself, giving shape to the episodic.

Mary, in *Another Year,* offers a telling counterpoint to the work of Poppy and Scott's driving lessons: flush with the initial thrill of owning a car for the first time in decades, she announces at a barbecue that "just driving here today, I felt like a whole person." So, without the car, Mary is a fragment of a person, or perhaps many fragments of a person. To some degree, this allows us to think about Poppy and Scott as fragments of people—or, more correctly, fragments of characters, who require the space of the car to become whole, as part of a centaur and as part of the system of plot. But Mary may in fact be more than a whole person when she gets behind the wheel. In a subsequent scene at the barbecue, she tells a friend that, now that she is driving a car, "I feel like Thelma and Louise." Direct allusions to other films are extremely rare in Leigh's cinema; this verbal gesture toward the most famously centaurical driving women in film history reminds us of a story that begins as a road movie—a meandering character drama—before suddenly swerving into the land of plot. It is worth noting that we also see Hannah and Annie drive around town in many of the contemporary scenes of *Career Girls*; Hannah's declaration that "if we could be a combination, we'd be the perfect woman," and the way that her film suddenly swerves into coincidence, offers a kind of antithesis to the perpetually drifting Mary. Mary feels plotless at this point of her life—bobbing along with a passable job and a passable flat, but with none of the centripetal force, or at least the sense of fitting into a system, that marriage or parenthood could entail. So, does driving a car make her feel like a whole person, or does it make her feel like two persons—or, more precisely, two fictional characters? The person to whom she makes the Thelma and Louise remark is Joe (Oliver Maltman), the adult son of Tom (Jim Broadbent) and Gerri (Ruth Sheen)—hosts of the barbecue and patient friends of the scattered Mary, the one focus for her fragmented life. "Tom and Gerri," of course, is a homonym for another celebrated cinematic centaur—one composed of what might be called two fragments of "real" people, in that they are animated, and in that they are animals. Mary believes, delusionally, that she and Joe "click," and she clearly imagines that "Joe and Mary" could

Figure 16. Whole and fragment, plot and character: Gerri and Mary in *Another Year*.

be a couple—a centaur with biblical overtones that makes Gerri, Joe's mother, recoil.

This recoiling occasions a crucial shift in the narrative of *Another Year*, which is narrated through four successive seasons—spring, summer, autumn, and winter. The system represented by a year gives shape to lives and events that might otherwise reside outside the realm of plot; in the case of *Four Days in July*—also divided into four calendrical units—the marching season exists to reinforce plot's ability to suffocate character. But the seasons of *Another Year* show the film not so much as an integrated story as a collection of disparate pieces, effectively four short films, a collection of mini-narratives yoked loosely together. The integrating force here is not itself an episodic system—the driving lessons of *Happy-Go-Lucky*—but rather a character system that serves as the episodes' hub. This system is Tom and Gerri, whose house is the epicenter of the film's action, and whose happy/lucky marriage represents the stability absent not only from Mary's life but from virtually every other life onscreen. Their groundedness is made explicit in the frequent visits they make to their beloved allotment, where they harvest the food that makes their kitchen the epicenter's epicenter; it is a garden plot in more ways than one, providing the order and structure that Mary so clearly wants. But it is also a plot that seems to have reached its end before the story has begun—since neither Tom nor Gerri explicitly "changes" over the course of the film, in terms either of plot or character. Contrasted with Tom and Gerri's static throughline are not only the other people we meet but the confederation of seasons themselves. Each season introduces a character whom we have never seen before. Spring, and the film itself, starts with Janet (Imelda Staunton), a woman complaining of insomnia to Gerri, her medical counselor; summer offers us Tom and Gerri's old friend Ken (Peter Wight), a lost soul who travels down from Derby for the barbecue; autumn introduces us to Katie (Karina Fernandez), Joe's new love interest; winter takes us to Derby, for the funeral of Tom's sister-in-law Linda, where we meet Tom's laconic brother Ronnie (David Bradley) and Ronnie's estranged son Carl (Martin Savage). The pitch and yaw of *Another Year* comes from the tussle between the system of Tom and Gerri and the scattering effect of people and characters temporarily yoked and then dispersed again. The signal exception in this sequence—the one new character whom we see again in a later season—is

Katie, who returns in winter as Joe's established girlfriend. The apparent entrenchment of Katie, a person whose constant enthusiasm and good humor remind us of Poppy, offers *Another Year*'s version of *Happy-Go-Lucky*'s girl-meets-boy narrative. The fact that this wandering spirit can be incorporated into the governing system of the film—most literally, Tom and Gerri's kitchen—makes Mary fully and tragically aware of her inability to enter the world of plot.

And now to the unbroken shots that conclude the films, with very different effects. It has been a central mission of this book to trace connections and continuities in Leigh's cinema; but we must be equally alert to what changes or varies. Among those recent changes have been, in the last three films, a central female character and, in the last two films, a girl-meets-boy riff. Another change, or more precisely an idiomatic variant with a much longer history, is the moving-camera long take to conclude a film. The rhetoric of absence noted in my introduction of the term "unbroken shot," manifest in the language of the "unmoving" or "unbudging" shot discussed by David Bordwell, has more recently in Leigh been joined by a rhetoric of presence at the moment of narrative departure. The first instance of this trope comes at the end of *Naked.* Johnny, after agreeing to rejoin Louise in a marriage plot (or relationship plot), instead leaves the house, after seizing the pile of money left by Jeremy/Sebastian. As he hobbles down the stairs and into the street—his body still battered by the beating those anonymous youths gave him in a dark alley—we get the antithesis, to use Eddie Marsan's term, of the shot with which the film began. *Naked* starts with the personal, a shaky handheld camera pursuing Johnny into the film's first dark alley; *Naked* ends with the mechanical, a smooth Steadicam drifting slowly away from Johnny as he limps toward us—the only Steadicam shot in Leigh's career, as he noted to Amy Raphael (Raphael 244). The human agent is replaced by the rationalizing system; and as Johnny abandons the plot he offered to Louise, so the camera abandons him, treading the line (to use Bordwell's lexicon) between watching and staging, of objective witness and authorial intervention. We could contextualize this move towards movement as part of a broader emphasis on reframing. In *Happy-Go-Lucky* and *Another Year,* Leigh for the first time deploys the screen at its most horizontal, stretching the picture to a 2.35:1 ratio—changing the parameters of the image on a graphic level, and not only on the level of movement.

The crane shot at the end of *Happy-Go-Lucky* recalls the crane shot at the end of *Topsy-Turvy*. In the earlier example, we had a woman on stage, and the camera's gradual sweep back and up turned her, however temporarily, into a central character—even if Leonora Braham is not that in *Topsy-Turvy*, and Yum-Yum is not quite that in *The Mikado*. That tour de force, over two minutes long, is matched with equal bravado by the later shot, also more than two minutes long; it begins perched at water level in the middle of a lake and ends up looking down from the top of trees. Poppy and Zoe row toward us, backs initially to the camera; when their movement takes them past the camera, it swivels responsively to reframe the pair, and we briefly get the familiar Leigh frontal side-by-side. The two women operate as a pair because they are so different; these two thirty-year-old girlfriends recall those two other thirty-year-old girlfriends, Hannah and Annie, that centaurical combination of women. Here we have the flighty, optimistic Poppy and the grounded, realistic Zoe—the imaginative and the practical, talking about luck, happiness, and the possible ends of life's plot. Thelma and Louise, in a boat on a lake.

The camera at first seems content to watch them glide past into the background, hovering on the surface of the lake, as their talk turns into idle chatter—as if dialogue itself has run its course in the film. Then Poppy's mobile phone rings. It is plot calling—as represented by Tim, her newly christened boyfriend, the avatar of the girl-meets-boy plot. As she talks merrily to him, the camera moves up and away from the

Figure 17. The side-by-side centaur,
in passing: Poppy and Zoe leave the camera
at the end of *Happy-Go-Lucky*.

boat, toward the sun whose rays Yum-Yum celebrates. It is as if the phone call has triggered the reframing, and a change of mind about how to gather together the film's strands. This movement away, like that in *Topsy-Turvy,* replaces the brutal refusal of *Naked*—which imitated a car refusing to aid the maimed Johnny—with what cinematically is sometimes called "God's eye view": an encompassing perspective. (It is perhaps the antithesis of the demonic "all-seeing eye" that Scott uses to characterize a car's rearview mirror.) As the shot reaches its apex, and the boat's occupants become smaller, Poppy's voice does not get any fainter; we can hear her conversation with Tim as clearly as if we were rowing alongside her. *Happy-Go-Lucky* in effect wants to have it both ways here, using image to evoke the broader perspective of the world, or the "room," to cite Leigh's cinematic language of context, and using sound to bring us to the particulars of the "man" (in this case, "woman"). This disjoining effect—far away visually and close phonically—is hardly radical, within the vocabulary of narrative cinema; but it does shows us cinema's ability to put us in two places at once, to be whole and double simultaneously. It is a simultaneity that Mary wishes for herself: to be a whole person and a couple at the same time.

Mary's end, and the moving shot that defines it, differs from all these narrative conclusions. At the beginning of this section, I identified Mary as the protagonist of *Another Year.* But this is a debatable claim—indeed, a claim that might seem implausible for most of the film's two hours. After all, Tom and Gerri occupy the central topography of the film; many other figures come into their orbit throughout; and we do not even meet Mary until eleven minutes in. (By contrast, Johnny and Vera and Poppy are our focal points from beginning to end, starting with the first shot of each film.) To some degree, this is a film that cannot make up its mind about whom it wants to privilege, and how; that is evidenced in the opening scene, which features the taciturn Janet, a character who will be abandoned before the end of the first of the four seasons. The film does two things in the final wintry section to drag Mary into the spotlight. The first of these is one of Leigh's greatest moments of character collision; it is less patently dramatic than Hortense at the barbecue in *Secrets and Lies,* or Detective Inspector Webster at the party in *Vera Drake,* because it is not about drama—narrative consequence—but about people and character. After his wife's funeral,

Ronnie comes down from Derby to visit his brother in London for a few days. It is he who answers the door when Mary unexpectedly rings the doorbell; at this point, Mary has essentially been abandoned by Tom and Gerri, after her ill-tempered response to Katie's arrival demonstrated an unseemly desire for Joe. Ronnie is reluctant to admit this stranger, until she demonstrates her knowledge of the house by describing its epicenter, and the film's: Tom and Gerri's kitchen. Her ability to describe a room is both pathetic, in showing how much the space from which she is now alienated means to her, and thrilling, in making us aware of how carefully Leigh's characters understand their material condition. Over the next thirteen minutes, while the owners are away at their allotment, Mary and Ronnie converse, have tea, and smoke cigarettes—although to say that they converse is misleading, since Ronnie is emotionally and psychologically impenetrable. If Mary has no filter between outside and inside, no way of regulating herself, Ronnie's exterior is a wall. In a way, Mary has found a plausible partner here, within the logic of centaur-characters—the Louise to her Thelma, or the Thelma to her Louise. But a centaur-character is not the same as a human lover; clearly, Ronnie will not become Mary's other romantic half. Like Poppy and Scott, they are mates as characters, as fictional constructs, but not as people.

The second gesture that makes Mary central is the final shot: again more than two minutes in length, here circling all the way around the table, where Katie is now a permanent member, as the family talks about vacations past and present. The camera starts on Joe—the partner that Mary cannot have—and moves its way around the group, including the mute and foreign Ronnie, before finally settling on Mary and pushing in to a medium close-up. We could say that the camera here enacts both Detective Inspector Webster's circumlocutory tactics and Johnny's probing curiosity. The shot asks, How's it going inside there? We have here neither the abandonment at the end of *Naked* nor the valediction at the end of *Happy-Go-Lucky*; rather, we have an approach that seems both welcome and unwelcome. Mary is silent, inattentive, and devastated as the chatter around her fades away. Then, for the final fifteen seconds of the film, we get the same divorce of sight and sound as with Poppy on the lake—but with very different means and effects. Leigh cuts out sound completely for those fifteen seconds, sundering the diegetic compact of narrative cinema. Even more forcefully than in *The Short and*

Curlies—where the penultimate shot shows Charlene's face and sound is limited to offscreen events—the very structure of cinema is under examination here. We get the woman and not the room—indeed, the woman sundered from the room. This omission, this sundering, shows just how nominal all connections are. Is this a real person, or is this a character? Is she a human being or a construct? A living entity or an image? As so often in Leigh's films, this moment fingers the difficult space between the one and the other.

Notes

1. An example of the latter would be John Hill's chapter on Leigh and Loach in *British Cinema in the 1980s,* wherein Leigh's *High Hopes* (1988) is criticized for "conforming to a conservative ideology of 'familialism' that is little different from that associated with Thatcherism" (198).

2. The problem of collapsing Leigh with Loach is a significant one. Most obviously, Loach's films regularly have teenagers or children as their central characters, a choice that I have just cited as being noticeably absent in Leigh's cinema. Among the aspects vital to Loach but irrelevant to Leigh are: the aggressive use of the camera, a variety of shooting locations across Britain and the world, crowd scenes, the diegetic significance of popular music, regional and physical humor (as opposed to Leigh's penchant for puns and jokes), the use of nonprofessional actors, and collaboration with screenwriters. Perhaps most starkly different is the attitude toward improvisation and surprise, as Loach often maintains the veil of ignorance for his actors throughout the shooting, to capture their spontaneous responses. By comparison, Leigh's actors carefully shape, for the camera, the surprise and spontaneity they have discovered in preparation. That contrast alone clarifies how theoretically and conceptually dissimilar these two directors are.

3. Leigh, of course, does not legislate the dialogue and emotional performance of his actors to the imperious degree that Gilbert does in this scene (as Leigh mentions in the DVD commentary). But the commitment to precision and clarity is a quality the two directors share.

4. The broader issue of major and minor characters in fiction is far too complex to explore fully here. For a compelling study of this topic, particularly in the work of Dickens, see Alex Woloch, *The One vs. the Many: Minor Characters and the Space of the Protagonist in the Novel.*

5. My compressed chronology of Leigh's life and career is indebted to Michael Coveney's extremely helpful critical biography, *The World According to Mike Leigh.*

6. For a completely different perspective, see Ray Carney and Leonard Quart's *The Films of Mike Leigh: Embracing the World.* Carney in particular argues that

the earlier films are the defining ones of Leigh's career and that everything since 1991 represents a significant decline from greatness. Whatever the merits of this energetically contrarian view, the most prominent oddity of this argument is that *Four Days in July,* one of the most complex and important works in this phase, is the only film from 1971 to 1993 in the book that does not receive its own chapter.

7. Two prominent examples of this genre would be Pat O'Connor's *Cal* (1984) and Neil Jordan's *The Crying Game* (1992).

8. The other two films cited by Sontag were Gianni Amelio's *Lamerica* and Fred Kelemen's *Fate.*

9. The final "yes" represents the last of many connections between *Naked* and James Joyce's *Ulysses*; in his epic wandering, Johnny plays the parts of both Stephen Dedalus and Leopold Bloom.

10. Andy Medhurst offers a somewhat typical argument about the contrasts between these films, asserting that *Career Girls* "did little more than mark time" between *Secrets and Lies* and *Topsy-Turvy* (37).

11. A train will also bring someone southward to London in the "Summer" section of *Another Year.* Ken's journey from Derby will have none of the success, or coincidental flourishes, of Annie's.

12. These two words are not an invention of Leigh's; these were indeed the cryptograms that Gilbert used to keep track of box-office receipts. See Baily, *Gilbert and Sullivan Book,* 320.

13. Penny's resistance to using any kind of surname extends to the moment of medical crisis itself, when she calls Phil's dispatcher looking for him. She identifies herself as "Phil's Penny," a term that implies both a sense of belonging and a fragility of connection—a way of announcing oneself, through someone else's name, that would break down in a social circle any wider than the tight space in which this family finds itself.

14. The karaoke bar presents another complication of the self, or the individual human being. Karaoke allows participants to blend their own, usually untrained, voice with the professional orchestration that accompanies a famous song. To perform karaoke, in other words, is to be oneself and not oneself, to be live and on tape, to be present and absent simultaneously—neither one thing nor another.

15. Ryan Gilbey also makes the link between Spall's rendition of Maurice and Phil as characters who are accompanied by a "series of brief sketches" of clients. But Gilbey accentuates merely the division, stating that "the crucial difference this time is that Spall has his back to his clients, and seems scarcely to notice them" (16). As I am suggesting, the lens and the mirror are complementary devices, and Phil does notice his passengers—through a different technology.

16. The particular application of "a Mike Leigh film" here comes from Leigh himself. In the DVD commentary, he addresses a scene in the middle of this coincidental sequence, after Penny has managed to get a lift from Ron. As they rush to the hospital, Ron swerves around a truck and smashes directly into a station wagon that is backing into the street. "This is a classic piece of film car

accident stuff," Leigh observes, "something you don't see in 'a Mike Leigh film'; but there it is. I just felt, you know, it can happen—you have an accident, you get your car fixed, and then you have another one. Unfortunately, this happens to happen at the wrong time. This is a film about things happening at the wrong time." Certainly, things happen at the wrong time; but until 1997, these things didn't happen in his art.

17. The only death and police inquiry, before *Vera Drake,* are those in *Kiss of Death.* But the baby is dead before we encounter it, the police inquiry is routine, and we never find out anything more about the case.

Interview with Mike Leigh |

The following represents a distillation of a series of interviews conducted by the author. Two of these took place in London in July 2004; the third took place in New York City in October 2004.

SEAN O'SULLIVAN: We often think about generations of film movements based in certain countries—such as Italian cinema during and after World War II, or German cinema in the twenties or later on in the seventies, or, obviously, French cinema in the sixties, or New Hollywood in the seventies. And these generations are often predicated on people who have similar attitudes or beliefs or experiences with cinema. So, let me name ten British filmmakers. They were all born within ten years of each other, and on the surface they may seem to be far apart, but I wonder whether we can think of them as being in some sort of dialogue about filmmaking. Between 1935 and 1945 we have: Adrian Lyne, Alan Parker, Ridley Scott, Tony Scott; Derek Jarman, Terence Davies, Peter Greenaway; Ken Loach, Stephen Frears, Mike Leigh. Can one talk about this, at all, as a generation of filmmaking?

MIKE LEIGH: Well, it's interesting that a group of people born, and growing up from different class backgrounds, in different parts of the U.K., exposed, broadly speaking, to the pre–World War/postwar culture, and movie culture presumably, should manage to wind up doing such a diverse collection of things. But my own view of these things—and indeed my actual hands-on practical experience of it—is that the Italian postwar neorealism and the *nouvelle vague,* for instance, are absolutely more at the center of movements in culture and film culture that I feel part of and inspired by and influenced by and motivated by as much as anything else. Normally I get asked the question, "Were you influenced by the Free Cinema?" And the answer to that is, "No." Because the truth of the matter is that as far as the Free Cinema was concerned, that is to say, the documentaries they were making, when that was happening I had no idea about it, because I was still tucked away in Manchester, ignorant of everything except what was on at the local picture house—i.e., commercial British and American movies. Certainly, for those who came from a provincial background, films were British and American cinema. I never really saw a film not in English until 1960, when I came to London at the age of seventeen. Then it was a massive liberating experience and a sort of massive opening-up. I knew about Eisenstein, I'd read about him, but I hadn't actually seen any of his films. I'd got Roger Manville's book, *Film,* and so I knew—if you'd showed me stills from the Odessa steps scene I could tell you what it was. But I hadn't seen it.

SO'S: What is interesting about that list, to me, is the way it doesn't seem to be a list at all. It seems to be all over the place. This suggests that British cinema is everywhere and nowhere at the same time. There are three clear clusters here. First, if you think of some of the signature eighties Hollywood films, the movies that seem to typify that period of American filmmaking—*Blade Runner, Fatal Attraction, Top Gun, Angel Heart*—they are made by British directors, by people on that list. Those would represent, somewhat polemically, a triumph of style over substance. Second, if you think of modernist, individualist approaches to filmmaking, that's something that clearly Jarman and Greenaway and in many ways Davies fit into. And then, something more contentious for you, there's this third group that would include you and Ken Loach and Stephen Frears. You would be designated, typically, as the realist cluster. So it's interesting that three radically different areas, three clusters of ideas or approaches, are represented there. These could be said to represent the three dominant movements in the history of cinema.

ML: Yes, that's right. And obviously, there are overlaps. What is interesting is that it was actually Ken Loach and Stephen Frears and I who worked inside the BBC. Frears made a huge number of films as part of the "Play for Today" series, and many of the Alan Bennett scripts. That's very important. Of that gang [of ten British directors], we're the three people with a background in making independent-minded movies but with a commitment to social content. Terence, he sits in a funny place. He's very near to me in age, a bit younger than I. We come from about thirty miles apart—he from Liverpool, and me from Manchester. That world which he does in *Distant Voices, Still Lives*—the actual world itself, not the private perspective on it, but the world itself—is the world you see in *Hard Labour* and *Vera Drake*. Although his source material is the pain of growing up in this repressive, working-class environment in the 1940s and '50s, in a way he's actually making movies about movies. He sits on an odd cusp, really.

SO'S: How do you feel about being placed in this realist cluster? There's a way in which this is a sort of ghetto—by putting you and Stephen Frears and Ken Loach together as people who make films "about things," as opposed to being visually oriented, as if there were this kind of inevitable split between those possibilities.

ML: If you break down Ken Loach, Stephen Frears, and me—obviously, of the three of us, by far and away the most eclectic is Stephen. He wouldn't deny it. And indeed Stephen is an extremely impressive filmmaker, because he really does achieve films of quite different kinds. *The Grifters* is a tremendous film. And in a way, the least eclectic is Ken, obviously. But then Ken is on an entirely different journey. Because Ken is, first and foremost, a Marxist propagandist, which is a fact, and he is entirely agenda-driven, which, I would say, is his obvious strength and in some ways his weakness, probably. Particularly when you are talking about what you would call film aesthetics, because Ken, curiously, but perfectly understandably, for his particular kind of political purist, in some ways seeks to eschew art. He's as sophisticated as the rest of us, but it's a kind of filmmaking that in some way wants to be in denial of artifice, which is fair enough. And in fact, he achieves the great moments in Ken Loach films, the great moments of conflict and argument and stuff, by insisting on not rehearsing it. My motivation and "agenda" are more complex and varied than probably anybody's on that list, in a certain sense. I have an absolute commitment to making films about the real world as we experience it, society as it is, men, women, and life and death and birth, and work, love, and sex, and food, and all the rest of it, and really dealing with it and looking at it—that's a commitment. I have a commitment to using this complex medium in a whole range of ways. My status in the triumvirate of Ken, Stephen, and me is in some ways totally accurate, but in some ways, once you analyze it closely, it sort of falls apart. I actually use film in a way that makes me more of a kinsman, despite everything, with Derek Jarman and Peter Greenaway and Terence Davies. In terms of the plastic, as it were, straight-onto-the-canvas, hands-on use of the medium.

so's: How does this connect to the broader question of being a British filmmaker, of being identified by nationality?

ML: It's beyond discussion that I am a British filmmaker who makes British films about British things. But at the same time, I regard myself absolutely without affectation as being a European filmmaker. And that is defined by a sense of cultural, spiritual, cinematic fraternity with Europe; and also, being part of European cinema, like being part of world cinema, is defined by being not-Hollywood, by being outside of Hollywood and in opposition to Hollywood. That's not an abstract intellectual position, that's a manifest fact. It's all about what happens to our cinema, not only the product but the means of distribution in relation to the world-control of Los Angeles, basically.

so's: So, in your mind, you, Almodóvar, Kiarostami, Wong Kar-wai, as vastly different from each other as you are, have more in common because of that.

ML: You go back to that list, and you tell me which group I've got more in common with, Almodóvar, Kiarostami, and Wong Kar-wai, or Adrian Lyne, Alan Parker, Ridley Scott? It answers itself.

so's: The ones you've admitted some kind of identification with were Terence Davies and Peter Greenaway.

ML: Yes, sure, of course. And that's why the question about regional identity is not a black-and-white issue. Of course I'm a British filmmaker; of course I'm an English filmmaker; of course I'm a northern filmmaker, if you want to say that; and actually, if you want to be totally thorough about it, in terms of Mel Brooks and Woody Allen, you could look at my films and say I'm a Jewish filmmaker. Because there's a tragic-comic element in my films that undoubtedly is all about that as well.

SO'S: About being a northern filmmaker, you've only made two films in the North: *Hard Labour* and *The Kiss of Death.* Have you felt the urge to be more literal about that, about being northern?

ML: Oh, yes, regular as clockwork. And we never get out of London because it costs too much. I mean, *Vera Drake,* when I first proposed to [producer] Simon [Channing Williams] that we make a film about an abortionist in the 1950s as it was then, I said I wanted to do it up in Manchester—go back to a world that I remember. But it is astronomically expensive to head off out of London with a whole team of people.

SO'S: So it's mainly a logistical hurdle.

ML: Yes, but think about my films—leaving out *Naked,* which did in effect go to Manchester. On the one hand, certainly *High Hopes* is very literally in London—and it's important that it is the big city. But the character who shows up at the beginning of *High Hopes* with the suitcase, Wayne: the big city that Wayne goes to, it could be Manchester or anywhere else, same as Johnny in *Naked. Life Is Sweet,* which is quite specifically somewhere in the south, it could be quite equally somewhere in the north. And that's true of most of the films. So what I am saying is, there's something in the spirit—it's about an outlook and attitude toward things.

SO'S: And also you have plenty of northern characters, such as Annie in *Career Girls.*

ML: There's loads of them, yeah. And also the interesting thing that research for *Vera Drake* revealed is that after the war the metropolitan police recruited in the provinces—they had this idea that if London was policed by people who didn't know the community, who weren't part of the community, they would be incorruptible. So all the coppers who show up in *Vera Drake* have all got regional accents, they are all from the North.

SO'S: You mentioned *Naked,* and maybe we could use that to transition to the larger issue of how you make your films—specifically, how you turn the improvisations into a story. On the DVD commentary of *Naked,* David Thewlis talks about the moment when he's lying on the bed, after being beaten up. He says, "In improvisations, in character, I kept waking up, and joining in the improvisations. And Mike said, 'Actually, that's not your decision. You can't choose when to wake up. That's my decision. Because you're in a coma.' And then I actually thought at that point, 'Oh, he's gonna kill me. He's gonna say, "You don't wake up, actually. That's how the film finishes. You're dead. That's not your decision, because death isn't your decision."' And then at some point he said, 'Okay, now you can wake up.'" How does this connect to the perception of the "organic" development of your films?

ML: The fact is that all character-driven films with plots have got to square the circle of character and plot. And what happens has to be feasible for character and feasible for plot and serve the needs of the story. One of the most ridiculous myths about my work is that what happens is what comes out of improvisations, and everything that happens is what the characters want to do. But, of course, hold on a minute, who's decided who the characters are, and which characters are with which characters, and all the rest of it? Somebody's made a decision somewhere along the line—there's quite an elaborate range of pretty sophisticated decisions—even before you get down to it. And you know, I have spent a lot of time and a lot of rehearsals doing what you would have to call negotiating with actors who are carrying out my instructions to the letter and being strict about the characters' motivation. There's no question about arguing with actors about what they, the actors, think should happen to the story. That's never in the equation. But by the time we get to construct a film, I've got actors on the go who are absolutely into their characters and are honest, truthful, and able to say what he or she would do.

SO'S: Could you give an example of your intervention or decision making?

ML: My decision-making and interventions inform every film, right across the board. But if you want an example: famously, with *Secrets and Lies,* when we did the improvisation of the big sequence at the end, Roxanne, the white daughter, rushed out with the boyfriend when she finds out. [Claire Rushbrook, the actress] left, disappeared completely, was off somewhere at the other end of three parks—that's where we found her. And she said she would bugger off, no way would she want to see them again. She's going to bugger off as far as she can get, and that is the end of it. I knew that dramatically it was 100 percent gilt-edged essential that she should come back in, that there was more to come out, and all the rest of it. And she said, "No, there's no way." I know I'm dealing with an actress of total intelligence and integrity. There's no question of her being obstructive, or obstinate. Now, just outside the house there's a short street, for real, and across the road there's a bus stop with a shelter. I said to her, "Well, if she's up here, she's come in the taxi, which Cynthia has paid for. Is it feasible that she could go to that bus stop?" "Yes, it's feasible." "So let's say that's what she does." Okay, fine, so they go to the bus stop. So then that puts it dramatically back in my control, because it's in my brief to say, "A bus doesn't arrive yet." She could say, "Then the bus comes, and she gets on it"—but that's not a character function, that's a *deus ex machina*. So, fine. Then we re-explore a bit, another improvisation. Out he [Maurice] comes, he sees them, he goes over, and he tries to persuade her. No way is she going to come. So we had an improvisation to investigate that. Then we analyzed it. "There's no way, simply no way," she said. And then I said, "What if Paul, the boyfriend, thought she should go back in?" And she thought about it very carefully, and she said she *would* go in, because she would be moved by the fact that he was asserting himself. Now this, of course, afforded a double bonus, because not only did it mean that we could now progress to the next stage of exploration, which was obviously what we did, and what we were working towards. But also it rounded out his character's journey dramatically, which I was looking for.

SO'S: There's a wonderful parallel near the end of *Vera Drake* when Reg says that this is the best Christmas he's had in a long time. Not that you don't expect him to say that, but here's a character who's roughly parallel to Paul in some ways. He's the shy outsider who's been brought into the family. And his character development helps square the circle.

ML: That's right. Exactly.

SO'S: So these things are as much found as they are structured, or you could say they are both structured and found.

ML: Yes, that's the whole point. And in the end, you know, it doesn't matter. What matters is that they're there. It's like a discussion today, this morning, at the film school [London Film School, of which Leigh is the chairman]. There was a very intelligent guy, but he couldn't get his head around the fact that, so far as the music was concerned—we were again talking about in *Secrets and Lies,* as it happens, and the way the music is placed and seems to be so organically placed and inextricably part of what's going on—he was really having a problem and getting his head around the fact that we didn't plan the music before we shot. I said that we don't, the fact is we don't, most people don't, some people occasionally do, Antonioni famously did—he had music going on in his head before he shot, and he sometimes made the most boring films in the world.

SO'S: Despite the importance, for your process, of finding things as you go along, I would contend that if someone had never heard of you . . .

ML: Which is the case, with a lot of people.

SO'S: (laughs) . . . and sat down and watched one of your films, this person would not have any way of knowing that the film had been created through your particular process, through improvisation.

ML: I think that's really important.

SO'S: As opposed to, say, a Cassavetes film, where I think one feels that the mood of improvisation is up on the screen, however much the film may or may not have been improvised.

ML: I think you're absolutely right, that is of fundamental importance. And you know, the truth of it is, so far as I'm concerned, I would be more than happy never to have to put up with any discussion whatever about how I do it. And the truth is, and you're going to be no exception, I don't really discuss what I really do, because what I really get up to is particular, esoteric, and profound, and comes under the general heading of "Zen and the Art of Filmmaking." I mean, things that really go on at a sort of actual level are extremely difficult to describe. Except that—if you look at, for example, the way the family is in *Vera Drake,* it's perfectly obvious that something has gone on beyond merely sitting around and saying, "Well, he's the brother, she's the sister, she's the mother." Plainly, something has gone on that has created something that's happening between the lines, under the surface. You know, when they suddenly talk about the war, you certainly know that whatever it is that's led to this, it's not just in the script or something that we've sat around for just half an hour discussing. Something has really happened. They are referring back to things that actually took place, for real: the actors have really had those experiences in character.

so's: Could you talk a little bit about how this worked in relation to *Topsy-Turvy,* when you were dealing, in large part, with people with actual pasts?

ML: The way the dialogue scenes came into existence is basically identical with all the other films. In some cases, like the scene with Gilbert and Sullivan on the sofa, the dialogue is partly distilled from improvisation at rehearsal, and partly from correspondence between them, stuff that was in letters. There, we constructed this thing, and the wheeze of seeing two famous people actually behaving in a real, natural way, somehow it lent something extra to do it in one shot—so that it was sort of documentary. But generally the dialogue came out of improvisation—it all came out of working on locations or sets, and going from improvisation and working up into precise fixed dialogue. Now, if you ask, "Hang on a minute, how did they improvise in Victorian English?" The answer to this is complex. And, if you say, "Hang on a minute, didn't you say in some scenes there are real lines for what they actually said?" then that simply makes it more complex. The fact is that in all these films, you get improvisations, and then pin down certain things and improvise more, and then I will stop and arrest it and pin things down, but also change things, suggest words, write lines myself, take things out, edit it, and gradually whittle it down. And that is what we call writing. And it happens through rehearsal—that's to say, I don't go off and write and bring it back the next day. Now, if it so happens that other factors come in when you are doing that process, so be it. Now in *Topsy-Turvy,* broadly speaking—and this varied to a greater or lesser extent depending on how much time the actor had worked on the project—all the actors had a jolly good stab at doing it in Victorian. I mean, nobody wasted time doing it in modern dialect. But in the middle of an improvisation, somebody might simply say, "Okay"—but it's only an improvisation. That's giving us the through line, the motivation, the raw version. My job as a writer always, in this context, is to challenge and improve and refine and define and distill and structure and get the dialogue written properly, to create the final draft, the real thing, always working in collaboration with the actor, on the floor, as it were.

so's: There's that great scene in the rehearsal for *The Mikado* where Gilbert is leading them through the lines, and he changes a line, and gives them emphases, and takes them very carefully through the language and mechanics of the scene as he wants it done. It strikes me as perhaps that's a little closer to the way your actual process works, instead of the perception of it being sort of all hanging out. I understand that you're not exactly like Gilbert in terms of that degree of control. [In his DVD commentary on *Topsy-Turvy*, Leigh terms Gilbert's approach "the most prescriptive kind of directing: showing the actors what to do and how to say it—the very thing that directors like me wouldn't dream of doing."] But there's a little more of that, of Gilbert, of exacting detail and specificity in the process than is usually acknowledged.

ML: Totally. I am in absolute precision mode. And that's what it's about. We walked around, our researcher and me, she had a shopping trolley full of books, and actually, one of the books I kept by my side all the time was the Savoy operas, because in fact I just constantly found myself referring to it. I would just simply pick up bits of the straight dialogue between the songs, just as points of reference. And it actually was quite useful. But then, when it came to fitting in bits of the actual, see, once you've improvised, and you've got the sort of shape of it, then you can start to add to it, to stitch into it with invisible stitching bits of things from letters and such.

so's: Something I especially want to talk about is the camera and the aesthetic. You've said in one or two places that when you compose a shot, you ask yourself, "Is this a man in a room, or a room with a man in it?" Could you elaborate?

ML: That's mainly a useful technical language for me and the cinematographer. All it means in practical terms is, if it's a man in a room, then you don't necessarily have to read the room as such. But if it's a room with a man in it, then the room and the sense of the room and the imagery of the room become more important. It's a matter of choice of shots in any film.

so's: That choice raises the issue of the individual and the social. Is it fair to say that your films, as opposed to, say, Hollywood films, tell stories that are equally about people and context? That is, where neither the man nor the room inherently predominates?

ML: Yes, it's true. Terence Davies is quoted as having once said that my films are all just talking heads. Now that's Terence Davies, bless him, occupying his extreme position of some kind. The truth is you can't say that my films are just a lot of talking heads. That's ridiculous. My films are very much about people, but they're about place. And if you start with *Bleak Moments* and work your way through, you can see it and feel it. And Harry Hook, a British film director, did an interview where he said, "I don't make films like Mike Leigh, I couldn't spend all my time filming in a suburban house." Again, a filmmaker being sort of perverse. Now, I *have* spent a huge amount of time with film crews inside houses and flats and rooms and bedrooms and on staircases and in kitchens and in lavatories, and the fact of the matter is, it is poetry to me. Because that is what life is all about, and I have no qualms or inhibitions or sense of it not really being cinema. And working as I do with, not only with brilliant cinematographers but with some very brilliant designers, the whole joy of creating and exploring an environment is tremendous. My point is that there are loads and loads of stuff in my films which are about environment—and it's not a backdrop, it's exploring the characters interfacing with the environment. The whole joy of creating and exploring an environment is tremendous—quite apart from the details and the minutiae of interior worlds. All of these are richly cinematic, to be explored in a richly cinematic way.

so's: I'm wondering how the visual, or cinematic, enters into your process. One angle on this might be to ask how you dealt with the "cinematic" in your television films.

ML: All the BBC films, even the ones that were shot with sophisticated cameramen like Remi Adefarasin—you would go in, and you'd make a film. But from the perception of the BBC, that film was just a television program. And the cameramen were people who would work the year round shooting documentaries, and feature programs, and educational programs, and farming programs, and news, and the occasional drama. So, they'd show up more or less at the time that we'd start shooting it, and you'd start shooting it. The notion at the BBC of sophisticated discussions between the director, the cameraman, the designer, the costume designer, and the makeup designer, and the shooting of tests with everybody contributing and sitting in a room and working, and sitting later in a preview theater and discussing palette—I mean, these things were just a million miles away because we weren't making feature films, we were just making films. Once you get into the territory of sophisticated features films—when we shot *Topsy-Turvy,* we did the most elaborate tests some six months before we started shooting.

SO'S: Is there anything you miss about working in television? Or how does the film-television distinction matter to you, aside from the obvious limitations you're talking about?

ML: In the days when we did telly—"we" meaning me and Ken Loach and Stephen Frears and everybody else—when we did those films that were called "Play for Today," you could score four, five, six, eight, nine, and in the case of *Abigail's Party,* sixteen million viewers at one sitting. Now, sixteen million people will not see *Vera Drake* in the U.K. in the cinema—that is the truth of it, tragically. So, in terms of the medium of television—missing out on any discussion about aesthetics, and also missing out on any question of discussion about differences between the big screen and the little one, or the collective experience of watching movies in the cinema as opposed to the isolated experience of watching television in your sitting room—playing the television was very good news. But I'm first and last a fundamentalist unreconstituted purist cinemaphile, and the bottom line is, going and sitting in a darkened place and the lights going down and getting stuck in to the movie with no distractions, it remains as exciting to me when the lights go down in the cinema and the thing starts as ever it was in the 1940s. And that's why I rejoice to think that I am privileged enough to make work that other people experience in that context. And the big screen and Dolby stereo and everything else is fantastic.

SO'S: Getting to some of your specific visual tendencies, you clearly use the long take a great deal. Is that something you think ahead of time as a film-by-film issue, or a scene-by-scene issue?

ML: Well, there are times when I will cover very extensively, and oftentimes I will be spare with the cover—depending on the dynamics of the scene, the style of the scene, the quality of the performance, et cetera, et cetera.

SO'S: So for you, the long take is not necessarily an ideological thing. For example, for Bazin, obviously, that's a crucial part of how he thinks cinema works. He believes in the long take as something that doesn't just work for the scene but has a kind of truth value.

ML: The truth of the matter is, the most extreme film of recent years, which I love—I think it's a wonderful film—is Roy Andersson's *Songs from the Second Floor.* It's a great, strange film—he spent about twenty-five years making it, I think. It's a full-length feature, and it's got fifty-two setups, or fifty-something setups, and they're all wide shots. And they're amazingly constructed. The thing about it is, first of all, I love single setups that go on for their own right, as long as they work. I think it's great, and sometimes when you do it, you are allowing the audience even subliminally to know that what they're seeing is really happening; it's not a trick. So there's that. But the real point about the long take . . . for example, the long single static shot in *Secrets and Lies* around the barbecue table. Now, for that scene, there was no cover, of course. I shot it, and if you look at it and analyze it, you see it could only have been done by it being meticulously directed and meticulously scripted to serve the shot. Everything that happens plainly is constructed and written in absolute gear with what is happening visually because the timing of everything—food, comings and goings—it's all meticulous. Now, the reason why it makes sense to have that is because I knew that in the next scene we would cut inside, and we were going to be around the table, and then the shit was going to hit the fan, and you're going to have all sorts of sparks going, so that the montage would do that. So therefore I felt to do that here was to let the audience do the work. It's important that you are always making choices about what the audience is doing, the work the audience is doing.

SO'S: Another recurring choice of yours, one that gets back to the man in the room—or in this case, the man in the street—is the way you have several movies that begin with a strong vertical. There's the static shot of the alley in *Four Days in July,* the graphically narrowed shot of the street in *High Hopes,* and of course the handheld pursuit in the alley in *Naked.* And parallel to that is the corridor at the beginning of *All or Nothing*—it's almost like a street effect. Is it sort of a predilection of yours?

ML: Yes, it is. It's very interesting, but it's sort of no big deal. It is what film is. Film is about capturing life going on. What's interesting about lots of the kind of shots that you're invoking there—actually, apart from anything else—is that there are certain kinds of things that I naturally like to do. The thing of foreshortening, looking that way at things, this all relates to one of my idiosyncrasies: VFF, vertical-frame format.

The thing is, for years, for many years I have always been interested in the fact that the convention is the lateral-screen format, but I'm fascinated by the idea of a vertical frame. And when I'm filming—this has gone on for years—particularly with [cinematographer] Dick Pope, with whom I've been working since 1990, I look through the viewfinder to find my shot, and the shape of the screen is matted off inside. I turn the viewfinder ninety degrees, and for a joke I say to Dick, "Well, actually, I think this is the shot," and he has a look. We always laugh, but we really think it is exciting. It would be fantastic to do a whole movie with a vertical frame. We've talked about this for years. Indeed, there's a guy who wants to build a camera for us. But the problem is, the real truth, you can lop off the side, which we matte off, which we did for a trailer for the London Film Festival. But then you lose a lot of area on the film—so you get a smaller image. So in an ideal world you'd have a cinema which could show a vertical frame.

I was walking through New York City one day with my friend Howard Feinstein, the film critic. We looked up at the skyscrapers, and I started talking about the vertical frame, and he said, "Oh, Eisenstein wrote an essay about this." So I tracked it down. He gave this lecture in 1931 or so in L.A. to the American Motion Picture Academy, because at that time, along with the whole thing about sound coming in, there was a lot of discussion about the definitive format. And he actually said that the horizontal screen is not logical. What he posited wasn't my notion but that the only natural shape should be square. I had to give a lecture, a few years ago, and I talked about this. It is a fascinating possibility, particularly if you want to make films about people in rooms and all the rest of it. We did this thing for the London Film Festival where we had a whole series of images in black and white of people, little momentary scenes shot this way, and then it suddenly went into color and widescreen with all these characters in bright colors, all walking across the bridge with Big Ben in the background, striking, and then they're all sitting in a cinema, which turns into the London Film Festival. And they showed it as a sort of thing in front of all the movies for several years. All of this relates to what we're talking about because, for example, to go back to the shot at the beginning of *Four Days in July,* and there are loads of shots like this—I find it really interesting to sort of look down things, and a lot of times I like to look into a room or look up a staircase, where what you're looking at is defined, is focused by vertical elements that compose away from that. It's hard to put into words, but you'll find that is a real characteristic of lots of shots.

so's: I'd like to connect this subversive attitude, if we can call it that, about the dominant orientation of the screen with your subversions of storytelling more broadly. There is something very subversive in the way you deal with assumptions about narrative—the assumptions we get from dominant genres and media. Part of this has to do with the tension between minor and major characters, or how much or little of the past we get to learn. Are you happy to be considered a subversive, in this regard?

ML: Well, I am certainly interested in challenging the status quo and challenging the expected. I mean, at a certain level, there are subversions on the go that really do resonate and relate to other movies. And there are times when things happen that are actual film references. For example, in *Bleak Moments,* there is this moment when you see Sylvia creeping downstairs with a bottle of sherry, and you see her feet and then the bottle. And I remember I said, "This is the Hitchcock shot in this film." Obviously, there are all sorts of levels—there is no way anyone can seriously argue that *Naked* is a film noir, because it isn't. But there is a kind of subtle underpinning and subversion of the conventions of film noir. And then there is the whole conceit of *Topsy-Turvy,* in that it takes a chocolate-box subject. It's a subversion of the expectations of a Mike Leigh film. People endlessly say it's a musical, but it's not a musical at all. It's a straightforward narrative in which sometimes people make music. But it takes the whole general notion of the Hollywood backstage musical, and a chocolate-box subject, and subverts it totally by taking it terribly seriously. And at the same time you are seeing an industrial process. You know, you see people backstage with electric wires and people sawing away in the pit and the audience sitting there and all that, so you are looking at it as a documentary about something happening in the theater, as it were. So there are all sorts of subversions going on at all those levels.

so's: There are two other issues I'd like to touch on. One has to do with endings. Given that there are always a number of different possibilities going on in your films, what about the issue of closure? Maybe we could talk about *Vera Drake* in particular—especially the last shot, or the last moment. You have some scenes in films that end with reconciliations, whether final or momentary, such as *Life Is Sweet,* or *Secrets and Lies,* and some films seem to end with a lack of reconciliation, say *Naked,* or that last moment in *Topsy-Turvy,* which is so complicated. What about the final moment of *Vera Drake,* the four-shot in the home, when Vera is gone from the household, and everyone is looking off in a different direction?

ML: I think the fundamental, philosophical overriding consideration is that, by instinct and impulse and by compulsion, I make films where you walk away from the film, and the film's still going on in your head. I mean, I don't make films that tie up so neatly and conclusively that you can walk away and forget the whole bloody thing and never think about it again. On the contrary. So, on another level, to express the same thing, I indeed do actually feel or think that these guys are still there, they go on existing. And just because the film comes to an end doesn't mean that it comes to an end. So a lot of the ends that you're talking about, all of them in some way are an expression of that fact. And when we cut *Vera Drake* . . . the shot where she walks up the clanking stairs and away into the distance in the prison was designed, we shot it as the last shot. Indeed, we shot a long take so that we could run credits over it. But when we got in the cutting room it occurred to me that that was somehow not interesting and rather predictable and also not very evocative—and somehow the logical thing would be to go back to them, really. And that's what we did, which, having shot that, it was just reversing the order of things a bit. And it seemed by far and away far more interesting, and it leaves people quite stunned really, and sort of with a great deal more to think about.

SO's: Finally, I'd like to ask you about names. How do you go about naming the characters?

ML: That's an interesting question. What do you want to know?

SO's: Well, you have a lot of twinned names of characters, like Maurice and Monica and Phil and Penny and Rachel and Rory. And obviously, Nicholas and Natalie—and even names that sound alike, like Shirley and Cyril?

ML: Is the question, are you saying is it an accident, or do I do it purpose? I always do it on purpose, everything is done on purpose.

SO's: Do the actors have a say in the names?

ML: They do—up to a point. A part of my art is that I collaborate, so I work with each actor, and I say, "Right, let's name." For a while in embryo form the character is going unnamed, and then I say, "Okay, let's think about it and make a long list of all the names it could be." We make a list of first names, and then we, select, if I'm smart, four, with reference to how they will go with other names. And I also carry a permanent index, a notebook which I have with me at naming sessions of all the names in all of my work. I think it's got up to something like four hundred and something. Even for the most minor characters. So I can double check and see if I'm going to have the same, or whatever. So it's never an accident when a name reappears.

(The celebrated *Abigail's Party* [1977] is a stage play that received a three-camera television studio recording; it belongs in a study of Leigh's drama rather than his cinema.)

Bleak Moments (1971)
Sylvia lives with her mentally handicapped sister Hilda and works as a secretary with maladroit, overbearing Pat. The movie presents a parade of awkward social moments, many involving Sylvia's would-be love interest, schoolteacher Peter, and hipster musician Norman; it has virtually no plot development. Leigh's only feature film until 1988 experimented with unbroken shots and unconventional editing; his first extended side-by-side narrates one of the most uncomfortable first dates in film history.
United Kingdom
Production: Autumn Productions, Memorial Enterprises, British Film Institute
Director: Mike Leigh
Scenario: Mike Leigh
Producer: Leslie Blair
Photography: Bahram Manoochehri
Editor: Leslie Blair
Art Director: Richard Rambaut
Music: Mike Bradwell
Sound Recordist: Bob Withey
Cast: Anne Raitt (Sylvia), Sarah Stephenson (Hilda), Eric Allan (Peter), Joolia Cappleman (Pat), Mike Bradwell (Norman), Liz Smith (Pat's Mother), Malcolm Smith (Norman's Friend), Donald Sumpter (Norman's Friend), Christopher Martin (Sylvia's Boss), Linda Beckett (Remedial Trainee), Sandra Bolton (Remedial Trainee), Stephen Churchett (Remedial Trainee), Una Brandon-Jones (Supervisor), Ronald Eng (Waiter), Reginald Stewart (Man in Restaurant), Susan Glanville (Enthusiastic Teacher), Joanna Dickens (Stout Teacher), Christopher Leaver (Wine Merchant)
106 min.

Hard Labour (1973)

Mrs. Thornley, a quiet Catholic housecleaner, and her truculent husband, a security guard, live with their daughter Ann in a terraced house in Salford (Greater Manchester). Mrs. Thornley's principal employer is Mrs. Stone, a solipsistic woman of considerable means. The Thornleys' son Edward is married and lives in a slightly rising part of town—the first in Leigh's series of families cleft by economic and social difference. The film's most significant plot event involves Ann's friend Julie, who gets pregnant by a married man and aborts the baby.

United Kingdom
Production: BBC
Devised and Directed by: Mike Leigh
Producer: Tony Garnett
Photography: Tony Pierce-Roberts
Editor: Christopher Rowlands
Designer: Paul Munting
Costumes: Sally Nieper
Sound: Dick Manton
Cast: Liz Smith (Mrs. Thornley), Clifford Kershaw (Jim Thornley), Polly Hemingway (Ann), Bernard Hill (Edward), Alison Steadman (Veronica), Vanessa Harris (Mrs. Stone), Cyril Varley (Mr. Stone), Linda Beckett (Julie), Ben Kingsley (Naseem), Alan Erasmus (Barry), Rowena Parr (June), June Whitaker (Mrs. Rigby), Paula Tilbrook (Mrs. Thornley's Friend), Keith Washington (Mr. Shaw), Louis Raynes (Tallyman), Alan Gerrard (Greengrocer), Diana Flacks (Mrs. Rubens), Patrick Durkin (Frank), Ian East (Dick), Dennis Barry (Old Man), Sonny Farrar (Publican), Surya Kumari (Sikh Lady), Irene Gawne (Sister), Hal Jeayes (Priest)
74 min.

The Five-Minute Films (1975)
United Kingdom
Production: BBC
Devised and Directed by: Mike Leigh
Producer: Tony Garnett
Camera: Brian Tufano
Editor: Chris Lovett
Sound: Andrew Boulton
27 min. total

The Birth of the Goalie of the 2001 F.A. Cup Final
Cast: Richard Ireson (Father), Celia Quicke (Mother)

Old Chums
Cast: Tim Stern (Brian), Robert Putt (Terry)

Probation
   A youth, arrested in a dispute over a cup of tea, is offered several cups of tea while waiting to meet a probation officer.
Cast: Herbert Norville (Arbley), Bill Colville (Sid), Antony Carrick (Mr. Davies), Theresa Watson (The Secretary), Lally Percy (Victoria)

A Light Snack
   In parallel stories, two men make sausage rolls in a factory, while a window washer eats a sausage roll offered by his employer.
Cast: Margaret Heery (Mrs. White), Richard Griffiths (The Window Cleaner), Alan Gaunt (The Talker), David Casey (The Listener)

Afternoon
   Three women drink, talking about children and married life.
Cast: Rachel Davis (The Hostess), Pauline Moran (The Teacher), Julia North (The Newly-Wed)

Nuts in May (1976)
   Irksome couple Keith and Candice Marie go on a camping holiday, only to be met with frustration. The officious Keith is particularly enraged by lower-class Honky and Finger, whose raucous behavior offends his desire to commune with nature. Leigh's first manifestly comic film represents a very rare foray out of the city and into the country.
United Kingdom
Production: BBC
Devised and Directed by: Mike Leigh
Producer: David Rose
Film Cameraman: Michael Williams
Editor: Oliver White
Designer: David Crozier
Costumes: Gini Hardy
Sound Recordist: John Gilbert
Dubbing Mixer: David Baumber
Cast: Roger Sloman (Keith), Alison Steadman (Candice Marie), Anthony O'Donnell (Ray), Sheila Kelley (Honky), Stephen Bill (Finger), Richenda Carey (Miss Beale), Eric Allan (Quarryman), Matthew Guinness (Farmer), Sally Watts (Farm Girl), Richard Ireson (Policeman)
84 min.

The Kiss of Death (1977)

Apprentice mortician Trevor learns his trade in Lancashire; his relationship to the death trade is bemused and ironic. The film interweaves scenes at work with scenes at play—primarily in clubs with girlfriend Linda, friend Ronnie, and his girlfriend Sandra—operating as a series of related sketches more than a dramatic construct. A crib death offers the one somber note; Trevor's occupational visit to the bereaved home troubles the deliberate weightlessness of the rest of the film.

United Kingdom

Production: BBC

Devised and Directed by: Mike Leigh

Producer: David Rose

Film Cameraman: Michael Williams

Editor: Oliver White

Designer: David Crozier

Costume Designer: Al Barnett

Sound Recordist: John Gilbert

Dubbing Mixer: Dave Baumber

Music: Carl Davis

Cast: David Threlfall (Trevor), John Wheatley (Ronnie), Kay Adshead (Linda), Angela Curran (Sandra), Clifford Kershaw (Mr. Garside), Pamela Austin (Trevor's Mum), Phillip Ryland (Froggy), Frank McDermott (Mr. Bodger), Christine Moore (Mrs. Bodger), Karen Petrie (Policewoman), Brian Pollitt (Doctor), Eileen Denison (Mrs. Ball), Marlene Sidaway (Christine), Elizabeth Hauck (Shoe Shop Customer), Elizabeth Ann Ogden (Bridesmaid)

75 min.

Who's Who (1978)

More densely populated than most of Leigh's early films, this extended lampoon of social status and aspiration is centered on a financial office, and particularly on Alan, a working-class enthusiast of the aristocracy; his interests and pretensions are regularly mocked by cheeky young office mate Kevin. A senior manager's visit to Kensington allows us to see bluebloods and poseurs in full flight. The film is a kind of partner to *Nuts in May* in the breadth and tone of its satire; the pastoral is replaced here by fields of wealth and social desire.

United Kingdom

Production: BBC

Devised and Directed by: Mike Leigh

Producer: Margaret Matheson

Photography: John Else

Editor: Chris Lovett

Designer: Austen Spriggs
Costume Designer: Robin Stubbs (uncredited)
Sound Recordist: John Pritchard
Dubbing Mixer: Alan Dykes
Cast: Richard Kane (Alan), Joolia Cappleman (April), Philip Davis (Kevin), Adam Norton (Giles), Simon Chandler (Nigel), Graham Seed (Anthony), Catherine Hall (Samantha), Felicity Dean (Caroline), Jeffry Wickham (Francis), Souad Faress (Samya), David Neville (Lord Crouchurst), Richenda Carey (Lady Crouchurst), Lavinia Bertram (Nanny), Francesca Martin (Selina), Geraldine James (Miss Hunt), Sam Kelly (Mr. Shakespeare), Angela Curran and Roger Hammond (Couple in Window)
76 min.

Grown-Ups (1980)

Mandy and Dick, a young working-class couple in Canterbury, move next door to their former and much-disliked schoolteacher, Mr. Butcher, and his wife. The film's central crisis occurs when Mandy's flighty, intrusive older sister Gloria—having been tossed out of their house by the fed-up couple—runs next door to the Butchers. Class and social conflict ensue. Like *High Hopes,* the film is narratively structured through the side-by-side device of adjacent homes.
Production: BBC
Devised and Directed by: Mike Leigh
Producer: Louis Marks
Photography: Remi Adefarasin
Editor: Robin Sales
Designer: Bryan Ellis
Costumes: Christian Dyall
Sound Recordist: John Pritchard
Dubbing Mixer: David Baumber
Cast: Philip Davis (Dick), Lesley Manville (Mandy), Brenda Blethyn (Gloria), Janine Duvitski (Sharon), Lindsay Duncan (Christine), Sam Kelly (Ralph)
97 min.

Home Sweet Home (1982)

The film focuses on the lives, loves, and families of three Hertfordhsire postmen: on-the-prowl Stan, slovenly Gordon, and socially inept Harold. The mood shifts from light to dark and back again, with domestic and sexual strife most prominent. A critical theme, explored repeatedly in later films, is the problem of having or not having children—of the persistent gap between the possible and the actual.
Production: BBC
Devised and Directed by: Mike Leigh

Producer: Louis Marks
Photography: Remi Adefarasin
Editor: Robin Sales
Designer: Bryan Ellis
Costume Designer: Michael Burdle
Sound Recordist: John Pritchard
Dubbing Mixer: Dave Baumber
Music: Carl Davis
Cast: Eric Richard (Stan), Lorraine Brunning (Tina), Kay Stonham (Hazel),
    Timothy Spall (Gordon), Su Elliott (June), Tim Barker (Harold), Frances
    Barber (Melody), Lloyd Peters (Dave), Sheila Kelley (Janice), Heidi
    Laratta (Kelly), Paul Jesson (Man in Dressing Gown)
92 min.

Meantime (1983)
Production: Channel Four, Central Independent Television, Mostpoint
Devised and Directed by: Mike Leigh
Producer: Graham Benson
Director of Photography: Roger Pratt
Editor: Lesley Walker
Art Director: Diana Charnley
Costume Designer: Lindy Hemming
Sound Recordist: Malcolm Hirst
Dubbing Mixer: Trevor Pyke
Music: Andrew Dickson
Cast: Marion Bailey (Barbara), Phil Daniels (Mark), Tim Roth (Colin), Pam
    Ferris (Mavis), Jeff Robert (Frank), Alfred Molina (John), Gary Oldman
    (Coxy), Tilly Vosburgh (Hayley), Paul Daly (Rusty), Leila Bertrand
    (Hayley's Friend), Hepburn Graham (Boyfriend), Peter Wight (Estate
    Manager), Eileen Davies (Unemployment Benefit Clerk), Herbert Norville
    (Man in Pub), Brian Hoskin (Barman)
103 min.

Four Days in July (1985)
Production: BBC
Devised and Directed by: Mike Leigh
Producer: Kenith Trodd
Photography: Remi Adefarasin
Editor: Robin Sales
Designer: Jim Clay
Costume Designer: Maggie Donnelly
Sound Recordist: John Pritchard
Dubbing Mixer: David Baumber

Music: Rachel Portman
Cast: Bríd Brennan (Collette), Des McAleer (Eugene), Paula Hamilton (Lorraine), Charles Lawson (Billy), Brian Hogg (Big Billy), Adrian Gordon (Little Billy), Shane Connaughton (Brendan), Eileen Pollock (Carmel), Stephen Rea (Dixie), David Coyle (Mickey), John Keegan (Mr. McCoy), John Hewitt (Mr. Roper), Ann Hasson (Sister Midwife), Geraldine Lidster, Stephen Lidster, Lisa Mullan, and Kerry O'Neill (Children), Emma Hamilton and Mark Lawless (Babies)
100 min.

The Short and Curlies (1987)
United Kingdom
Production: Channel Four, Portman Productions
Written and Directed by: Mike Leigh
Producer: Victor Glynn
Director of Photography: Roger Pratt
Editor: Jon Gregory
Production Designer: Diana Charnley
Costume Designer: Lindy Hemming
Sound Recordist: Malcolm Hirst
Music: Rachel Portman
Cast: Alison Steadman (Betty), Sylvestra Le Touzel (Joy), David Thewlis (Clive), Wendy Nottingham (Charlene)
18 min.

High Hopes (1988)
Progressive, post-hippie Cyril and Shirley work, respectively, as a courier and a parks employee; they take care of Cyril's elderly mother, Mrs. Bender, who is becoming increasingly detached from the world. Next door to Mrs. Bender are the snobbily yuppie Booth-Braines, who revel in Thatcherist excess; the Booth-Braines are an aspirational model for Cyril's consumerist sister Valerie and her entrepreneurial husband Martin. The film is structured around such Leigh techniques as side-by-side architectural narrative, a traumatic birthday party, and the socially bifurcated family.
United Kingdom
Production: Film Four, British Screen, Portman Productions
Distributor: Skouras Pictures
Written and Directed by: Mike Leigh
Producers: Simon Channing Williams and Victor Glynn
Director of Photography: Roger Pratt
Editor: Jon Gregory
Production Designer: Diana Charnley

Costume Designer: Lindy Hemming
Sound: Billy McCarthy
Music: Andrew Dickson
Cast: Philip Davis (Cyril), Ruth Sheen (Shirley), Edna Doré (Mrs. Bender),
    Philip Jackson (Martin Burke), Heather Tobias (Valerie Burke), Lesley
    Manville (Laetitia Boothe-Braine), David Bamber (Rupert Boothe-Braine),
    Jason Watkins (Wayne), Judith Scott (Suzi), Cheryl Prime (Martin's
    Girlfriend), Diane-Louise Jordan (Chemist Shop Assistant), Linda Beckett
    (Receptionist)
113 min.

Life Is Sweet (1990)
    Industrial chef Andy and dance instructor Wendy live with twin daughters
    Natalie, a sensible trainee plumber, and Nicola, a stay-at-home malcontent
    and secret bulimic. Andy's delusional friend Aubrey opens his own bistro,
    with a bizarre menu and disastrous consequences. Nicola is teased about
    her political inertia by an occasional and clandestine lover; finally, her
    secret is revealed, and the final shot offers a reconciliation of sorts between
    the two dissimilar sisters.
United Kingdom
Production: Film Four, British Screen, Thin Man Films
Distributor: October Films (U.S.)
Written and Directed by: Mike Leigh
Producer: Simon Channing Williams
Director of Photography: Dick Pope
Editor: Jon Gregory
Production Designer: Alison Chitty
Costume Designer: Lindy Hemming
Sound Recordist: Malcolm Hirst
Music: Rachel Portman
Cast: Alison Steadman (Wendy), Jim Broadbent (Andy), Claire Skinner
    (Natalie), Jane Horrocks (Nicola), Stephen Rea (Patsy), Timothy Spall
    (Aubrey), David Thewlis (Nicola's Lover), Moya Brady (Paula), David
    Neilson (Steve), Harriet Thorpe (Customer), Paul Trussel (Chef), Jack
    Thorpe Baker (Nigel)
103 min.

A Sense of History (1992)
    A mockumentary short film in which the Twenty-third Earl of Leete narrates
    the story of his estate; as he walks the grounds and tells stories of the past,
    it becomes clear that he is the criminally insane murderer of his brother,
    his wife, and his two young children. This satire was written by its star, Jim
    Broadbent; it is the only film that Leigh has directed but not scripted.

United Kingdom
Production: Thin Man Films, Film Four
Distributor: October Films (U.S.)
Director: Mike Leigh
Writer: Jim Broadbent
Producer: Simon Channing Williams
Director of Photography: Dick Pope
Editor: Jon Gregory
Production Designer: Alison Chitty
Sound Recordist: Tim Fraser
Music: Carl Davis
Cast: Jim Broadbent (Twenty-third Earl of Leete), Stephen Bill (Giddy),
    Belinda Bradley and Edward Bradley (Earl's Children)
26 min.

Naked (1993)
United Kingdom
Production: Film Four, British Screen, Thin Man Films
Distributor: Fine Line (U.S.)
Written and Directed by: Mike Leigh
Producer: Simon Channing Williams
Director of Photography: Dick Pope
Editor: Jon Gregory
Production Designer: Alison Chitty
Costume Designer: Lindy Hemming
Sound Recordist: Ken Weston
Music: Andrew Dickson
Cast: David Thewlis (Johnny), Lesley Sharp (Louise), Katrin Cartlidge
    (Sophie), Greg Cruttwell (Jeremy/Sebastian), Claire Skinner (Sandra),
    Peter Wight (Brian), Ewen Bremner (Archie), Susan Vidler (Maggie),
    Deborah Maclaren (Woman in Window), Gina McKee (Café Girl),
    Carolina Giammetta (Masseuse), Elizabeth Berrington (Giselle),
    Darren Tunstall (Poster Man), Robert Putt (Chauffeur), Lynda Rooke
    (Victim), Angela Curran (Car Owner), Peter Whitman (Mr. Halpern), Jo
    Abercrombie (Woman in Street), Elaine Britten (Girl in Porsche), David
    Foxxe (Tea Bar Owner), Mike Avenall and Toby Jones (Men at Tea Bar),
    Sandra Voe (Bag Lady)
131 min.

Secrets and Lies (1996)
United Kingdom
Production: CIBY 2000, Channel Four Films, Thin Man Films
Distributor: October Films (U.S.)

Written and Directed by: Mike Leigh
Producer: Simon Channing Williams
Director of Photography: Dick Pope
Editor: Jon Gregory
Production Designer: Alison Chitty
Costume Designer: Maria Price
Sound Recordist: George Richards
Music: Andrew Dickson
Cast: Timothy Spall (Maurice), Phyllis Logan (Monica), Brenda Blethyn (Cynthia), Claire Rushbrook (Roxanne), Marianne Jean-Baptiste (Hortense), Elizabeth Berrington (Jane), Michele Austin (Dionne), Lee Ross (Paul), Lesley Manville (Social Worker), Ron Cook (Stuart), Emma Amos (Girl with Scar), Brian Bovell and Trevor Laird (Hortense's Brothers), Clare Perkins (Hortense's Sister-in-Law), Elias Perkins McCook (Hortense's Nephew), June Mitchell (Senior Optometrist), Janice Acquah (Junior Optician), Keeley Flanders (Girl in Optician's), Hannah Davis (First Bride), Terence Harvey (First Bride's Father), Kate O'Malley (Second Bride), Joe Tucker (Groom), Richard Syms (Vicar), Grant Masters (Best Man), Jonathan Coyne (Fiancé), Mia Soteriou (Fiancée)
142 min.

Career Girls (1997)
United Kingdom
Production: Channel Four Films, Matrix Films, Thin Man Films
Distributor: October Films (U.S.)
Written and Directed by: Mike Leigh
Producer: Simon Channing Williams
Director of Photography: Dick Pope
Editor: Robin Sales
Production Designer: Eve Stewart
Sound Recordist: George Richards
Music: Marianne Jean-Baptiste and Tony Remy
Cast: Katrin Cartlidge (Hannah), Lynda Steadman (Annie), Kate Byers (Claire), Mark Benton (Ricky), Andy Serkis (Mr. Evans), Joe Tucker (Adrian), Margo Stanley (Ricky's Nan), Michael Healy (Lecturer)
87 min.

Topsy-Turvy (1999)
United Kingdom
Production Company: Thin Man Films, Greenlight Fund, Newmarket Capital
Distributor: USA Films (U.S.)
Written and Directed by: Mike Leigh

Producer: Simon Channing Williams
Cinematography: Dick Pope
Editor: Robin Sales
Production Designer: Eve Stewart
Costume Designer: Lindy Hemming
Sound Recordist: Tim Fraser
Music: Carl Davis, from the works of Arthur Sullivan
Cast: Jim Broadbent (William Schwenk Gilbert), Allan Corduner (Arthur
    Sullivan), Timothy Spall (Richard Temple), Lesley Manville (Lucy
    Gilbert [Kitty]), Ron Cook (Richard D'Oyly Carte), Wendy Nottingham
    (Helen Lenoir), Kevin McKidd (Durward Lely), Shirley Henderson
    (Leonora Braham), Dorothy Atkinson (Jessie Bond), Martin Savage
    (George Grossmith), Eleanor David (Fanny Ronalds), Sam Kelly (Richard
    Barker), Andy Serkis (John D'Auban), Charles Simon (Gilbert's Father),
    Vincent Franklin (Rutland Barrington), Cathy Sara (Sibyl Grey), Nicholas
    Woodeson (Mr. Seymour), Jonathan Aris (Wilhelm), Stefan Bednarczyk
    (Frank Collier), Mark Benton (Mr. Price), Eve Pearce (Gilbert's Mother),
    Lavinia Bertram (Florence Gilbert), Theresa Watson (Maude Gilbert),
    Kenneth Hadley (Pidgeon), Dexter Fletcher (Louis), Kate Doherty
    (Mrs. Judd), Michael Simkins (Frederick Bovill), Louise Gold (Rosina
    Brandram), Sukie Smith (Clothilde), Mia Soteriou (Mrs. Russell), Alison
    Steadman (Madame Leon), Adam Searle (Shrimp), Katrin Cartlidge
    (Madame), Heather Craney (Miss Russell), Bríd Brennan (Mad Woman)
160 min.

All or Nothing (2002)
United Kingdom
Production Company: Studio Canal, Alain Sarde, Thin Man
Distributor: United Artists (U.S.)
Written and Directed by: Mike Leigh
Producers: Simon Channing Williams, Alain Sarde
Cinematography: Dick Pope
Editor: Lesley Walker
Production Designer: Eve Stewart
Costume Designer: Jacqueline Durran
Sound Recordist: Malcolm Hirst
Music: Andrew Dickson
Cast: Timothy Spall (Phil), Lesley Manville (Penny), Alison Garland (Rachel),
    James Corden (Rory), Ruth Sheen (Maureen), Marion Bailey (Carol), Paul
    Jesson (Ron), Sam Kelly (Sid), Kathryn Hunter (Cécile), Sally Hawkins
    (Samantha), Helen Coker (Donna), Daniel Mays (Jason), Ben Crompton
    (Craig), Gary McDonald (Neville), Diveen Henry (Dinah), Robert Wilfort
    (Doctor), Valerie Hunkins (Nurse), Jean Ainslie (Old Lady), Badi Uzzaman

and Parvez Qadir (Passengers), Russell Mabey (Nutter), Thomas Brown-Lowe, Oliver Golding, Henri McCarthy, and Ben Wattley (Small Boys), Leo Bill (Young Man), Peter Stockbridge (Man with Flowers), Brian Bovell (Garage Owner), Timothy Bateson (Harold), Michele Austin (Care Worker), Alex Kelly (Neurotic Woman), Alan Williams (Drunk), Peter Taylor (MC), Dawn Davis (Singer), Emma Lowndes and Maxine Peake (Party Girls), Matt Bardock and Mark Benton (Men at Bar), Dorothy Atkinson, Heather Craney, and Martin Savage (Silent Passengers), Joe Tucker (Fare Dodger), Martha (Edna Doré), Georgia Fitch (Ange), Tracy O'Flaherty (Michelle), Di Botcher (Supervisor)

128 min.

Vera Drake (2004)
United Kingdom
Production: Studio Canal, Alain Sarde, U.K. Film Council, Inside Track, Thin Man Films
Distributor: Fine Line (U.S.)
Written and Directed by: Mike Leigh
Producers: Simon Channing Williams, Alain Sarde
Cinematography: Dick Pope
Editor: Jim Clark
Production Designer: Eve Stewart
Costume Designer: Jacqueline Durran
Sound Recordist: Tim Fraser
Music: Andrew Dickson
Cast: Imelda Staunton (Vera), Phil Davis (Stan), Alex Kelly (Ethel), Daniel Mays (Sid), Adrian Scarborough (Frank), Heather Craney (Joyce), Eddie Marsan (Reg), Ruth Sheen (Lily), Sally Hawkins (Susan), Fenella Woolgar (Susan's Confidante), Peter Wight (Det. Inspector Webster), Martin Savage (Det. Sergeant Vickers), Helen Coker (WPC Best), Lesley Manville (Mrs. Wells), Simon Chandler (Mr. Wells), Sam Troughton (David), Marion Bailey (Mrs. Fowler), Allan Corduner (Psychiatrist), Leo Bill (Ronny), Gerard Monaco (Kenny), Lesley Sharp (Jessica Barnes), Liz White (Pamela Barnes), Anthony O'Donnell (Mr. Walsh), Sinéad Matthews (Very Young Woman), Sid Mitchell (Very Young Man), Tilly Vosburgh (Mother of Seven), Elizabeth Berrington (Cynical Lady), Emma Amos (Cynical Lady), Vinette Robinson (Jamaican Girl), Rosie Cavaliero (Married Woman), Richard Graham (George), Anna Keaveney (Nellie), Sandra Voe (Vera's Mother), Wendy Nottingham (Ivy), Joanna Griffiths (Peggy), Chris O'Dowd (Sid's Customer), Jim Broadbent (Judge), Paul Jesson (Magistrate), Robert Putt (Station Sergeant), Eileen Davies (Prison Officer)

125 min.

Happy-Go-Lucky (2008)
United Kingdom
Production: Miramax, Summit Entertainment, Ingenious Film Partners,
    Film4, U.K. Film Council, Thin Man Films
Distributor: Miramax (U.S.)
Written and Directed by: Mike Leigh
Producer: Simon Channing Williams
Cinematography: Dick Pope
Editor: Jim Clark
Production Designer: Mark Tildesley
Costume Designer: Jacqueline Durran
Sound Recordist: Tim Fraser
Music: Gary Yershon
Cast: Sally Hawkins (Poppy), Eddie Marsan (Scott), Alexis Zegerman (Zoe),
    Sylvestra Le Touzel (Heather), Stanley Townsend (Tramp), Kate O'Flynn
    (Suzy), Caroline Martin (Helen), Oliver Maltman (Jamie), Sarah Niles
    (Tash), Samuel Roukin (Tim), Karina Fernandez (Flamenco Teacher),
    Nonso Anozie (Ezra), Sinéad Matthews (Alice), Andrea Riseborough
    (Dawn), Ayotunde Williams (Ayotunde), Jack MacGeachin (Nick), Charlie
    (Charlie Duffield), Elliot Cowan (Bookshop Assistant), Joseph Kloska
    (Suzy's Boyfriend), Anna Reynolds (Receptionist), Trevor Cooper (Patient)
119 min.

Another Year (2010)
United Kingdom
Production: Focus Features International, U.K. Film Council, Film4
Distributor: Sony Pictures Classics (U.S.)
Written and Directed by: Mike Leigh
Producer: Georgina Lowe
Cinematography: Dick Pope
Editor: Jon Gregory
Production Designer: Simon Beresford
Costume Designer: Jacqueline Durran
Sound Recordist: Tim Fraser
Music: Gary Yershon
Cast: Jim Broadbent (Tom), Ruth Sheen (Gerri), Lesley Manville (Mary),
    Oliver Maltman (Joe), Peter Wight (Ken), David Bradley (Ronnie),
    Martin Savage (Carl), Karina Fernandez (Katie), Michele Austin (Tanya),
    Phil Davis (Jack), Imelda Staunton (Janet), Stuart McQuarrie (Tom's
    Colleague), David Hobbs (Vicar), Badi Uzzaman (Mr. Gupta), Meneka Das
    (Mr. Gupta's Friend), Ralph Ineson (Drill Worker), Edna Doré (Allotment
    Lady), Gary Powell (Man in Bar), Lisa McDonald (Girl in Bar)
129 min.

Ashby, Justine, and Andrew Higson, eds. *British Cinema, Past and Present.* New York: Routledge, 2000.

Auty, Martyn, and Nick Roddick, eds. *British Cinema Now.* London: British Film Institute, 1985.

Baily, Leslie. *The Gilbert and Sullivan Book.* Rev. ed. London: Spring Books, 1966.

Bazin, André. *"Bicycle Thief."* In *What Is Cinema?* Vol. 2. Ed. and trans. Hugh Grey. Berkeley: University of California Press, 1971. 47–60.

———. "The Evolution of the Language of Cinema." In *What Is Cinema?* Vol. 1. Ed. and trans. Hugh Grey. Berkeley: University of California Press, 1971. 23–40.

Bordwell, David. *Figures Traced in Light: On Cinematic Staging.* Berkeley: University of California Press, 2005.

Bradley, Ian, ed. *The Complete Annotated Gilbert and Sullivan.* New York: Oxford University Press, 1996.

Brooks, Xan. "All or Nothing." *Sight and Sound* 12.11 (2002): 38.

Buruma, Ian. "The Way They Live Now." *New York Review of Books* 41.1–2 (1994): 7–10.

Carney, Ray, and Leonard Quart. *The Films of Mike Leigh: Embracing the World.* Cambridge: Cambridge University Press, 2000.

Clarke, Peter. *Hope and Glory: Britain 1900–1990.* London: Penguin, 1996.

Clements, Paul. *"Four Days in July."* In *British Television Drama in the 1980s.* Ed. George W. Brandt. Cambridge: Cambridge University Press, 1993. 162–77.

———. *The Improvised Play: The Work of Mike Leigh.* London: Methuen, 1983.

Coveney, Michael. *The World According to Mike Leigh.* London: HarperCollins, 1996.

Dargis, Manohla. "Johnny in the City: Mike Leigh's *Naked.*" *Artforum* 32.5 (1994): 54–57, 113.

———. "A Motherly Abortionist Gets Tangled With the Law." *New York Times,* October 8, 2004, E1.

Denby, David. "*Vera Drake.*" *New Yorker*, October 18, 2004, 50.

Eaton, Michael. "Not a Piccadilly Actor in Sight." *Sight and Sound* 3.12 (1993): 32–33.

Edelstein, David. "Grand Finale." *Slate,* January 7, 2000; accessed March 24, 2011. http://slate.com/id=68313/.

Fried, Michael. *Courbet's Realism.* Chicago: University of Chicago Press, 1990.

Friedman, Lester, ed. *Fires Were Started: British Cinema and Thatcherism.* Minneapolis: University of Minnesota Press, 1993.

Gilbey, Ryan. "Reasons to be Cheerful." *Sight and Sound* 12.10 (2002): 14–17.

Goodridge, Mike. *Screencraft: Directing.* Boston: Focal Press, 2002.

Gunning, Tom. "The Cinema of Attractions: Early Film, Its Spectator, and the Avant-Garde." In *Early Cinema: Space, Frame, Narrative.* Ed. Thomas Elsaesser. London: British Film Institute, 1990. 56–62.

Higson, Andrew. "Space, Place, Spectacle: Landscape and Townscape in the 'Kitchen Sink' Film." In *Dissolving Views: Key Writings on British Cinema.* Ed. Andrew Higson. London: Cassell, 1996. 133–56.

Hill, John. *British Cinema in the 1980s.* Oxford: Clarendon Press, 1999.

Holden, Stephen. "First-Rate Acting in Secondary Roles." *New York Times,* December 31, 2004, E1.

Jones, Edward Trostle. *All or Nothing: The Cinema of Mike Leigh.* New York: Peter Lang, 2004.

Kael, Pauline. "Circles and Squares." *Film Quarterly* 16.3 (1963): 12–26.

Laprevotte, Gilles. *Mike Leigh.* Amiens: Trois Cailloux, 1993.

Lay, Samantha. *British Social Realism.* London: Wallflower, 2002.

Leigh, Mike. *All or Nothing.* London: Faber and Faber, 2002.

———. *Career Girls.* London: Faber and Faber, 1997.

———. *Naked and Other Screenplays.* London: Faber and Faber, 1995.

———. *Secrets and Lies.* London: Faber and Faber, 1997.

———. *Topsy-Turvy.* London: Faber and Faber, 1999.

Leigh, Mike, dir. *All or Nothing* (2002). DVD. UGC Films/Momentum Pictures, 2003. Region 2.

———. *Happy-Go-Lucky* (2008). DVD. Miramax. 2009.

———. *Naked* (1993). DVD. Criterion Collection. 2005.

———. *The Short and Curlies* (1987). On *Naked* DVD. Criterion Collection. 2005.

———. *Topsy-Turvy* (1999). DVD. Criterion Collection, 2011.

Macnab, Geoffrey. "*Secrets and Lies.*" *Sight and Sound* 6.6 (1996): 51–52.

———. "*Happy-Go-Lucky.*" *Sight and Sound* 18.5 (2008): 65.

Malcolm, Derek. "Mike Leigh at the NFT." *The Guardian,* October 7, 2002; accessed March 24, 2011. http://www.guardian.co.uk/film/2002/oct/07/features.mikeleigh.

McFarlane, Brian. *An Autobiography of British Cinema.* London: Methuen, 1997.

Medhurst, Andy. "Mike Leigh: Beyond Embarrassment." *Sight and Sound* 3.11 (1993): 7–10.

———. "The Mike-ado." *Sight and Sound* 10.3 (2000): 36–37, 55.

Monk, Claire. "*Naked.*" *Sight and Sound* 3.11 (1993): 48–49.

Movshovitz, Howie, ed. *Mike Leigh: Interviews.* Jackson: University Press of Mississippi, 2000.

Murphy, Robert, ed. *The British Cinema Book.* 2d ed. London: British Film Institute, 2001.

Noller, Matt. "Cannes Film Festival 2010: *Another Year.*" May 16, 2010; accessed March 24, 2011. http://www.slantmagazine.com/house/2010/05/canne-film-festival-2010-day-four/.

Porton, Richard. "Entertainment and Empire: An Interview with Mike Leigh." *Cineaste* 25.2 (2000): 34–37.

———. "*Secrets and Lies.*" *Cineaste* 22.4 (1997): 51–52, 54.

———. "*Topsy-Turvy.*" *Cineaste* 25.2 (2000): 57–59.

Quart, Leonard. "Raising Questions and Positing Possibilities: An Interview with Mike Leigh." *Cineaste* 22.4 (1997): 53.

Raphael, Amy, ed. *Mike Leigh on Mike Leigh.* London: Faber and Faber, 2008.

Romney, Jonathan. "'Me? Miserable? Nonsense!'" *Independent on Sunday: New Review,* April 13, 2008, 34.

Rosenbaum, Jonathan. "Shotcuts to Happiness." *Chicago Reader,* October 24, 1996; accessed March 24, 2011. http://www.chicagoreader.com/chicago/shotcuts-to-happiness/Content?oid=891895.

Sontag, Susan. "The Decay of Cinema." *New York Times Magazine,* February 25, 1996, 60–61.

Truffaut, François. *Hitchcock.* Rev. ed. New York: Simon and Schuster, 1984.

Watson, Garry. *The Cinema of Mike Leigh: A Sense of the Real.* London: Wallflower, 2004.

Whitehead, Tony. *Mike Leigh.* Manchester: Manchester University Press, 2007.

Williams, Carolyn. "Intimacy and Theatricality: Mike Leigh's *Topsy-Turvy.*" *Victorian Literature and Culture* (2000): 471–76.

Woloch, Alex. *The One vs. the Many: Minor Characters and the Space of the Protagonist in the Novel.* Princeton, N.J.: Princeton University Press, 2003.

songs. *See* music and songs

Songs from the Second Floor (Andersson), 157

Sontag, Susan, 56–57, 143n8

Sorcerer, The (Gilbert and Sullivan), 95

sound, split from sight: and *Another Year*, 141–42; and cinema as centaur, 90; and *Happy-Go-Lucky*, 140; and *Meantime*, 47, 55; and *The Short and Curlies*, 31–33; and *Topsy-Turvy*, 32, 90–92, 102–3

Spall, Timothy, 105, 113, 143n15

Spiderman (comics character), 49

Steadicam, 138

Steadman, Alison, 34

stenciling, 77–80, 116

Sullivan, Arthur: and character, 36; and Leigh, 9–11; and Romanticism, 11, 103; and sound, 90, 92

"Sun, Whose Rays Are All Ablaze, The" (song from *The Mikado*), 97, 102–4

Tarkovsky, Andrei, 57

television: and Leigh's cinema, 11, 22, 34, 39, 155–56; and *Meantime*, 46, 49; and *The Short and Curlies*, 27; and *Vera Drake*, 121

Thatcher, Margaret, 8, 39, 142n1

theater and theatricality: and *Career Girls*, 87; and cinema, 102, 105; and contrivance, 10, 91; and *Four Days in July*, 37; and Leigh's career, 3, 34; and *Naked*, 62; and *Topsy-Turvy*, 10, 21, 37, 91–93, 96, 99, 102, 104–5, 159

Thelma and Louise (Scott), 136, 139, 141

theoretical cinema and art, 1–3, 11, 25, 32, 37, 65, 72, 142n2

Thewlis, David, 65, 105, 149–50

Times (London), 102

Top Gun (Scott), 146

Topsy-Turvy (1999): and abortion, 107, 122; analysis of, 80–105; and artist-figure, 66; and *Career Girls*, 80–95, 114, 143n10; and centaur, 19–21, 36, 54, 90–91, 93, 94, 104, 105, 121; and central characters, 133; and character/plot, 36; closing shot of, 160; and coincidence, 114; and couch scene, 19–21, 25, 54, 91–92; 153; and face-to-face, 99; final word of, 77, 101; and *Four Days in July*, 36–37, 42; and *Happy-Go-Lucky*, 139–40; Leigh's cinema, 9–11, 156, 159; and Leigh's process, 153–54; and motherhood, 46, 77, 100–104; narrative structure, 110, 121; and pregnancy, 68, 107; and realism ("human emotion and probability"), 10–11, 21, 88, 98, 102; *Secrets and Lies*, 19–21, 60, 110, 121; and side-by-side, 19–21, 36–37, 91–93, 97–98, 102, 105; sound split from sight in, 32; and theater, 37; title of, 26; and unbroken shot, 16, 19–21, 36–37, 91, 98–100, 153

topsy-turvydom: and *All or Nothing*, 115; and *Career Girls*, 89, 94; as plot, 36, 89, 115; and *Secrets and Lies*, 19, 127; and *Vera Drake*, 119

Touch of Evil (Welles), 15

train, as cinematic device: 83–85, 143n11

Two Thousand Years (2005), 34

Ulster Defence Regiment (UDR): and *Four Days in July*, 40, 44–45

Ulysses (Joyce), 143n9

unbroken shot (long take), 33, 35, 80; and absence, 15, 138; and alley shot, 44, 71; and *All or Nothing*, 110, 128–29; and *Another Year*, 133, 141–42; and *Bleak Moments*, 163; and centaur, 17–18, 19–21, 36, 53–54, 66, 131; and closing shots, 16, 53–55, 99–100, 133, 138–42; defined, 15–16; and *Four Days in July*, 16, 36–37, 44, 53–54; and *Happy-Go-Lucky*, 133, 139–40; and Leigh's cinema, 156–57; and *Life Is Sweet*, 54, 78–80; and *Meantime*, 42, 47, 54–55; and *Naked*, 59–65, 71, 138; and opening shots, 16; and plot, 106; and realism, 16, 62, 91, 98; and *Secrets and Lies*, 19–21, 54, 62–63, 66, 74, 78–80, 157; and *The Short and Curlies*, 26, 31; and side-by-side, 16, 19–21, 36, 53, 54–55, 63, 66, 71, 78–80, 91, 98, 128; and *Topsy-Turvy*, 16, 19–21, 36–37,

91, 98–100, 153; and *Vera Drake*, 110, 119–20, 128, 129–31, 160

Vera Drake (2004), 11, 34, 35, 156; and abortion, 19, 33, 36, 100, 149; and *All or Nothing*, 70, 94, 105–32; analysis of, 105–32; and *Another Year*, 132, 140; and centaur, 26, 109, 121, 128, 131; and central character, 93, 132, 140; and closing shot, 159–60; and coincidence, 28, 94, 110, 115–18, 122–23; and contrivance, 10; and death, 122, 144n17; and face-to-face, 110, 129–31; final word of, 77, 131–32; and *Happy-Go-Lucky*, 132, 134; and interiority, 80; and Leigh's cinema, 10; and Leigh's process, 5, 68–69, 152; and mini-narratives (abortion clients), 15, 16, 24, 48, 70, 108–9, 117–19, 125; and motherhood, 102; and names, 26, 117, 120–21, 122, 126–27, 131–32; and narrative structure, 151; and north of England, 147, 149; and parallel families, 38, 110, 116; and party scene, 10, 65, 68–69, 119–20, 123, 129, 134, 140; as "perfect," 7–8; and plot, 36, 94, 110, 121–23, 125–27, 134; and pregnancy,

19, 33, 100, 102; and realism, 9, 94, 119, 126; and side-by-side, 110, 117, 129–31; title of, 26, 117; and topsy-turvydom, 119; and unbroken shot, 110, 119–20, 128, 129–31, 160
verticality: and alley shot, 30, 43–44, 157; and *All or Nothing*, 157; as character, 44; and *Four Days in July*, 37, 43–44, 96, 157–58; and the grid, 37, 43–44, 96; and *High Hopes*, 157; and horizontality, 30; and Leigh's cinema, 157–59; and *Naked*, 157; and opening shots, 157; and pregnancy, 107; and *The Short and Curlies*, 30, 32; and side-by-side, 107; and *Topsy-Turvy*, 37, 96
Vertov, Dziga, 57
Vicious, Sid, 49
Visconti, Luchino, 35
von Stroheim, Erich, 9

Weekend (Godard), 37
Welles, Orson, 15, 57
William of Orange, 40, 53
Wise, Ernie, 49, 50
Woloch, Alex: 142n4
Wong, Kar-wai, 148
Wuthering Heights (Brontë), 88

Sean O'Sullivan is an
assistant professor of English at
The Ohio State University.

Books in the series
Contemporary Film Directors

The University of Illinois Press
is a founding member of the
Association of American University Presses.

Designed by Paula Newcomb
Composed in 10/13 New Caledonia LT Std
with Helvetica Neue LT Std display
by Barbara Evans
at the University of Illinois Press
Manufactured by Cushing-Malloy, Inc.

University of Illinois Press
1325 South Oak Street
Champaign, IL 61820-6903
www.press.uillinois.edu